BIOGRAPHICAL ESSAYS
ON TWENTIETH-CENTURY PERCUSSIONISTS

Geary Larrick

The Edwin Mellen Press
Lewiston/Queenston/Lampeter

Library of Congress Cataloging-in-Publication Data

Larrick, Geary, 1943-
  Biographical essays on twentieth-century percussionists / Geary
Larrick.
      p.   cm.
  Includes bibliographical references and index.
  ISBN 0-7734-9559-2
  1. Percussionists--Biography. I. Title.
ML399.L35   1992
786.8'092'2--dc20
  [B]   92-18731
                                                              CIP
                                                              MN

A CIP catalog record for this book
is available from the British Library.

The Edwin Mellen Press   The Edwin Mellen Press
        Box 450   Box 67
   Lewiston, New York   Queenston, Ontario
      USA 14092   CANADA L0S 1L0

The Edwin Mellen Press, Ltd.
Lampeter, Dyfed, Wales
UNITED KINGDOM SA48 7DY

Printed in the United States of America

Contents

Acknowledgments

The author is most appreciative of the knowledge and efforts of many people who have helped produce this volume. The musicians whose careers are detailed on these pages took time from their busy performance schedules to provide specific information about their music, education and experiences. The Percussive Arts Society, with its international membership, has provided the author with much information, motivation and good humor. Several publishers of percussion music, and manufacturers of percussion instruments, have sent complimentary materials containing a wealth of data. Certainly, the author recognizes the great assistance of his family, friends and colleagues.

Preface

The musical art forms involving percussion instruments have been present in society since prehistoric times. In the twentieth century, the field of percussion music has been receiving considerable written treatment accompanied by prolific activity around the world. Literary reporting of this activity is currently an occupation of numerous scholars in the United States of America; articles have been appearing in magazines, journals and books during recent decades, though few large-scale reference projects have been effected. A major focus of the present volume is to offer factual material and individual analysis concerning the careers of a significant number of professional percussionists who have performed, written and taught in the twentieth century. References are included regarding source materials and sound recordings. Discographies and selective publication lists follow the subject entries, in addition to references about that subject.

The eighty subjects mentioned here are in several instances known to the author professionally. Each person's artistry is well documented either in live performance or on recordings. An effort has been made to encompass various genres and styles. However, many deserving percussion artists have not been included in this book. It is hoped that this can be remedied with a future edition. Still, the subjects detailed in this volume are for the most part successful, important and immensely productive.

Introduction

The present volume details career highlights of eighty contemporary professional percussionists who have performed and are performing in the twentieth century. The instrument with which these people work, however, is quite unique and should be described. By definition, percussion instruments are those that produce music by being hit together or struck with a stick or mallet. Categorically, the percussion include drums, keyboards, rattles, and many other types of noise makers. It is the percussionist's prerogative to utilize the instruments to produce not just noise but a musical sound. Traditionally, the percussion have been especially effective at emphasizing rhythm and tone color in musical performance. Given the variety of instruments within this category, some produce a definite pitch while others produce a sound of indefinite pitch. One of the problems faced by writers for percussion, in addition to occasional unfamiliarity with specific aspects of notation, is the fact of unpredictability with some of the instruments. For example, a composer may request a tom-tom of indefinite pitch, only to hear a performance with a tom-tom of defined, though unpredictable, pitch. Additionally, the percussion are capable of numerous reiterated sounds as in the drum roll: notation and expectations regarding specifics of the roll are not always practical or generally understandable. Further, because of the many instruments, names and ranges vary from place to place.

Examples of these difficulties and challenges are the names for the vibraphone, also called the vibraharp, vibe, or vibes, and that keyboard percussion instrument's varying ranges from instrument to instrument. In addition, the vibraphone may have a variable speed tremolo, no tremolo, an electronically produced vibrato, and a sustaining pedal. The resulting challenges in detail and notation are not made any easier by individual preferences for certain kinds of mallets that may or may not be in agreement by the composer or conductor.

Some twentieth century composers, for example Harry Partch, John Cage, Lou Harrison and Yannis Xenakis, have written for unusual percussion instruments that may have to be constructed or borrowed for a particular performance. It is this kind of variety, however, that makes the percussion exciting and fresh. The performers described in this book have added much to their art form, based on good decision making daily in their work. These choices have resulted in many publications and beautiful sounds in recorded form that may be enjoyed by audiences around the world.

Abe, Keiko
Born c. 1943, Tokyo, Japan

Keiko Abe's specialization within the field of percussion involves the keyboard percussion instrument called the marimba. With the marimba, Abe has performed internationally and taught the instrument's technique to students. She has also composed music for the instrument, and caused several works to be written by others for the marimba with or without accompaniment.

Abe earned both baccalaureate and master's degrees at Gakugei University in Tokyo. At that school, she enrolled in the regular course of music study, and studied the xylophone with Eiichi Asabuki, the piano with Nobuko Honda, music composition with Shosuke Ariga, and general percussion with Yusuke Oyake. In her international travels as soloist, she has met and worked with various artist percussionists.

As a proponent for marimba literature, Keiko Abe has motivated the composition of several new works for the instrument. Examples of these include <u>Time for Marimba</u> by Minoru Miki, <u>Torse III</u> by Akira Miyoshi, <u>Mirage pour Marimba</u> by Yasuo Sueyoshi. In addition, Abe served as editor for an important collection of solo marimba compositions created by Miyoshi, Toshiya Sukegawa and Shin-ichiro Ikebe. Her own compositions, for example <u>Frogs</u> and <u>Michi</u>, have received performances at universities by both students and faculty.

Abe's marimba music utilizes a traditional four-mallet grip, as well as improvisatory characteristics. Likewise, her master classes and teaching incorporate improvisation in both tonal and modal harmonic/melodic languages. Her pedagogical repertoire includes music of Johann Sebastian Bach in addition to contemporary music literature.

In the 1970s, Abe performed as a leader in the Tokyo Quintet. Since 1975, she has served as a professor at the Toho-Gakuen School of Music. Since 1980, Keiko Abe has been a lecturer in the music department of Sohai University. In the mid-1980s, she worked as a visiting professor at Utrechts

Conservatorium in Holland. Auxiliary appointments include the board of directors for the Percussive Arts Society, and activity with the Japan Xylophone Association. She has shared her expertise literally in published articles and interviews, in addition to serving as the creative source for detailed musical analysis.

Significant presentations of Keiko Abe include the first performance of Akira Miyoshi's <u>Concerto for Marimba and String Ensemble</u> (1971), an appearance as featured soloist with the Concertgebouw Orchestra of Amsterdam (1984), and the premiere performance of *Marta Ptaszynska's <u>Marimba Concerto</u> (1986). Other important presentations were the world premiere of Jorge Salmientos' <u>Marimba Concertino</u> at Osaka Symphony Hall (1989), and solos at Percussive Arts Society International Conventions.

Festival Participation

Freibourg International Festival, Germany
Kuhmo Chamber Music Festival, Finland
New Harmony Town Festival, United States of America
New Music Concerts, Canada
Percussion Forum at Pompidou Center, France
Sevenoaks Summer Festival, England
Strasbourg International Percussion Festival, France
Taipei International Music Festival, Taiwan

Master Class Presentations

American University, United States of America (U.S.A.)
Baylor University, U.S.A.
Brooklyn College, U.S.A.
California State University, U.S.A.
Carnegie Mellon University, U.S.A.
Denmark - Fnen Conservatory, Holstebro Musick School, Music Conservatory Aalborg, Music Conservatory Arhusw, Royal Academy of Music
Drake University, U.S.A.

---

*M. Ptaszynska is a subject in this book.

Eastern Carolina University, U.S.A.

Eastman School of Music, U.S.A.

England - Leicester Polytechnic, Royal College of Music

Germany - Konservatorium der Stadt Nurnberg, Music Conservatory Berlin, Music School Stuttgart

Indiana University, U.S.A.

Ithaca College, U.S.A.

Netherlands - Sweelinck Conservatory Amsterdam

New England Conservatory, U.S.A.

Norway - East Norway Music Conservatory, State Academy of Music

Oberlin College, U.S.A.

State University of New York, U.S.A.

Sweden - Music-Akademie Stockholm

Switzerland - Music-Akademie der Stadt Basel

Temple University, U.S.A.

University of Cincinnati, U.S.A.

University of Illinois, U.S.A.

University of Massachusetts, U.S.A.

University of Michigan, U.S.A.

University of North Texas, U.S.A.

University of Wisconsin, U.S.A.

Demonstrably, Keiko Abe has served as an influential performer and teacher with the marimba around the world. She has been an important promoter of new music for the instrument and has shared her art with many people in various places. At the same time, Abe has represented traditional techniques and music in a respectful manner.

DISCOGRAPHY

Dyna Sound 45 Noctrne. CBS Sony 28AG165.

Japanese Poetic Scenes. Walter van Hauwe, recorder. Denon OF-7163.

Keiko Abe: Art of Marimba. Columbia JX-9-11.

Keiko Abe: Marimba Fantasy. Wergo WER 60177-50.

Keiko Abe: Marimba Selections. Columbia OQ-7466.

4

Keiko Abe: Marimba Selections II. Denon OX-1332.
Keiko Abe: Marimba Selections III. Denon 30CO-1729.
Kroumata and Keiko Abe. BIX CD-462.
Marimba Spiritual. Denon CO-4219.
The Tokyo Quintet. Denon 38C37-7280.

COMPOSITIONS

Ancient Vase. Germany: Schott.
Dream of the Cherry Blossoms. Germany: Zimmerman.
Frogs. U.S.A.: Studio 4.
Little Windows. Germany: Schott.
Memories of the Seashore. Germany: Schott.
Michi. U.S.A.: Music for Percussion.
Variations on Japanese Children's Songs. Germany: Schott.
Wind in the Bamboo Grove. Germany: Schott.

BOOKS

Abe, Keiko, editor. Modern Japanese Marimba Pieces. Tokyo: Ongaku No Tomo, 1969.

Abe, Keiko, editor. Modern Japanese Marimba Pieces 2. Tokyo: Ongaku No Tomo, 1978.

ARTICLES

"Keiko Abe." Master Technique Builders for Vibraphone and Marimba. Compiled and edited by *Anthony J. Cirone. U.S.A.: Belwin-Mills, 1985.

"Percussion Education at Japanese Universities." Percussive Notes 29/2 (December 1990), 31.

---

*A. Cirone is a subject in this book.

ARTICLES ABOUT SUBJECT

Helmig, Martina. "Virtuose Schlagwerkerin." Germany: <u>Berliner Morgenpost</u> (Oktober 1988).

"Keiko Abe: Marimba Fantasy." <u>Modern Percussionist</u> III/2 (March 1987).

Kotschenreuther, Hellmut. "Virtuosin und viel mehr: Keiko Abe im Kammermusiksaal." Germany: <u>Der Tages Spiegel</u> (Oktober 21, 1988).

Lang, Morris.* "A Talk with Marimba Virtuoso Keiko Abe," Interview, Part 2. <u>Percussive Notes</u> 21/5 (July 1983), 20.

Sabins, Jany. "Keiko Abe: Expanding the Marimba." <u>Modern Percussionist</u> II/4 (September 1986), 14.

Wolin, Kenneth S. "Focus on Research: An Analytical Approach to Keiko Abe's 'Dream of the Cherry Blossoms'." <u>Percussive Notes</u> (Fall 1989), 59.

REFERENCE SOURCE

Information supplied by the subject (January 1990).

---

*M. Lang is a subject in this book.

Bailey, Elden C.

Born April 22, 1922, Portland, Maine

"Buster" Bailey is one of the finest orchestral snare drummers in the world. As a member of the percussion section of the New York Philharmonic, he has received wide recognition in addition to the opportunity to travel to more than fifty countries with that organization.

Bailey's early education took place in the schools of Portland, Maine, where he earned a diploma from Deering High School in 1940. After graduation from secondary school, Elden Bailey enrolled at the New England Conservatory in Boston, Massachusetts, studying percussion with Boston Symphony Orchestra percussionist Lawrence White. From 1931 to 1941, Bailey studied different musical instruments with various teachers, including the percussion with Howard N. Shaw in Portland, and the piano, the clarinet and music theory with Frank J. Rigby also in Portland. Bailey's collegiate attendance was interrupted by World War II, and in 1943 he enlisted in the United States Army, serving as a member of the 154th Army Ground Forces Band. His early musical training in versatility enabled him to play the clarinet in the Army's concert band, the snare drum in the marching band, and the piano in the dance band. He also wrote arrangements and led the dance band. In 1946, Bailey left the military and enrolled at the Juilliard School of Music in New York City, graduating from that conservatory in 1949.

The year that he graduated from Juilliard, Elden Bailey joined the percussion section of the New York Philharmonic, where he has remained. With that symphony orchestra, he has had the opportunity to work with famous conductors including Leonard Bernstein, Pierre Boulez and Zubin Mehta. His colleagues in the percussion and timpani section of that orchestra have included Walter Rosenberger, Saul Goodman, Arthur Layfield, *Morris Lang, Roland Kohloff and *Chris Lamb. As a college student, Bailey had studied with timpanist Saul Goodman and percussionist author Morris

---

*M. Lang and C. Lamb are subjects in this book.

Goldenberg in New York. Elden Bailey has said that his "other teachers included almost every drummer that I ever say play. I watched and I listened, and learned from them all."

Bailey's playing experience has encompassed chamber music and wind ensembles, in addition to orchestral performance. He has appeared as guest drummer with the circus bands of Ringling Brothers and Barnum and Bailey Circus, with the Clyde Beatty-Cole Brothers Circus, the Mills Brothers Circus, and Circus Kingdom. As a teenager, he performed in the Portland Symphony Orchestra and with other groups in that region. Later he worked as a freelance percussionist in New York City. Jobs have included work as percussionist with The Little Orchestra Society, and with modern dance ensembles led by Sophie Maslow, Richard Bales, Jane Dudley and Jose Limon. In 1953, Bailey was one of the original members of the Sauter-Finegan Jazz Orchestra. In October, 1977, Elden Bailey served as a featured percussionist in the premiere performances of *Michael Colgrass's Deja Vu for percussion quartet and orchestra that was commissioned by the New York Phlharmonic.

As a teacher of percussion, Bailey has written a popular method book titled Mental and Manual Calisthenics for the Modern Mallet Player (1963). He has been a part of the percussion faculty at The Juilliard School since 1969. Earlier teaching appointments were with the Greenwich House Music School, the New York College of Music, and New York University.

In the several decades of a very successful career, Elden Bailey has consistently performed at a high level of quality. The technical discipline and perseverance required to obtain and maintain steady employment as a professional percussionist has, in this instance, given his music listening audience many, many hours of enjoyment and meditation. As a member of the New York Philharmonic, Bailey has performed on more than twenty-five foreign concert tours plus numerous concerts and recordings since 1949. His early training and experience helped prepare him for this work: between

---

*M. Colgrass is a subject in this volume.

1934 and 1941, Bailey appeared as a featured xylophonist more than a hundred times at a variety of musical events in Maine, building his stamina for later years.

DISCOGRAPHY

Carl Nielsen: Concerto for Clarinet and Orchestra. New York Philharmonic conducted by Leonard Bernstein. MS-7028.

Carl Nielsen: Symphony No. 5, Op. 50. New York Philharmonic conducted by Leonard Bernstein. MS-6414, 1963.

Dmitri Shostakovich: Fifth Symphony. New York Philharmonic conducted by Leonard Bernstein. CBS Records MYK-37218, 1959 and 1981.

Duke Ellington Jazz Party. Columbia Records Collectors Series JCS-8127.

Footlifters--A Century of American Marches. The Incredible Columbia All-Star Band conducted by Gunther Schuller. Columbia Records XM-3353, 1975.

Ludwig van Beethoven: Symphony No. 9. New York Philharmonic conducted by Leonard Bernstein. CBS Records MK-42224, 1969 and 1986.

Miles Davis: Sketches of Spain. Arranged and conducted by Gil Evans. Columbia Jazz Masterpieces, CBS Records CD-40578, 1986.

Other recordings of the New York Philharmonic since 1949.

Sousa Forever. Symphonic Band conducted by Morton Gould. RCA Records LSC-2569, 1961.

BOOK

Mental and Manual Calisthenics for the Modern Mallet Player. Miami, Florida: Belwin-Mills, 1963.

REFERENCE SOURCES

Information supplied by the subject (October 1989).

Live from Lincoln Center. New York Philharmonic conducted by Zubin Mehta. Wausau: Wisconsin Public Television, December 31, 1990.

Beck, John H.

Born February 16, 1933, Lewisburg, Pennsylvania

One of the most accomplished professional percussionists in the twentieth century is Professor John H. Beck, percussion teacher at the University of Rochester's Eastman School of Music in Rochester, New York. Concurrently, he has served as timpanist for the Rochester Philharmonic Orchestra since 1962, and was president of the international Percussive Arts Society from 1987 through 1990.

Beck graduated from Lewisburg High School in 1951. He earned a baccalaureate degree at the Eastman School of Music in 1955, studying percussion with *William Street. In 1962, Beck earned the Master of Music degree at the Eastman School, majoring in percussion performance.

After receiving his Bachelor's degree, John Beck joined the United States Marine Band in Washington, District of Columbia. With that organization, he performed and toured as a featured marimba soloist and timpanist. After four years of military service, Beck returned to Rochester where he became principal percussionist in the Rochester Philharmonic.

In 1959, Beck became an instructor in the Eastman School's Preparatory Department. He became Eastman's full time percussion teacher in 1967. In this capacity, he has performed frequently as an artist percussionist in solo appearances, chamber music and large ensembles. Associated presentations have included performances with drum set at Eastman and in freelance work, in addition to playing timpani and general percussion. Beck has taught the percussion methods course at Eastman and conducted the Eastman Percussion Ensemble in many concerts and on tour. This percussion ensemble, under his direction, has performed for recordings and clinic presentations. Each of the percussion ensemble's performers studies privately with Professor Beck at the Eastman School of Music.

---

*W. Street is a subject in this book.

John Beck has appeared as featured percussion soloist with the Rochester Philharmonic, the Eastman Wind Ensemble, the Syracuse University Wind Ensemble, and the Chautauqua Band in western New York. He has also performed in that capacity with the Rochester Chamber Orchestra and the Memphis State University Wind Ensemble.

From 1965 to 1972, Beck was percussion columnist for the <u>National Association of College Wind and Percussion Instructors Journal</u>. As president of the Percussive Arts Society, he regularly wrote a column for the magazine <u>Percussive Notes</u>. He has contributed an article about the percussion ensemble to the <u>Grove Dictionary of American Music</u>, and has revised the percussion portion of <u>World Book Encyclopedia</u>. Beck has written a method book for drum set and composed several works for solo percussion and percussion ensemble.

In 1976, John Beck directed the first international convention of the Percussive Arts Society in Rochester. The organization had been meeting annually in Chicago previously, at the same time as the Mid-West Band and Orchestra Clinic. Beck has served as chairperson of percussion for the New York State School Music Association, and has presided on the Board of Directors for the Percussive Arts Society. Also within the Percussive Arts Society, he has served in the capacities of New York state chapter president, second vice president and first vice president for the parent organization. During his tenure as president, he led conventions in Saint Louis, Nashville, San Antonio and Philadelphia.

Beck has recorded numerous orchestral and chamber music compositions. He has toured South America with the Aeolian Consort, and has performed with the Eastman Chamber Players in New York City. In summer of 1990, Beck performed solo recitals for the Third International Percussion Workshop in Bydgoszcz, Poland. In the early 1990s, Beck accompanies the Rochester Philharmonic in its guest appearances in the Colorado mountains.

In summary, John H. Beck has worked as an important teacher of percussion, as well as an adept performer and lecturer. His students occupy significant positions in major orchestras and universities. Beck has set a good example visibly as writer, performer and instructor.

DISCOGRAPHY

Bela Bartok: Sonata for Two Pianos and Percussion. Musical Heritage Society 3679.

Eastmontage. Eastman Percussion Ensemble conducted by John H. Beck. University of Rochester ES-72001, 1969.

Lou Harrison: Concerto for Violin and Percussion Orchestra. Carroll Glenn, Violin, and the Eastman Percussion Ensemble conducted by J.H. Beck. Turnabout 34653.

Mozart Piano Concerto No. 26, K. 537. Barry Snyder, Piano, and the Rochester Philharmonic Orchestra conducted by David Zinman. Canada: Moss Music Group MWCD-7120, 1986.

Nola. Eastman Marimba Band directed by J.H. Beck. Golden Imports 75108.

Robert Hall Lewis: Combinazioni II for Percussion Ensemble and Piano. Eastman Percussion Ensemble conducted by J.H. Beck. Orion 79363.

Verne Reynolds: Concertare I for Brass Quintet and Percussion. Mark Records.

COMPOSITIONS

Alpine Slide for Timpani. Kendor Music, 1985.

Colonial Capers. Kendor, 1975.

Colonial Drummer. Kendor, 1975.

Concerto for Drum Set and Percussion Ensemble. Kendor, 1979.

Concerto for Timpani and Percussion Ensemble. Kendor, 1984.

Episode for Solo Percussion. Studio 4 Productions, 1977.

Episodes for Percussion Trio. Wimbledon Music, 1980.

Grand Teton for Timpani. Kendor, 1985.

Jazz Miniatures for Percussion Ensemble. Columbia Pictures, 1985.

Jazz Variants for Percussion Ensemble. Boston Music, 1971.

Latin Fantasy. Columbia Pictures, 1986.

Little March for Percussion Ensemble. Columbia Pictures, 1985.

Overture for Percussion Ensemble. Kendor, 1976.

14

Rhapsody for Percussion and Band. Kendor, 1970.

Snake River for Timpani. Kendor, 1985.

Sonata for Timpani. Boston Music, 1969.

Three Episodes for Timpani. Kendor, 1980.

Three Movements for Five Timpani. Meredith Music, 1985.

Triptych Motif for Timpani. Kendor, 1983.

BOOKS

A Practical Approach to the Drum Set. New York: MCA Music, 1967.

Flams, Ruffs and Rolls for Snare Drum. Fort Lauderdale, Florida: Meredith Music Publications, 1984.

ARTICLES

"President's Message." Percussive Notes 29/1 (Fall 1990), 3.

"President's Message." Percussive Notes 29/2 (December 1990), 3.

REFERENCE SOURCES

Egart, Richard. "Critique." Modern Percussionist II/3 (June 1986), 54.

"Faculty and Student Notes." Notes 20/6 (January 1990), Eastman School of Music of the University of Rochester.

Information supplied by the subject (September 1989).

"Officers." Percussive Notes 29/1 (October 1990), 2.

Regal Snare Drum Sticks, "John Beck" model. Niagara Falls, New York: J.D. Calato Manufacturing Company.

Beck, John R.
Born November 24, 1960, Rochester, New York

John Richard Beck, son of *John H. Beck, has worked as a freelance musician since 1987, residing in Fairfax, Virginia. John R. Beck, like his father, attended the Eastman School of Music and performed in the U.S. Marine Band in Washington, D.C. He has been an active performer and teacher.

Beck earned a diploma from the Preparatory Department of the Eastman School of Music in Rochester in 1978. His teachers there were Ernest Muzquiz, *Gordon Stout, David Mancini, *Niel DePonte, and *Ruth Cahn. For his undergraduate study, Beck enrolled at Oberlin College in northern Ohio, studying at that school in the Conservatory of Music with percussionist *Michael Rosen. John R. Beck earned the degree Bachelor of Music at Oberlin in 1982.

After receiving his baccalaureate degree, Beck returned to upstate New York and enrolled at the Eastman School of Music, working toward a Master's degree which he received in 1983. Along with his graduate degree, Beck earned a Performer's Certificate as a particularly accomplished percussionist. His percussion teacher at the Eastman School was his father, John H. Beck.[1]

After earning his graduate degree, John R. Beck was accepted as a percussionist in the U.S. Marine Band in Washington, serving as percussionist and featured soloist at keyboard percussion. Beck's enlistment period was four years in Washington and on tour. With this professional level wind ensemble, Beck served as principal cymbalist and received much valuable playing experience.

Beginning in 1985, John R. Beck performed as an extra percussionist with the National Symphony Orchestra in Washington. He took on the same role in 1987 with the Baltimore Symphony Orchestra. Other orchestral work

---

*J.H. Beck, G. Stout, N. DePonte, R. Cahn and M. Rosen are subjects in this book.

that Beck has performed has included appearances with the Fairfax Symphony Orchestra since 1984, the Maryland Symphony Orchestra and the National Gallery Orchestra since 1985, and the Washington Opera Orchestra since 1987. Beck has performed as extra percussionist with the Annapolis Symphony Orchestra in 1989, has played with the Baltimore Opera Orchestra since 1989, and was a featured percussion soloist with the Alexandria Symphony Orchestra also in 1989.

Auxiliary positions as a professional percussionist for Beck have included participation at the Grand Teton Music Festival in 1988, and presentation of a clinic at a Percussive Arts Society International Convention in Washington, D.C. Beck has performed as a set drummer in concert at the Kennedy Center in Washington, and has played at the White House. In addition to touring with the U.S. Marine Band, Beck has also toured with the Paris Opera and Ballet Orchestra. He has presented master classes and served as a percussion clinician at the Grand Teton Music Festival, at the University of Miami, and at the Eastman School of Music.

John R. Beck received a John Philip Sousa Award in 1978 for excellence in participation in his high school music program. He has served as president of the District of Columbia chapter of the Percussive Arts Society. As a percussion music teacher, Beck has worked at George Washington University and at the Shenandoah College Conservatory of Music in Winchester, Virginia.

As a freelance percussionist on the east coast of the United States, John Beck has ample opportunity to perform with several ensembles in different cities. His versatility and high level of quality allow him to perform in various musical situations, in addition to auxiliary work as a teacher and clinician.

DISCOGRAPHY

Dmitri Shostakovich: Symphony No. 7. National Symphony Orchestra conducted by Rostrapovich. In preparation.

Orchestral Music of Sir Edward Elgar. Baltimore Symphony Orchestra. In preparation.

Recordings with the United States Marine Band from 1983 to 1987.

ARTICLE ABOUT SUBJECT

Skelly, Anne. "The President's Percussionists." <u>Modern Percussionist</u> III/4 (September 1987), 18.

REFERENCE SOURCE

Information supplied by the subject (November 1989).

Becker, Bob
Born June 22, 1947, Allentown, Pennsylvania

North American xylophone virtuoso Bob Becker leads a varied career in a multicultural approach to his music. His background includes Western classical music, military music, twentieth century popular music and musics of India, Africa and Indonesia.

Becker's early percussion study was with James Betz in Pennsylvania from 1954 to 1965. In 1965, Becker enrolled at the Eastman School of Music, earning a baccalaureate degree in performance in 1969. His teachers at this time included *William Street, *John Beck and *Warren Benson. During his undergraduate study, Becker performed in the Rochester Philharmonic Orchestra, and received the prestigious Performer's Certificate at the Eastman School. Becker's ensemble performance at Eastman involved participation in the Eastman Philharmonia, the Eastman Wind Ensemble, and the Eastman Percussion Ensemble.

In 1969, Bob Becker joined the United States Marine Band in Washington, D.C., as percussionist and marimba soloist. He then returned to Rochester and entered graduate study at the Eastman School, earning the Master's degree in percussion performance and music literature in 1971. He served as the Eastman School's graduate assistant in percussion at this time.

From 1971 to 1975, Becker studied in the graduate ethnomusicology program at Wesleyan University in Middletown, Connecticut. Working in the world music program, he took lessons from various teachers acquainted with drumming and percussion within a variety of cultures from around the world. Becker had begun his study of Hindustani music in 1970, then eventually studied Ghanaian drumming with Abraham Adzenyah, Gideon Alorwoye, and Freeman Donkor. Becker studied Javanese gamelan music with Prawotosaputro and Sumarsam. Further study included mrdangam lessons with Ramnad Raghavan, and the tabla drums with Pandit Sharda Sahai.

---

*W. Street, J. Beck and W. Benson are subjects in this book.

Becker has since appeared professionally with several of India's leading artists, including Ram Narayan, Amjad Ali Khan, Vijay Raghav Rao, Laksmi Shankar, Jitendra Abisheki and Salamat Ali Khan. Continuing education for Bob Becker includes attendance at Percussive Arts Society International Conventions, where he occasionally performs as part of the featured program.

In 1971, Becker was a founding member of the percussion ensemble Nexus. He continues to perform and record with this chamber music group. One of his specialties with Nexus is performing arrangements of George Hamilton Green's music on the xylophone with marimbas and percussion accompaniment. In the middle 1970s, Bob Becker migrated to Toronto, Ontario, Canada, and began performing part-time with the Toronto Symphony in 1976.

In 1972, Becker became a member of Steve Reich and Musicians ensemble. From 1972 to 1975, Becker was percussionist with Paul Winter Consort. In 1968 and 1972, he performed at the Marlboro Music Festival. He has also performed as timpanist of the Festival Orchestra conducted by Pablo Casals. Since 1983, Becker has been proprietor of Xylomusic Publishing in Toronto. As a member of Nexus, he has toured worldwide and recorded several times. With Nexus, Becker has performed at Percussive Arts Society International Conventions. Beginning in 1986, he has been a featured performer at World Drums conventions. In 1988, Becker performed in eastern Asia at the Tokyo Music Joy Festival.

The range of Bob Becker's professional music activities is impressive. His work encompasses improvisation, composition, publishing, ensemble performance, solo presentations and writing. Becker received Canada Council Grants in 1982 and 1983 as encouragement for his active professional endeavours.

DISCOGRAPHY

Changes. Nexus. NE-04, 1982.
Dance of the Octopus. Nexus. CBC SM-5000, 1989.
Drumming. Steve Reich and Musicians. Nonesuch, 1987.
Eastman Wind Ensemble. Deutsche Grammophon 2530-063, 1969.
Eastmontage. University of Rochester ES-72001, 1969.

Jo Kondo - Under the Umbrella. Nexus. CP2-11, 1980.

Music For A Large Ensemble. Steve Reich and Musicians. ECM, 1981.

Music for Eighteen Musicians. Steve Reich and Musicians. ECM, 1978.

Music of Nexus. NE-01, 1981.

Nexus and Earle Birney. NE-02, NE-03, NE-04, 1982.

Nexus Now. Holcomb, New York: *William L. Cahn Publishing, 1989.

Nexus Plays the Novelty Music of George Hamilton Green. Cassette, 1986. CD, 1989.

Nexus Ragtime Concert. Toronto: Nimbus 9 Productions, 1976.

Paul Horn + Nexus. Epic LP KE-33561, Black Sun CD 15002-2, 1975.

Sextet/Six Marimbas. Steve Reich and Musicians. Nonesuch 9 79138-1, 1986.

Tehillim. Steve Reich and Musicians. ECM, 1981.

The Best of Nexus. Denon CD-10251, 1989.

The Desert Music. Brooklyn Philharmonic. Nonesuch, 1984.

COMPOSITIONS

"Cymbal." Nexus Now. Holcomb: *W.L. Cahn, 1989.

Lahara. Toronto: Xylomusic Publishing, 1977.

Valse Brillante for xylophone and piano by George Hamilton Green, edited with cadenza by B. Becker. Fort Lauderdale, Florida: Meredith Music Publications.

ARTICLES

"Introduction." Modern Improvising and Application of Ideas to Melody by George Hamilton Green. Fort Lauderdale: Meredith.

Record Jacket Notes. Nexus Ragtime Concert. Toronto: Nimbus 9, 1976.

---

*W.L. Cahn is a subject in this book.

Technique Article. <u>Master Technique Builders for Vibraphone and Marimba</u>, compiled and edited by *Anthony J. Cirone. Miami, Florida: Belwin-Mills Publishing, 1985.

ARTICLES ABOUT SUBJECT

Larrick, Geary. <u>Analytical and Biographical Writings in Percussion Music</u>. New York: Peter Lang Publishing, 1989.

Larrick, Geary. "Biography and Analysis of Bob Becker's 'Lahara'." <u>National Association of College Wind and Percussion Instructors Journal</u> XXXIV/4 (Summer 1986), 26.

Larrick, Geary. "Multicultural Music: Bob Becker's 'Lahara'." <u>National Association of College Wind and Percussion Instructors Journal</u> XXXIX/1 (Fall 1990), 10.

Mattingly, Rick. "Nexus." <u>Modern Percussionist</u> I/3 (June 1985), 8.

REFERENCE SOURCES

Information supplied by subject (October 1989).

Miller, William F. "Critique." <u>Modern Percussionist</u> III/2 (March 1987), 60.

Program. Eastman School of Music of the University of Rochester. Rochester, New York: Sunday, January 12, 1969.

---

*A.J. Cirone is a subject in this book.

Bellson, Louis
Born July 26, 1924, Rock Falls, Illinois

Louis Bellson is an internationally acclaimed artist of the drum set. In a career that has spanned several decades, Bellson's abilities at communicating his art remain relevant, refreshing and always rhythmical.

In 1940, Bellson won a national drumming contest sponsored by Gene Krupa. One of Bellson's early teachers was Roy Knapp, with whom he studied as a teenager. He entered military service during the Second World War and, after 1946, became an important big band drummer. Leaders with whom Bellson performed include Count Basie, Duke Ellington, Benny Goodman, Harry James and Tommy Dorsey. Other jazz musicians with whom Bellson has performed include Red Norvo, Benny Carter, Teddy Wilson, George Duvivier, Oscar Peterson and Ray Brown. At a relatively young age, Bellson received the opportunity to write musical arrangements. Other professional activity for Bellson has included serving as music director for his wife, Pearl Bailey, and leading his own big bands.

Special performances during Bellson's career have included Duke Ellington's sacred concert in 1965, and two "swing reunion" concerts in 1985 at Town Hall in New York City with Carter, Wilson, Norvo and Duvivier. As a composer, Bellson wrote a jazz ballet titled The Marriage Vows in 1962, and has contributed several scores for his big bands.

A rather unique aspect of Louis Bellson's approach is to play two pedal-operated bass drums, instead of the standard single pedal-operated bass drum included in most drum sets. Bellson learned tap dance at an early age and was able to transfer some of his acquired abilities of coordination toward competent performance of the double bass drums.

Writer Whitney Balliett has referred to Bellson as a child prodigy as a youth and a "virtuoso drummer" in maturity. Authority J. Bradford Robinson has written about Bellson's "precise technique" and "flamboyant solo style." Bellson has displayed impressive technical control, speed capability and musical talent. Bellson's activities in recent years have included educational appearances with amateur big bands, and serving on the planning committee for the 1991 Percussive Arts Society International Convention. Associated professional involvements include serving as a vice president and advisor for a percussion company in North Hollywood, California, and sharing his expertise as a designer of drum mallets for a company in Northbrook, Illinois.

DISCOGRAPHY

Big Band Jazz from the Summit. Roulette 52087, 1962.

Cool, Cool Blue. Pablo 2310-899, 1982.

Duke's Big 4. Pablo 2310-703, 1973.

Ellington Uptown. Columbia ML-4639, 1952.

For the First Time. Pablo 2310-712, 1974.

Louie Bellson Jam. Pablo 2310-838, 1978.

Louis Bellson Quintet. EPN 70-3, 1954.

Side Track. Concord 141, 1979.

Sunshine Rock. Pablo 2310-813, 1977.

The Best of Louie Bellson. Pablo 2310-851, 1980.

The London Gig. Pablo 2310-880, 1982.

ARTICLES ABOUT SUBJECT

Balliett, Whitney. "Profiles: First and Last." The New Yorker, June 19, 1989.

Robinson, J. Bradford. "Bellson, Louie." The New Grove Dictionary of Jazz, Volume One. Edited by Barry Kernfeld. London: Macmillan Press. New York: Grove's Dictionaries of Music, 1988.

REFERENCE SOURCES

"Bellson Joins PASIC '91 Planning Committee." Percussion News, January, 1991.

"Bellson To Play in Point on November 6." Stevens Point Journal, Accent Section, Monday, October 20, 1989.

Green, Benny. Record Jacket Notes. For the First Time: Count Basie Trio. Pablo 2310-712, 1974.

Benson, Warren

Born January 26, 1924, Detroit, Michigan

Composition professor Warren Benson has put together a career marked by a high level of performance. His attendance at top quality schools helped prepare him for an ascent at a relatively young age to important professional positions, followed by a maturity in influential jobs and roles in the percussion field.

Benson earned a secondary school diploma at Cass Technical High School in Detroit in 1943. He then enrolled at the University of Michigan, receiving the opportunity to teach percussion part-time while studying toward an undergraduate degree. His baccalaureate degree was received in 1949 emphasizing the area of music theory, followed by a Master of Music in theory earned in 1951 at the University of Michigan. Benson's teaching at the Ann Arbor school included work with undergraduate percussion students and classroom experience in a graduate percussion methods course.

Important professional performance experience for Warren Benson occurred from 1946 to 1954. During this time, he performed as timpanist with the Detroit Symphony Orchestra, the Ford Sunday Evening Hour Orchestra, and the Brevard Festival Orchestra. Some of the conductors with whom he worked included Fritz Reiner, Eugene Ormandy and Leonard Bernstein.

In 1952, Benson was a Fulbright teacher of music at Anatolia College in Salonica, Greece. During the 1952-53 school term, he served as director of large ensembles at Mars Hill College in North Carolina. From 1953 to 1967, Warren Benson was a teacher of percussion at Ithaca College in New York, where he concentrated on serious composition. Since 1967, Benson has served as a composition professor at the Eastman School of Music in Rochester, New York.

In addition to performing with well known organizations, Warren Benson has received several grants and commissions to compose music. Awards have come from the National Endowment for the Arts, the New York State Council on the Arts, and the Ford Foundation. Commissions have come from the United States Air Force Band, the Kronos Quartet, the University of Michigan Symphony Band, the Chestnut Brass Company, the International Horn Society, the Cantata Singers, and the Rochester Philharmonic. Benson has written articles for publication, lectured and conducted his own compositions at leading educational centers and festivals in North America, South America and Europe.

Professor Benson, who was named a University Mentor at the University of Rochester in 1984, is an important influence of music with a percussive orientation during the latter half of the twentieth century. This influence includes not only "noisy" music but lyrical music as well, as evidenced by his success with the vocal medium. The breadth and variety of his production is consistent with a similar orientation in the percussion field, given worldwide activity in numerous cultural environments. Additionally, Benson's work as an educator is significant, far reaching and musical.

DISCOGRAPHY

"American Primitive." <u>Songs of America</u>. Jan DeGaetani, mezzo-soprano, and Gilbert Kalish, piano. Elektra-Nonesuch 9-79178-2.

<u>Dawn's Early Light</u>. United States Air Force Band, conducted by Col. J.M. Bankhead, 1989.

<u>Symphony for Drums and Wind Orchestra</u>. Lawrence University Wind Ensemble, conducted by Robert Levy. Golden Crest ATH-5085.

<u>The Leaves Are Falling</u>. Eastman Wind Ensemble, conducted by Donald Hunsberger. Centaur CRC-2014.

COMPOSITIONS

<u>Cancionitas de las Calles</u> for baritone, viola, clarinet, guitar and percussion, 1982.

<u>Canon</u> for tuba and hand drum, 1974.

<u>Concertino for Flute, Strings and Percussion</u>, 1983.

<u>Earth-Sky-Sea</u> for chorus, flute, trombone and marimba, 1975.

<u>How Do I Love Thee</u> for soprano and marimba, 1976.

<u>Invocation and Dance</u> for saxophones and percussion, 1958.

Picnic Music for carillon, 1981.

Polyphonies for Percussion and Band, 1960.

Rondino for handclappers, 1967.

Songs of O for chorus, brass quintet and marimba, 1974.

Streams, percussion ensemble, 1961.

Symphony for Drums and Wind Orchestra, 1962.

The Red Lion, vibraphone and piano, 1988.

Three Dances, snare drum, 1962.

Three Pieces, percussion quartet, 1960.

Trio for Percussion, 1957.

Variations on a Handmade Theme, handclappers, 1957.

Winter Bittersweet, percussion ensemble, 1981.

ARTICLES ABOUT SUBJECT

A Comprehensive Biographical Dictionary of American Composers. Compiled by David Ewen. New York: G.P. Putnam, 1982.

ASCAP Biographical Dictionary, Fourth Edition. New York: Jacques Cattell Press, 1980.

Contemporary American Composers: A Bibliographical Dictionary. Compiled by E. Ruth Anderson. Boston: G.K. Hall, 1976.

Hunsberger, Donald. "Discussion with Warren Benson." CBDNA Journal I/1, 1984.

International Who's Who in Music and Musician's Directory, Tenth Edition. Cambridge, England: International Biographical Centre, 1975.

The New Grove Dictionary of Music and Musicians, Sixth Edition. Washington, D.C.: Grove's Dictionaries of Music, 1980.

Tonkunstler-Lexicon, Volume II. Wilhelmshaven, Germany: Edition Heinrichshofen.

*Udow, Michael. "Focus on Performance: An Interview with Warren Benson." Percussive Notes (Winter 1989).

Who's Who in the World, Fifth Edition. Chicago: Marquis Publications.

---

*M. Udow is a subject in this book.

REFERENCE SOURCES

Information supplied by the subject (March 1990).

"New Releases from Eastman." <u>Notes</u> 20/6 (January 1990).

Bergamo, John
Born May 28, 1940, Palisades Park, New Jersey

John Bergamo has specialized in hand drumming in recent years, though his background includes utilization of his talents in various capacities. Bergamo's range has been associated primarily with the east coast and the west coast of the United States.

His Bachelor of Music was earned in 1961 at the Manhattan School of Music in New York City. A year later he received the Master of Music degree from that conservatory. While studying at the Manhattan School, Bergamo's major emphases were in percussion and composition. Other work has included composition study at Darmstadt Summer Institute in 1962, contemporary music study at Tanglewood in 1963, 1964 and 1965, and work at the State University of New York in Buffalo from 1964 to 1966. Additional study was at Ali Akbar College of Music from 1966 to 1969, and at the Lenox School of Jazz in 1978.

Bergamo has received several awards and scholarships, including the Mayor's Scholarship in Composition at Darmstadt, Fromm Fellowships at Tanglewood, a Rockefeller Foundation grant at Buffalo, and awards from the American Society of Composers, Authors and Publishers in 1985 and 1987. He has also received a Mellon Foundation Grant for Creative Study, and a scholarship at the Lenox School.

John Bergamo's teachers include Joseph Girratano, *Max Roach, Paul Price, Fred Albright, Ali Akbar Khan, Mahapurush Misra, Shankar Ghosh, Allah Rakha, T. Ranganathan, P.S. Venkateshan, K.R.T. Wasitodiningrat, I. Nyomen Wenten, Alfred Ladzekpo, Kobla Ladzekpo, and teachers at the Manhattan School of Music. Musicians with whom Bergamo has collaborated include Lukas Foss, Arthur Weisberg, Charles Wuorinen, Gunther Schuller and *John Wyre. Ensembles with whom Bergamo has performed include the

---

*M. Roach, J. Wyre and S. Gadd are subjects in this book.

Cal Arts Twentieth Century Players, the Guarneri Jazz Quartet, and the Maelstrom Percussion Ensemble.

Since 1970, Bergamo has been percussion area coordinator in the School of Music at the California Institute of the Arts in Valencia. Previously he taught at the University of Washington in Seattle, and at Ali Akbar College Summer Institute. He has also taught at Naropa Summer Institute in Boulder, Colorado.

As a performing artist, John Bergamo has offered presentations at Percussive Arts Society International Conventions, and has worked with New Music America. Other organizations for which Bergamo has performed include the Cal Arts Contemporary Festival, and Monday Evening Concerts in California and Colorado. He has participated in the World Drum Festival in Vancouver, at Expo '86 with the percussion ensemble Nexus, with Glen Velez, and with drum set specialist *Steve Gadd.

Bergamo has studied Western music, Asian Indian music, Indonesian music, and African music. Professional associations have included Chamber Music America, the American Gourd Society, Composers' Forum, and Independent Composers Association. From 1979 to 1988, he served on the Board of Directors for the Percussive Arts Society.

The scope of John Bergamo's professional activity is wide and at the same time specific. His knowledge of the intricacies of ethnic percussion, added to his foundation in traditional musics, produce an artist performer of exceptional ability. Bergamo's early composition for solo timpanist, "Four Pieces for Timpani," is a very successful work written at a time when such publications were rare.

DISCOGRAPHY

Bracha. CMP Records.

In Need Again. Repercussion Unit. CMP Records.

Lou Harrison: Suite for Violin and American Gamelan. Conducted by J. Bergamo. New Albion Records.

On the Edge. CMP Records.

COMPOSITIONS

Blanchard Canyon. Talamala.

Boffondaghoul. Talamala.

Faropace. Talamala.

Five Miniatures. Talamala.

Four Pieces for Timpani. Music for Percussion, 1963.

Gupta Sloka Chand. Talamala.

Interactions for Vibes and Percussion. Music for Percussion.

Like Be-bop. Talamala.

Little Smeg. Talamala.

Piru Bole. Talamala.

Remembrance. Talamala.

Shradhanjali. Talamala.

Startime. Talamala.

Tanka. Talamala.

Three Pieces for the Winter Solstice. Talamala.

Totally Hip. Talamala.

5 x 5 x 5. Talamala.

#33. Talamala.

EDUCATIONAL VIDEO

On the Art and Joy of Hand Drumming. Co-presented with Glen Velez. Brattleboro, Vermont: Interworld Music Associates.

BOOK

Style Studies for Mallet-Keyboard Percussion Instruments. Fort Lauderdale, Florida: Music for Percussion.

ARTICLES

"Exploring Tambourine Technique." Co-authored with Janet Bergamo. Percussive Notes (Spring 1990), page 12.

"Faropace." Perspectives of New Music.

"On the Edge." Percussioner International I/3 (1986).

"South Indian Drumming." <u>Percussive Notes,</u> Research Edition (1985).

"The Rhythm Scale." <u>Percussioner International</u> I/4 (1987).

"The Tavil of South India." <u>Percussioner International</u> I/2 (1986).

REFERENCE SOURCES

Information supplied by the subject (December 1989).

Bergamo, John. <u>Four Pieces for Timpani.</u> Fort Lauderdale, Florida: Music for Percussion, 1963.

Blades, James
Born September 9, 1901, Peterborough, England

James Blades has led a various and illustrious career as a performer, teacher and author. His detailed text book about the percussion from a historical and a performer's points of view, remains one of the most important productions in the area of serious percussion in the twentieth century. The book is currently in its first published revision, and was completed when its author was past the age of sixty.

Blades' early musical education included singing in a church choir prior to age ten, playing a harmonica that was purchased for the price of six and one-half pence, and performing with drum and bugle while serving as a member of the Boy Scouts. James Blades received his first percussion lessons from an uncle in 1919, and soon learned to improvise on the drum. His early schooling included attendance at Saint John's School in Peterborough.

James Blades became an accomplished performer first, then taught others to perform. In 1919, Blades became a member of the Blades-Hitchborn Duo, and soon after played circus jobs. From circus work at The Hippodrome in Wisbech, the young artist moved on to orchestral percussion and sound effects performance with silent films and moving pictures. Early work in this area included playing at The Oxford Picture House in Workington, Cumberland, and playing in a dance band. Instrumentalists with whom he performed in this period of his career included a pianist and a violinist.

By 1927, Blades was performing at The Kinnaird Picture House in Dundee, and his first radio broadcast occurred a year later in Dundee where he played xylophone solos during the Children's Hour. From 1929 to 1931, the artist performed with Gerald Bright's dance band at the Hotel Majestic, St. Annes-on-Sea, with Al Davison's Claribel Band at The Villan Marina in Douglas, recorded featured xylophone solos with the Nat Star Band for several 78-rpm records, and worked as drum set performer and featured xylophonist with Jerry Hoey's ensemble at London's Piccadilly Hotel. He remained with the Hoey group until 1939, including regular BBC broadcasts from the hotel. Other similar work was at Gaumont British Film Studios with conductor Louis Levy, and at London Film Studios in Denham. From 1935 to 1980, James Blades recorded the superimposed gong sounds for Rank Films trademark.

In 1935, a long association with composer Benjamin Britten began, with Blades recording the composer's film music for The Night Mail and Coalface at G.P.O. London studio. During the Second World War, Blades performed in France, then returned to London, becoming a percussionist with the London Symphony Orchestra. His first full length broadcast was made in 1947 for a BBC Forces program entitled "The Orchestral Instruments of Percussion."

In 1947, Blades presented his first lecture recital, "The World of Percussion," with assistance by his wife. Blades' lecture recitals eventually became a regular presentation for music interest organizations, public schools and universities in Great Britain. Blades served as orchestral percussionist for the coronation of Queen Elizabeth II in Westminster Abbey, and in 1953 began an important association with The English Opera Group and The English Chamber Orchestra.

Institutional teaching by Blades has included instruction at The Royal Academy of Music in London and at the University of Surrey, in addition to being a private teacher for everyone who has read his books. He was for several years a regular performer with The Melos Ensemble, and has been cited for honor by numerous organizations. Some of these honors include an honorary membership in The Royal Academy of Music, a diploma for Men of Achievement, an honorary Master of Music from the University of Surrey, an honorary member of The Royal Society of Musicians, and a Fellow of The Royal Society of Arts. James Blades has toured England and Europe as a percussionist, and has attended festivals in Germany, Austria, Sweden, Greece, Poland, Russia, Australia and Canada.

Blades has consistently displayed originality and creative energy in addition to high quality performance in several forms. His courage to assert himself and his art has aided his profession in countless ways.

DISCOGRAPHY

As with Gladness and Ring Out Wild Bells. London Hospitals Massed Choirs, Farncombe, FWSC-U01.

Blades on Percussion. Discourses ABK-13.

Britten: Albert Herring. English Chamber Orchestra, Decca 274/6.

Britten: 'Cello Symphony. Rostropovich. English Chamber Orchestra. Decca SXL-6641.

Britten: Curlew River. English Chamber Orchestra. Decca 301.

Britten: Serenata Notturna. English Chamber Orchestra. Decca K-239.

Britten: The Prodigal Son. English Chamber Orchestra. Decca 438.

Britten: The War Requiem. English Chamber Orchestra. Decca 252-3.

Britten: Turn of the Screw. English Chamber Orchestra. Decca LXT-5053.

Britten: Violin Concerto. Lubotsky. Britten: Piano Concerto. Richter. English Chamber Orchestra. Decca SXL-6512.

Bruch: Concerto No. 1. Heifetz. Conducted by Sargent. RCA LSB-4061.

Carols for Choirs. Bach Choir, Willcocks. Philip Jones Brass Ensemble. O.U.P. 150.

Don Giovanni. English Chamber Orchestra. Bonynge, Sutherland. Decca 412-5.

Excerpts from Handel's "Messiah." Little Orchestra of London. EM1 MFP-2108.

Handel Coronation Anthems. Argo 1BBA-1001/4.

Harp, Celeste and Percussion. HMV 7EG-8675.

Holst: Capriccio. Conducted by Imogen Holst. Lyrita SRCS-44.

J.S. Bach: Suites No's. 2 and 3. English Chamber Orchestra. Phillips 6500-068.

Music of the Crusades. Early Music Consort of London, Munrow. Argo ZRG-673.

Peter and the Wolf. Little Orchestra of London. EM1 MPF-2126.

Songs for Children. Argo ZDA-4061.

36

Walton: <u>Facade</u>. ECS-566.
Walton: <u>Facade 1 and 2</u>. O.U.P. 210.
Walton: <u>The Bear</u>. English Chamber Orchestra. EM1 SAN-92.

BOOKS

<u>Drum Roll</u>. Autobiography. Faber and Faber, 1977.

<u>Drums and Drumming Today</u>. Boosey and Hawkes, 1964.

<u>Early Percussion Instruments</u>. Co-authored with Jeremy Montagu. Oxford University Press, 1976.

<u>How To Choose An Instrument</u>. Fountain Music Series No. 5, 1954.

<u>How To Play Drums</u>. Co-authored with J. Dean. Elm Tree Books, 1985.

<u>Orchestral Percussion Technique</u>. Oxford University Press, 1961. Also in Japanese.

<u>Percussion Instruments and Their History</u>. Praeger, 1970. Faber and Faber, 1984.

<u>Percussion Year Book</u>. Boosey and Hawkes, 1939.

<u>Play Tuned Percussion</u>. Co-authored with Michael Skinner. Faber Music, 1981.

ARTICLES

Articles on percussion. <u>The New Grove Dictionary of Music and Musicians</u>. Macmillan, 1980.

ARTICLES ABOUT SUBJECT

Goodwin, Simon. "James Blades: A Life of Percussion." <u>Modern Percussionist</u> I/1 (December 1984), 18.

REFERENCE SOURCES

Information supplied by the subject (July 1990).

Blakey, Art
Born October 11, 1919, Pittsburgh, Pennsylvania
Died October 16, 1990, New York, New York

Art Blakey, long-time leader of The Jazz Messengers, has been recorded many times. As a mentor and leader of young talent, he helped numerous jazz musicians get started in their careers, in addition to communicating the "jazz message" to audiences worldwide.

Blakey studied the piano during his elementary school years, and was primarily self taught at the drum set. He probably was a band leader as early as his secondary school years. In autumn, 1942, Blakey performed with Mary Lou Williams at Kelly's Stable in New York City. In 1943 and 1944, Blakey performed with the Fletcher Henderson Orchestra, including a lengthy tour of the southern region of the United States.

In 1955, Art Blakey formed the ensemble The Jazz Messengers with Horace Silver. In the early version of this group, other performers were Kenny Dorham and Hank Mobley. Silver left the ensemble in 1956, and Blakey continued as leader until 1990. Notable musicians who have passed through the Blakey bands include JoAnne Brackeen, Freddie Hubbard, Keith Jarrett, Chuck Mangione, Wynton Marsalis, and Woody Shaw. This author had the pleasure of hearing the Messengers with Blakey at a jazz festival in the Colorado Rocky Mountains in the early 1980s.

In retrospect, Art Blakey's professional maturity from 1940 to 1990 witnessed several important changes such as the proliferation of air travel, the invention of many electronic machines used in the music business, and a considerable growth of population worldwide. Still, the drum set of 1940 remained essentially unchanged in 1990, though musical styles were invented, developed and discovered during that period. Blakey and his music have had "staying power" in that his musical performance contained a certain level of quality and substance that is not always present elsewhere. In addition, Blakey's versatility in the broader arena along with consistency within the drum set and learned fundamentals allowed him to achieve continued success within the scope of an original aesthetic.

DISCOGRAPHY

Album of the Year. Timeless 155, 1981.

A Night at Birdland. Blue Note 5037-9, 1954.

Horace Silver and the Jazz Messengers. Blue Note 5058, 1954.

Jazz Messengers '70. Catalyst 7902, 1970.

Message from Kenya. Blue Note 1626, 1953.

Miles Davis: Weirdo. Blue Note 45-1650, 1954.

Recorded Live at Bubba's. Who's Who in Jazz 21019, 1980.

The Freedom Rider. Blue Note 84156, 1961.

Thelonius Monk: Who Knows? Blue Note 1565, 1947.

VIDEO RECORDING

Jazz at the Smithsonian: Art Blakey and the Jazz Messengers. Kultur, 1982.

ARTICLES ABOUT SUBJECT

"Art Blakey and the Jazz Messengers." Swing Journal XXXIII/2, 1979.

Frost, H. "Art Blakey in St. Louis." Metronome LXIII/2, 1947.

Humphrey, T. "The Art of Blakey Considered." Jazz Beat III/7, 1966.

Lovett, H. "Art Blakey." Metronome LXXII/6, 1956.

Porter, Lewis. "Blakey, Art." The New Grove Dictionary of Jazz, Volume One, 1988.

Stewart, Z. "Art Blakey in His Prime." Down Beat LII/7, 1985.

Tynan, J. "The Jazz Message." Down Beat XXIV/21, 1957.

REFERENCE SOURCES

Keezer, Ronald. Biographical information supplied about the subject (September 1990).

Buda, Fred
Born May 25, 1935, Boston, Massachusetts

Fred Buda, drum set performer for the Boston Pops Orchestra, has combined professional percussion performance in the classical and the popular music arenas. As a regular performer in an ensemble that receives national television coverage, Buda can be seen and heard at the drum set, or at other percussion instruments like the concert bass drum and the concert snare drum.

Buda graduated from the United States Navy School of Music in 1953, then played in the U.S. Navy Band for four years. After serving in the U.S. Navy Band, Buda enrolled at Boston University. At Boston University, he studied for ten years while earning a Bachelor of Music degree and a Master of Music degree. Private percussion teachers of Fred Buda included George L. Stone, Sonny Igoe and Charlie Smith, a member of the Boston Symphony Orchestra.

Fred Buda has performed variously as a freelance percussionist. Performance experience has included playing timpani in the Boston Ballet Orchestra and percussion at the Marlboro Music Festival. Buda has performed in various theaters as percussionist, and as staff percussionist for WGBH television station. He has performed with the Herb Pomeroy Jazz Orchestra and with the Boston Opera Orchestra. Buda is a charter member of the Boston Philharmonia. He has performed various types of shows such as Vaudeville and Ice Capades. Some of the major jazz figures with whom Buda has performed are Buddy DeFranco, Stan Getz and Mel Torme. Since 1968, Fred Buda has performed drum set and percussion with the Boston Pops Orchestra.

As a teacher, Buda is a former chairperson for the percussion area at the Berklee College of Music in Boston. He has taught at the New England Conservatory and the University of Lowell, serving as leader of the Jazz Pops Ensemble.

Fred Buda is an example of the modern percussionist who can perform competently on various instruments within the percussion family, in addition to performing with versatility in a selection of musical styles. Fortunately, he finds time to share his expertise with students and other interested persons in the Boston area and nationwide through the medium of television.

DISCOGRAPHY

Aisle Seat: Great Film Music. Boston Pops Orchestra, conducted by John Williams. Phillips 6514-328, 1982.

American Classics: Great Moments of Music. Boston Pops Orchestra, conducted by Arthur Fiedler. Time-Life Records STLS-7001.

Beethoven: Symphony No. 7. Marlboro Symphony Orchestra, conducted by Casals.

Other recordings with the Boston Pops Orchestra since 1968.

Stravinsky: Les Noces. Conducted by Robert Craft. Columbia Records.

REFERENCE SOURCES

Evening at Pops. Madison and Wausau: Wisconsin Public Television, August 17, 1991.

Information supplied by the subject (September 1989).

Burton, Gary
Born January 23, 1943, Anderson, Indiana

Vibraphone specialist Gary Burton is known as an effective educator and virtuoso performer. His primary positions have been recording artist, clinician, soloist, and college administrator.

Burton's higher education was received at the Berklee College of Music in Boston, Massachusetts, from 1960 to 1962. In 1963, Burton served as vibist with George Shearing Quintet. From 1964 to 1966, he played vibes with Stan Getz Quartet. Since 1967, Burton has led his own groups on tour and in recording sessions. An early award of Burton's was recognition as jazz player of the year by Down Beat magazine in 1968. Since 1971, Gary Burton has worked as a teacher and administrator at the Berklee College of Music in Boston.

Other professional endeavours of Burton have included music composition, arranging, and writing articles for publication. He also endorses vibraphone mallets that are manufactured within the music industry. Gary Burton is very talented and disciplined in an art form that allows creativity combined with technology.

DISCOGRAPHY

Alone at Last. ATL S-1598.
Concert in Zurich. ECM 1-1182.
Country Roads. VIC LSP 4908.
Crystal Silence. ECM 1024-ST.
Dreams So Real. ECM 1072-ST.
Duet. ECM 1-1140.
Duster. RCA LSP 3835.
Easy as Pie. ECM 1-1184.
Good Vibes. ATL S-1560.
Hotel Hello. ECM 1055-ST.
In Concert. VIC LSP 3985.

In the Public Interest. Polydor 6503.

Lyric Suite for Sextet. ECM 1-1260.

Paris Encounter. ATL S-1597.

Passengers. ECM 1092-ST.

Picture This. ECM 1-1226.

Reunion. GRP.

Ring. ECM 1051-ST.

Seven Songs for Quartet and Chamber Orchestra. ECM 1040-ST.

Slide Show. ECM.

Tennessee Firebird. RCA LSP 3719.

The New Quartet. ECM 1030-ST.

Times like These. GRP-9569.

Times Square. ECM 1-1111.

Whiz Kids. ECM.

With Keith Jarrett. ATL S-1577.

COMPOSITIONS

Solo. Glenview, Illinois: Creative Music, 1966.

BOOKS

Four Mallet Studies. Glenview: Creative Music, 1968.

ARTICLES

"Evolution of Mallet Techniques--1973." Percussionist X/3 (Spring 1973), 74.

ARTICLES ABOUT SUBJECT

Howland, Harold. "Gary Burton: The Enfant Terrible at Forty," Part 2. Percussive Notes 21/5 (July 1983).

Larrick, Geary. Analytical and Biographical Writings in Percussion Music. New York: Peter Lang, 1989, page 177.

Larrick, Geary. "Gary Burton: 'The Sunset Bell'." Percussionist XIII/2 (Winter 1976), 48.

Mattingly, Rick. "Gary Burton." <u>Modern Percussionist</u> I/1 (December 1984), 6.

REFERENCE SOURCES

Information supplied by the subject (September 1989).

Cahn, Ruth Patricia McLean
Born March 17, 1946, McKeesport, Pennsylvania

As a member of a major symphony orchestra since graduation from college, Ruth Cahn has specialized in keyboard percussion, cymbals and committee work. In addition, she has taught and performed chamber music.

After graduation from secondary school, Cahn attended the University of Rochester's Eastman School of Music. At the Eastman School, her emphases were percussion performance and music education. She received the Bachelor of Music degree in 1968. From 1966 to 1968, Ruth Cahn studied percussion with *Stanley Leonard, timpanist in the Pittsburgh Symphony Orchestra. While at Eastman, she studied percussion with *William Street and *John Beck. From 1974 to 1978, Cahn studied classical music of northern India with Kahmud Rhanjan Banarjee at the Chautauqua Institution in western New York.

Since 1970, Ruth Cahn has worked as a percussionist in the Rochester Philharmonic Orchestra following a year as a part-time performer. During the summer of 1966, Cahn performed as timpanist with the New Hampshire Music Festival Orchestra. From 1967 to 1979, she was percussionist with the Chautauqua Symphony Orchestra and Chautauqua Opera Orchestra. From 1968 to 1975, Ruth Cahn was timpanist for Disney Parade Presentations. Since 1968, she has recorded sound tracks for the National Museum of Space in Washington, D.C. From 1968 to 1972, Cahn served as co-founder of New Diaphony, a flute and percussion duo that specialized in the performance of contemporary classical music. Since 1968, she has performed frequently as recitalist in ensemble, including several first performances of new music compositions. From 1974 to 1980, she was a member of the Rochester Marimba Band. Regular performances since 1976 for Ruth Cahn have included appearances with the Society for Chamber Music, the Rochester

---

* S. Leonard, W. Street and J. Beck are subjects in this book.

Chamber Orchestra, the Hochstein at Noon recital series, and the Unitarian Church recital series in Rochester, New York.

As a recording artist, Ruth Cahn has played for radio and television broadcasts with the Rochester Philharmonic since 1966, and recorded for both radio and television with the Chautauqua Symphony Orchestra from 1966 to 1978. In 1986, she served as interim principal percussionist with the Rochester Philharmonic for four months. Also in that year, Cahn performed as both actor and musician in a production by Rochester Classical Videos of a theater arrangement of Hector Berlioz's "March to the Scaffold." In 1987, she performed as marimbist with Roger Williams Show. She has been an artist-in-residence for the Rochester City School District since 1985.

As a teacher of music and percussion, Ruth Cahn's experience has been varied. She has worked in the Community Education Division of the Eastman School of Music since 1975, where she founded the organization's percussion ensemble. She is a senior associate with that department. From 1972 to 1975, Cahn taught at Nazareth College in Rochester. Since 1984, she has been director of the Music Horizons summer program for high school students at the Eastman School, and has served as coordinator of the Careers in Music seminar for secondary school students. Programs that she has presented as a musical artist for the Rochester City School District include "Instruments around the World," "Drumming," "Meet the Composer," and "Friends of the Philharmonic." As a part-time faculty member in music therapy in the late 1960s, she taught for the Board of Cooperative Educational Services serving Rochester area schools. In 1989, she was a featured soloist with the Philharmonic on a concert series entitled "Drummer's Delite." In 1990, she presented a solo percussion recital at the Unitarian Church.

Besides performance and teaching, Ruth Cahn has worked with numerous committees in Rochester. Since 1976, she has been a member of search committees for the Philharmonic for positions of president, marketing director and chief executive director. Other Philharmonic committees with which she has served include groups for nominations, development, operations and development, pensions, and a future endowments committee. With the Community Education Division, she has served on various committees as well as participated in various forums regarding alumni, women's issues and the music education department. For the Philharmonic, she has also served on the Youth Orchestra board, the finance committee, and as chairperson of a conductor search committee.

In her native state of Pennsylvania, Ruth Cahn received the Hall of Fame award in 1988 at McKeesport High School for her many achievements in music performance and education. In 1989, she helped to present music programs in public schools of Pennsylvania for the Mon-Yough Valley Educational Consortium.

Ruth Cahn's professional associations include the Percussive Arts Society, International Conference of Symphony and Opera Musicians, Arts for Greater Rochester, Mu Phi Epsilon Music Sorority, American Federation of Musicians, and the Rochester Philharmonic League. In 1982, Cahn collaborated with Dr. Ellen Koskoff, ethnomusicologist at the Eastman School, supported with a grant from the New York State Council on the Arts. The project was entitled "Music for Wood" and included research at the Rochester Museum and Science Center, public lectures for children and adults, and creation of a music composition titled "Music from Wood." This piece featured wooden instruments from various cultures.

Professional percussionist Ruth Cahn has made her presence known in several areas. She has worked in both leadership and supporting roles as an artist musician, teacher, performer and humanitarian.

DISCOGRAPHY

Adler, Samuel. Flute Concerto. Rochester Philharmonic.

Beethoven Classics. Canadian Brass and others.

Leroy Anderson Pops. Rochester Philharmonic conducted by Erich Kunzel.

Other recordings with the Rochester Philharmonic Orchestra and the Rochester Pops Orchestra since 1968.

"William Walton: Facade Suite." Society for Chamber Music, Rochester, New York, 1985.

COMPOSITIONS

<u>Music from Wood</u>. Collaborated with Ellen Koskoff, 1982.

REFERENCE SOURCES

Information supplied by the subject (September 1989).

Cahn, William L.
Born November 11, 1946, Philadelphia, Pennsylvania

William Cahn serves his profession as an orchestral percussionist, as a chamber music performer, as a composer, and as a publisher. This multiple approach to his work has allowed him to participate in the public performance of historically important music, and to be active in contemporary approaches to his art.

Cahn began playing percussion instruments in elementary school in the Philadelphia schools. One of his early teachers was Joseph Huttlin, with whom he began study in the seventh grade, continuing until 1964. From 1960 to 1964, Cahn studied percussion with *Fred Hinger, timpanist in the Philadelphia Orchestra. During this time, Cahn received the opportunity to attend symphony orchestra concerts. Another of Cahn's important experiences during secondary school was studying music appreciation with Dr. Saul Feinberg, and learning music theory and composition. Other activities during his Philadelphia school years included the band, orchestra and dance band at Lincoln High School, in addition to performing in all-city bands and orchestras. For four years, Cahn performed in the Settlement Music School Percussion Ensemble directed by Philadelphia Orchestra percussionist Alan Abel.

Also at Settlement Music School, William Cahn studied the horn with Anton Ryva; at this time he was a member of the Philadelphia Youth Orchestra under the direction of Joseph Primavera. Cahn composed his first work for percussion ensemble in 1963, titled "Miniature Suite." As a student, he organized a school percussion ensemble and appeared on Philadelphia Orchestra young people's concerts. He also played a featured marimba solo on an NBC-TV affiliated station in Philadelphia, performing J.S. Bach's "Concerto in A Minor." In 1964, Cahn performed at the Marlboro Music Festival, and as timpanist for the Ventnor Music Festival Orchestra.

*F. Hinger is a subject in this book.

After secondary schooling, William Cahn enrolled at the Eastman School of Music, studying percussion there with *William Street and *John Beck. Cahn graduated from Eastman School in 1968 with a Bachelor of Music degree including a Performer's Certificate. One of his peers at Eastman School was *Bob Becker, who later joined Nexus ensemble with Cahn.

In September, 1968, William Cahn became principal percussionist in the Rochester Philharmonic where he has remained. From 1968 to 1970, Cahn taught percussion in the Eastman School of Music's preparatory department. As the principal percussionist in the Rochester Philharmonic, he has been responsible for performance of difficult parts, assignment of parts, and selection of extra players.

Besides performing regularly with the Philharmonic and touring with Nexus chamber percussion ensemble, William Cahn has performed various engagements during the past few decades. Cahn has performed as percussionist in the Chautauqua Symphony Orchestra, the Toronto Symphony, Paul Winter Consort, Chuck Mangione Orchestra, the Rochester Chamber Orchestra, at the Grand Teton Festival, and for the Ice Capades. As a drum set performer, Cahn has played in miscellaneous shows featuring artists Chet Atkins, Carman Cavallero, Judy Collins, Jimmy Durante, Tony Martin, Al Martino and Marian McPartland. He has performed with the New Moog Quartet and at the Pocono Playhouse. Cahn has also performed in shows featuring artists Carol Channing, Rowan and Martin, "Doc" Severensen, and The Supremes.

As a featured percussionist and soloist, William Cahn has performed many times with Nexus ensemble, at the CBC Towne Hall Series, the Corning Symphony Orchestra, the New Hampshire Music Festival, the Rochester Philharmonic, the Rochester Chamber Orchestra, and the Detroit Symphony Orchestra. Cahn has also performed as a featured percussionist with the Toledo Symphony Orchestra, the Buffalo Philharmonic, the National Arts Center Orchestra, and with the Toronto Symphony. William Cahn is married to Rochester Philharmonic percussionist Ruth Cahn.

---

*W. Street, J. Beck and B. Becker are subjects in this volume.

William Cahn has composed a considerable number of works and publishes some of them through his own firm called William L. Cahn Publishing. In 1985, he wrote and produced a classical music video recording entitled "March to the Scaffold," featuring the Rochester Philharmonic Orchestra. This six minute video has been played over public television stations in the United States and in Australia. In August, 1987, the video was featured on CBS News Sunday Morning. His works have been performed in various countries and at schools in North America. In addition to percussion compositions, Cahn has written for symphony orchestra as accompaniment to featured percussion ensemble.

With the ensemble Nexus, Cahn has toured worldwide and performed at Percussive Arts Society International Conventions. Nexus has performed with several orchestras including the major ones in Toronto, New York City, Cleveland and at Tanglewood. With Nexus, Cahn has constructed various percussion instruments for presentation in chamber music environments in addition to his usual performance of the standard percussion instruments such as snare drum, timpani and xylophone. His activity with Nexus since its formation in the early 1970s has included, besides tours and featured solo appearances, recordings and sound tracks. Nexus's original film score accompaniments include music for an Academy Award winning documentary entitled "The Man Who Skied Down Everest." With the Nexus ensemble, Cahn has played novelty music, improvised music and composed music, in a variety of styles including avant garde, minimalistic, ragtime, in combinations of diverse cultural influences like African, Asian and American.

William Cahn's urban background has allowed him to be around major symphony orchestras for all of his career and early education. He has studied with masters in the field, and worked with some of the most successful professionals performing in the twentieth century. His impressive technique is accompanied by a sense of humor and a variety of musical interests.

DISCOGRAPHY

Compact disc recordings with the Rochester Pops, conducted by Erich Kunzel.

Eastman Wind Ensemble. Decca LP DL-710157, DL-710163.

John Teleska. Cassette HPCS-2.

Nexus. Black Sun CD-15002-2, Epic LP KE-33501, Nexus CD 10251, 10262, 10273, Nexus NE-01, NE-02, NE-03, NE-04, NE-05, Umbrella DD-2.

Paul Winter Consort. A & M LP SP-4698, Living Music LP LMR-1.

Rochester Philharmonic Orchestra. Bainbridge LP BT-6241, Pantheon LP PFN2041, RCA LP ARL1-0459, RPO LP TT-001, Vox LP TV-34705, Vox LP VCL9001, Vox LP TV-34705.

VIDEO RECORDING

Supercussion. Nexus. Necavenue A88V-3.

COMPOSITIONS

Arrangements for marimba ensemble. W.L. Cahn Publishing.

A Walk in the Garden of Earthly Delights for female voices and percussion. W.L. Cahn.

Changes for percussion trio. W.L. Cahn.

Etude for Taperecorder and Percussion for percussionist with taped accompaniment. W.L. Cahn.

In Ancient Temple Gardens for featured percussionist with four percussion accompanists. W.L. Cahn.

Miniature Suite for six percussionists. W.L. Cahn.

Nara for solo percussion. W.L. Cahn.

Partita for solo percussion. W.L. Cahn.

Perplexus for percussionist with taped accompaniment. W.L. Cahn.

Quiet Music for tuba, timpani and percussion. W.L. Cahn.

Raga No. 1 for solo timpani. Wimbledon Music.

Six Pieces for Percussion for three percussionists. W.L. Cahn.

Sonata for Trombone and Percussion for trombone and three percussion. W.L. Cahn.

Ten Pieces for Flute and Percussion for flutist and percussionist. W.L. Cahn.

The Recital Piece for solo xylophonist with self-prepared taped accompaniment. W.L. Cahn.

Tides for ten percussionists. W.L. Cahn.

BOOKS

Cartoons of George Hamilton Green. William L. Cahn Publishing.

The Xylophone in Acoustic Recordings (1877-1929), with tape recorded examples. W.L. Cahn.

REFERENCE SOURCES

Information supplied by the subject (September 1989 and April 1991).

Chenoweth, Vida
Born c. 1929, Enid, Oklahoma

Vida Chenoweth is known worldwide as a concert marimbist, scholar and ethnomusicologist. Chenoweth earned an associate diploma in arts at William Woods College in 1949. In 1950, she earned a certificate in French language at L'Alliance Francaise in Paris, France. She earned a Bachelor of Music degree in music literature and percussion performance at Northwestern University in 1951. In 1954, Chenoweth earned a Master of Music degree in music theory and percussion at American Conservatory of Music in Chicago. She studied Spanish in 1957 at the Instituto Guatemalteco-Americano in Guatemala City. In 1962-63, Chenoweth studied Greek language and Biblical "New Testament" literature at Asbury Theological Seminary. In 1974, she earned a Doctor of Philosophy degree in ethnomusicology and linguistics at the University of Auckland in New Zealand. Chenoweth has been a music professor in the Conservatory of Music at Wheaton College in Illinois since 1975.

Dr. Chenoweth's teaching experience began as an instructor of marimba at Phillips University in Enid, Oklahoma, in 1946. In 1954, she taught marimba in a private studio in Evanston, Illinois, and in 1972 taught likewise in Auckland, New Zealand. As a concert artist, Vida Chenoweth began performing in 1951 in New York and worldwide for Epic Records. Other recital locations have included Wheaton College in 1979, and Alice Tully Hall at Lincoln Center in New York City in 1980. She has also taught in Papua New Guinea, at the University of Queensland in Australia, at Bible College of New Zealand, and at the University of Oklahoma.

In 1957, Vida Chenoweth worked as a Fulbright Scholar. She has contributed to Grove's Dictionary of Music and Musicians, and to the Journal of the Society for Ethnomusicology. She has also served as a reviewer for the Journal of the Polynesian Society, for the Yearbook of the International Folk Music Council, and the Yearbook for Traditional Music. Chenoweth is an honorary member of the Japan Xylophone Association.

Vida Chenoweth's travels in the pursuit of scholarship have taken her to various places around the United States and into foreign countries. Some of her scholarly work has taken place in Africa at various places, and in South America, as well as in Asia, Australia and North America. Her recorded interpretations of some of *Clair Musser's marimba etudes probably will not be surpassed. Similarly, her scholarly accomplishments and writings have been and are important, forward looking and relevant.

DISCOGRAPHY

"Concertino for Marimba and Orchestra by Paul Creston and Concertino for Marimba and Orchestra by Jorge Alvaro Sarmientos." Wheaton, Illinois: The College Bookstore, CMP-VC1, 1987.
Vida Chenoweth: Classic Marimbist. CBS Epic P-17808.

BOOKS

Information of the Marimba by David Vela, translated by V. Chenoweth. Auckland, New Zealand: Institute Press, 1978.
Musical Instruments of Papua New Guinea, edited by V. Chenoweth. Papua New Guinea: Summer Institute of Linguistics, 1976.
New Testament. Translated into Usarufa language of Papua New Guinea by V. Chenoweth. South Holland, Illinois: Park Press, 1980.
The Marimbas of Guatemala. Lexington: University of Kentucky Press, 1964. Second edition, Hong Kong: Christian Communications, 1978.
The Usarufas and Their Music. Dallas: Museum of Anthropology, 1979.

ARTICLES

"Defining the Marimba and the Xylophone Inter-Culturally." Percussionist 1/1 (1963).
"Four-Mallet Technique." Percussionist 1/2 (1963).
"Mallet Position with Two Mallets." Percussionist 1/2 (1963).

---

*C. Musser is a subject in this book.

"Musicianship." Percussionist 1/4 (1964).

"Pioneering the Marimba." Percussive Notes (December 1964).

"Song Structure of a New Guinea Highlands Tribe." Ethnomusicology 10:285-97 (1964).

"The Differences among Xylophone-Marimba-Vibraphone." The Instrumentalist (June 1961).

"The Marimba." International Musician (November 1959).

"The Marimba: A Challenge to the Composer," Part I. Ludwig Drummer 4/1 (1964).

"The Marimba and the Xylophone." School Musician (February 1971).

"The Marimba Comes into Its Own." Music Journal (May 1957).

"Vida Chenoweth: Practicing Hints, Marimba (four-mallet etudes) and 'Wachet Auf by Philipp Nicolai," c. 1600, (transcribed for marimba)." Master Technique Builders for Vibraphone and Marimba compiled and edited by *Anthony J. Cirone. Miami: Belwin-Mills, 1985.

ARTICLES ABOUT SUBJECT

Bergdall, Calvin. "Marimbist Swaps Careers." Wichita Eagle, December 12, 1964.

Diehl, Oliveira. "Unique Concert at Taman Ismail Marzuki." Indonesian Observer, Djakarta, September 11, 1969.

James, Henry C. "Asbury Seminary Student Is Leading Marimba Artist." Lexington Leader, January 24, 1962.

Kammerer, Raphael. "Marimba." Musical America, March, 1961.

McCardell, Antony, reviewer. "Melodic Perception and Analysis." The Australian Journal of Music Education, October, 1973.

McLean, Mervyn, reviewer. "Musical Instruments of Papua New Guinea." Polynesian Journal, 1976.

Milmore, Eleanor. "Master of the Marimba." Young Keyboard, October, 1964.

Nelson, Mary Jo. "Carnegie Hall Beckons Sooner." Oklahoma City Times, November 7, 1959.

_____

*A.J. Cirone is a subject in this book.

58

North, William. "College Professor Inducted into Oklahoma Hall of Fame." <u>Wheaton Leader</u>, December 11, 1985.

*Stevens, Leigh Howard. "An Interview with Vida Chenoweth." <u>Percussive Notes</u> 15/3, 1977.

Thomas, Allan, reviewer. "The Usarufas and Their Music." <u>Journal of the Polynesian Society</u>, June, 1982.

"Two by Americans." <u>Time</u>, November 23, 1959.

"Vida Chenoweth, Concertista de la Marimba en Guatemala." <u>El Imparcial</u>, Guatemala, July 13, 1957.

"Vida Chenoweth's Debut in Europe Slated This Fall." <u>Daily Oklahoman</u>, Oklahoma City, September 2, 1962.

REFERENCE SOURCES

Information supplied by the subject (August 1990).

---

*L.H. Stevens is a subject in this book.

Cirone, Anthony J.
Born November 8, 1941, Jersey City, New Jersey

Anthony Cirone is one of a few orchestral percussionists whose influence in his field has reached beyond the symphony hall into the educational publishing industry. His contacts with major orchestra performers have allowed him to widen his scope beyond mere production toward practical artistry.

Cirone studied at The Juilliard School in New York City, earning a Bachelor of Science degree in 1964 and a Master of Science degree in 1965. Following graduation from Juilliard, he became percussionist in the San Francisco Symphony Orchestra in California, where he has remained. Since 1983, Cirone has served as a lecturer in percussion at Stanford University. Other teaching has been at San Jose State University. Additionally, Anthony Cirone has served as a consultant for CPP/Belwin Publications, and as a percussion clinician for the Zildjian cymbal company.

As a composer, Cirone has written several works for percussion musical instruments. As an author, he has written numerous articles and method books. Cirone's snare drum method book entitled Portraits in Rhythm is one of the most effective stylistic study collections published in this century. His method book entitled Master Technique Builders for Vibraphone and Marimba incorporates master lessons by several important percussionists, including *Keiko Abe, *Bob Becker, *Vida Chenoweth, *David Friedman, *Bobby Hutcherson, William Moersch, *Bill Molenhof, *Ted Piltzecker, Ed Saindon, *Dave Samuels, and *Gordon Stout. In Cirone's method book, each master lesson includes a photograph of the artist, some biographical information about that person, an essay by the performer regarding his or her philosophy of performance, and several etudes or exercises composed by that performer. This fine publication is an example of

---

*K. Abe, B. Becker, V. Chenoweth, D. Friedman, B. Hutcherson, B. Molenhof, T. Piltzecker, D. Samuels and G. Stout are subjects in this volume.

the kind of sharing of information, ideas and music that has been effected by Cirone in the latter half of the twentieth century.

DISCOGRAPHY

Carnival of the Animals. New York Philharmonic Orchestra conducted by Leonard Bernstein. Columbia ML-5768, 1962.

Music Makers. Standard School Broadcast, Percussion. SOCAL M-21, 1974.

76 Pieces of Explosive Percussion. Sonic Arts LS-11, 1976.

VIDEO RECORDINGS

Concert Percussion - A Performer's Guide. Masterplan Video Series #4514 and #4515, 1989.

COMPOSITIONS

Assimilation. Percussion ensemble, 1964. Miami, Florida: Belwin-Mills.

Dichotomy. Percussion ensemble. Miami: Belwin-Mills.

Double Concerto for Two Percussion and Orchestra. Miami: Belwin-Mills.

Five Items for Soprano and Percussion. Soloist and percussion ensemble. Miami: Belwin-Mills.

Japanese Impressions. Percussion ensemble. Miami: Belwin-Mills.

Sonata No. 1. Timpani and piano. Miami: Belwin-Mills.

Sonata No. 2. Percussion and trumpet. Miami: Belwin-Mills.

Sonata No. 3. Clarinet and percussion. Miami: Belwin-Mills.

Sonata No. 4. Violin, piano and percussion. Miami: Belwin-Mills.

Triptych. Percussion quartet. Miami: Belwin-Mills.

4/4 for Four. Percussion quartet. Miami: Belwin-Mills.

BOOKS

Master Technique Builders for Snare Drum. Miami: Belwin-Mills.

Master Technique Builders for Vibraphone and Marimba. Miami: Belwin-Mills.

Orchestral Techniques of the Standard Percussion Instruments. Miami: Belwin-Mills.

Portraits for Timpani. Miami: Belwin-Mills.

Portraits in Melody. Miami: Belwin-Mills.

Portraits in Rhythm. Miami: Belwin-Mills, 1966.

The Logic of It All. Co-authored with Joe Sinai. Miami: Belwin-Mills.

The Orchestral Mallet Player. Miami: Belwin-Mills.

The Orchestral Series Score. Miami: Belwin-Mills.

The Orchestral Snare Drummer. Miami: Belwin-Mills.

The Orchestral Timpanist. Miami: Belwin-Mills.

ARTICLES

"Portraits in Rhythm: Etude #3." Modern Percussionist II/3 (June 1986), 36.

"Portraits in Rhythm: Etude #4." Modern Percussionist II/4 (September 1986), 46.

"Portraits in Rhythm: Etude #5." Modern Percussionist III/1 (December 1986), 50.

"Portraits in Rhythm: Etude #6." Modern Percussionist III/2 (March 1987), 24.

"Portraits in Rhythm: Etude #8." Modern Percussionist III/4 (September 1987), 32.

"3/8 Etude." Modern Percussionist II/2 (March 1986), 50.

REFERENCE SOURCES

Information supplied by the subject (September 1989).

Clark, Owen
Born July 16, 1938, Winnipeg, Manitoba, Canada

Owen Clark has worked in the field of percussion as a teacher, performer, composer and consultant. Clark received his post-secondary education in both Canada and the United States. At McGill University in Montreal, Quebec, he was awarded a Licentiate Diploma in Performance, with high distinction in percussion. In 1971, Clark received a Bachelor of Music degree at McGill. In 1974, he earned a Master of Science in Education with an emphasis in music at Moorhead State University in Minnesota. During the 1978 school year, Clark studied privately in Chicago, Illinois, with Geraldo di Olivera, from whom he learned about percussion techniques in music of Brazil. In 1989, Clark participated in private study at the University of Delaware in the areas of laser video disk technology and CD-ROM technology. An example of Clark's continuing education in his career is his attendance at a conference in Toronto in 1990 on the subject of North American music.

An important position of Owen Clark has been his service as a faculty member at the University of Manitoba in Winnipeg since 1977. At the University of Manitoba, Clark has taught percussion and computer applications, and conducted the percussion ensemble. Since 1984, he has served as a digital arts consultant for the Seven Oaks School District.

Clark has participated in his art form in several ways, including work as a drummer, percussionist, singer, bass player, composer, music arranger, teacher, computer music specialist, and businessperson. He has displayed ability at moving from one style of music to another, such as jazz music, classical music, and various popular forms like rock, country, Latin American and musical theater. Clark has performed for CBC television and radio stations, as well as recorded numerous jingles, films, documentaries, albums and video recordings in Winnipeg recording studios.

As a freelance musician in the Winnipeg area since 1975, Owen Clark has performed with several ensembles. He has played with the Ice Capades in

1975 and 1977-79, the Owen and Barbara Clark Band since 1978, and the Winnipeg Symphony Orchestra from 1975 to 1983--including the position of principal percussion in 1980 and 1981. Other ensembles in which Clark has played include the CBC Montreal Opera Orchestra, Les Grande Ballets Canadienne, the National Arts Centre Orchestra in Ottawa, the Fargo-Moorhead Symphony Orchestra, the Royal Winnipeg Ballet Orchestra, the Manitoba Opera Company Orchestra, and the CBC Winnipeg Orchestra. He has also performed with the Manitoba Chamber Orchestra from 1975 to 1983.

As a teacher in addition to his specialty, Owen Clark has lectured in music history on the topics of popular music and film music. In the 1980s, he worked as an electronic music consultant for Infotech of Manitoba, as an educational consultant for Roland Canada Music in Vancouver, as an educational consultant for Apple/Canada, and as an educational consultant for Commodore Business Machines. As a leader in electronic music in his region, Clark has been active with the Manitoba Arts Council's artist visitation programs around Manitoba, and has participated in curriculum development in cooperation with the Seven Oaks Schools. His many collaborations include work with poets, dancers, school music teachers, composers and other percussionists. He has been a member of the board for the Winnipeg Musicians Association, president of the Manitoba Percussive Arts Society, and has worked with Tourism Industries Association of Winnipeg. His multitalented abilities and willingness to share his expertise have been an important facet of music in Manitoba in the twentieth century.

DISCOGRAPHY

Recordings with CBC.
Recordings with Winnipeg Symphony Orchestra.

MUSIC AND SOUND-EFFECTS RECORDINGS

Apple/Canada MIDI demonstration. Education tour, 1988.
Astronomers at the Leading Edge. Manitoba Planetarium, May, 1988.
Christmas Magic - Christmas Lights. Manitoba Planetarium, December, 1987.

Galaxies. Manitoba Planetarium, March, 1988.

Music of the Spheres. Manitoba Planetarium, November, 1988.

Return to Mars. Manitoba Planetarium, September, 1988.

Supernova. Manitoba Planetarium, October, 1987.

The Unseen Hand. MTC Warehouse Theatre, March, 1988.

The Visitors. Manitoba Planetarium, March, 1989.

Windhammen. Ghost Town Productions, 1988.

COMPOSITIONS

Batucada I. Percussion ensemble. Winnipeg: Clark Percussion, 1978.

Haiku. Percussion duo written to complement dance choreography by Rachel Brown based on selected Haiku poetry, 1980.

Halflight. Percussion quartet. Winnipeg: Clark Percussion, 1969.

Nite of the Bocor. Octet for voice, narrator and percussion. Winnipeg: Clark Percussion.

Quasi-Bossa Nova. Percussion quintet. Cleveland: Ludwig Music Publishing, 1965.

Right Hand Swing, Left Hand March. Solo drum set. Winnipeg: Clark Percussion.

The Cat. Trio for percussion, tape and dance. Winnipeg: Clark Percussion, 1977.

The Opener. Percussion septet. Winnipeg: Clark Percussion.

REFERENCE SOURCES

Information supplied by the subject (February 1990).

Colgrass, Michael
Born April 22, 1932, Chicago, Illinois

Michael Colgrass has earned a reputation for excellence in music composition following an emphasis on professional percussion performance earlier in his career. Colgrass received a Bachelor of Music degree at the University of Illinois in 1956. One of his major teachers there was percussionist Paul Price. The university percussion ensemble at the University of Illinois that included Colgrass was one of the early pedagogical ensembles in higher education in America. Colgrass's composition titled Three Brothers was first performed by that university ensemble in 1951, was later published, and became an often performed work nationwide. Other teachers of Colgrass were Darius Milhaud, Eugene Weigel, Lukas Foss, Wallingford Riegger and Ben Weber. During his undergraduate study, Colgrass studied at the Aspen Music School in Colorado and at Tanglewood in Massachusetts.

After graduation from college, Colgrass moved to New York City where he worked as a freelance percussionist while building his skills as a composer. Two of his published articles appeared during this period in the New York Times. As a resident of New York, Colgrass performed part-time with the New York Philharmonic, with an orchestra conducted by Igor Stravinsky, and several opera, ballet and musical theater orchestras. One of the musical theater orchestras that Colgrass performed in was an ensemble performing for Leonard Bernstein's West Side Story. In 1967, Colgrass quit performing in order to devote more time to music composition. He moved to Toronto, Ontario, Canada, in 1974.

As a successful composer, Colgrass has received the Pulitzer Prize, a Ford Foundation grant, Guggenheim Fellowships, a Fromm Foundation commission, and a Rockefeller grant. At various times, Colgrass has conducted his own works and performed narrations during the presentation of his compositions. Three of his popular percussion works besides the previously mentioned Three Brothers, are Inventions on a Motive, Percussion

Music and <u>Variations for Four Drums and Viola</u>. He has received many commissions to compose music for major orchestras and chamber ensembles. Michael Colgrass represents a type of success that was not achieved prior to the twentieth century by percussionists. Previously, most composers were specialists on another instrument. In this century, however, classical art forms involving the percussion have matured. Therefore, or perhaps coincidentally, percussionists have become successful composers at the highest level of achievement.

DISCOGRAPHY

"Fantasy Variations." <u>Percussion at Fredonia</u>. Fort Lauderdale, Florida: Music for Percussion, ADP-075S.

<u>Variations for Four Drums and Viola</u>. Fort Lauderdale: Music for Percussion, MGM E-3714.

COMPOSITIONS

<u>As Quiet As</u>, 1966.

<u>Auras</u>, 1977.

<u>Chamber Piece for Percussion Quintet</u>, Music for Percussion.

<u>Concert Masters</u>, 1976.

<u>Concertino for Timpani</u>, with brass and percussion accompaniment, Music for Percussion.

<u>Divertimento</u>, 1960.

<u>Fantasy-Variations for Eight Chromatic Drums and Percussion Sextet</u>, Music for Percussion.

<u>Inventions on a Motive</u>, Music for Percussion.

<u>Light Spirit</u>, 1963.

<u>Percussion Music</u>, Music for Percussion.

<u>Rhapsodic Fantasy</u>, 1965.

<u>Theatre of the Universe</u>, 1977.

<u>Three Brothers</u>, 1951, Music for Percussion.

<u>Variations for Four Drums and Viola</u>, Music for Percussion.

ARTICLES

"Then I Stood on my Head." <u>New York Times</u>, May 28, 1972.

"Wanted: Music for the Young." <u>New York Times</u>, August 3, 1969.

ARTICLES ABOUT SUBJECT

Baldwin, John. "Chapter News and Membership News." <u>Percussion News</u> (February 1990).

"Colgrass, Michael Charles." <u>Who's Who in America</u>, Volume One, 45th edition. Wilmette, Illinois: Macmillan Directory Division, 1988.

<u>International Musician</u> 89/6 (December 1990), 15.

Stone, Kurt. "Colgrass, Michael." <u>The New Grove Dictionary of Music and Musicians</u>, Volume Four, edited by Stanley Sadie. Macmillan, 1980.

REFERENCE SOURCES

Colgrass, Michael. <u>Inventions on a Motive</u>. Music for Percussion, 1969.

Parks, Walter. "The Origin of the Percussion Program in the American University: The University of Illinois." <u>National Association of College Wind and Percussion Instructors Journal</u> XXXIV/3 (Spring 1986), 4.

Culp, Paula N.
Born 1941, Fort Smith, Arkansas

Paula Culp's career as an orchestral percussionist has been characterized by a high level of performance technique in major symphony orchestras. In 1963, Culp received a Bachelor of Music degree at Oberlin College in northern Ohio. Her private study there in the Conservatory of Music was with Cleveland Orchestra timpanist *Cloyd Duff. During her undergraduate study, Culp attended the Mozarteum in Salzburg, Austria, for a year. After graduating from Oberlin, Culp enrolled at Indiana University in Bloomington, where she received the opportunity to study with George Gaber. As a graduate student, Paula Culp taught percussion part-time. In 1965, she received a Master of Music degree at Indiana University, also earning a Performer's Award.

After graduation from Indiana, Culp became timpanist for the Metropolitan Opera National Company for two years. In 1967, she became principal percussionist with the Indianapolis Symphony Orchestra for one season. She became a percussionist in the Minnesota Orchestra in 1968, serving presently as associate principal timpanist and assistant principal percussionist.

Conductors with whom Paula Culp has performed include Leonard Slatkin, Stanislaw Scrowaczewski, and Edo de Waart. She has biographical listings in The International Who's Who in Music, Who's Who in Entertainment, and the World Who's Who of Women.

DISCOGRAPHY

Recordings with the Minnesota Orchestra since 1968.
World's Greatest Overtures. The Minnesota Orchestra conducted by Leonard Slatkin. Pro Arte DDD CDM-813, 1987.

---

* C. Duff is a subject in this book.

ARTICLES

"Questions and Answers: Mounting and Adjusting the Plastic Timpani Head."

REFERENCE SOURCES

Information supplied by the subject (1989).

Dahlgren, Marvin
Born September 8, 1924, Minneapolis, Minnesota

Orchestral percussionist Marv Dahlgren is known for an equal competence as an improvisatory vibraphone player. He received his early education in secondary school, in the Naval Reserve as a pilot, and at MacPhail College of Music. Dahlgren earned a Bachelor's degree in 1950 at MacPhail, majoring in music composition. At MacPhail, he studied snare drum and keyboard percussion with Merv Ellefson, and timpani with Minneapolis Symphony Orchestra timpanist Henry Denecke. Dahlgren joined the Minneapolis Symphony in 1951, staying with that organization since that time. His position title with the presently named Minnesota Orchestra is Principal Percussion and Assistant Timpani.

Besides performing with the Minnesota Orchestra, Dahlgren has performed as a freelance percussionist in both classical and jazz music. From 1954 to 1959, he performed timpani and percussion with the Minneapolis Pops Orchestra. From 1959 to 1967, he was staff percussionist at the Guthrie Theatre. He has performed with the Ice Capades ensemble in Minneapolis four times, and has recorded many commercials and music for dance groups and theaters with Herb Pilhofer at Sound 80 Recording Studio. Since 1987, Dahlgren has performed with the Minneapolis Percussion Trio especially for young audience concerts.

Marv Dahlgren, in addition to performing, has served as a percussion clinician and teacher. He has taught at MacPhail College of Music, at the University of Minnesota, at Saint Olaf College, at Mankato State University, and at Macalester College. From 1946 to 1979, Dahlgren taught in a studio in his own drum shop in Minneapolis. One clinic in which he participated as an instructor was at the University of Wisconsin - River Falls for a North American percussion workshop, directed by *Terry Smith. Dahlgren has written several method books for publication.

---

*T. Smith is a subject in this volume.

With the Minnesota Orchestra, Dahlgren has received the opportunity to perform with conductors Antal Dorati, Stanislaw Skrowaczewski, Sir Neville Marriner and Edo de Waart. As a vibraphone performer, Dahlgren has performed at the Emporium of Jazz in Mendota among numerous other places. His versatile background in composition and all the major percussion concert instruments helped prepare him for one of the most prestigious percussion positions in the world. Honors and awards that Dahlgren has received include a certificate of appreciation for musical performance from the University of Minnesota - Morris in 1980, a Twin Cities Jazz Society Appreciation Award in 1982, and awards for high quality performance of percussion keyboard instruments granted by the Minnesota Music Academy in 1987, 1988 and 1989.

DISCOGRAPHY

"Donald Erb: Concerto for Solo Percussion." Featured soloist. Dallas Symphony Orchestra conducted by Donald Johanos. Turnabout Vox TV-S 34433.

"Gene Gutche: Bong Divertimento." Featured soloist. St. Paul Chamber Orchestra, St. Paul, Minnesota.

Recordings of the Minneapolis Symphony Orchestra since 1951, and recordings of The Minnesota Orchestra since 1968.

"Strauss: Die Fledermaus Overture." The Minnesota Orchestra conducted by Leonard Slatkin. Pro Arte DDD CDM-813, 1987.

BOOKS

Drum Set Control. Glenview, Illinois: Creative Music, 1971.
4-Way Coordination. Co-authored with Elliott Fine. Belwin.

ARTICLES ABOUT SUBJECT

Fisher, Thomas R. Review of M. Dahlgren clinic at North American Percussion Workshop. Newsletter of the Wisconsin Percussive Arts Society, edited by *James Latimer, 1980.

Showcase. June, 1982, page 14.

"Symphony Drummer Jazzes It Up." St. Paul Pioneer Press and Dispatch. Thursday, October 23, 1986, page 5-D.

REFERENCE SOURCES

Feldman, Mary Ann, editor. Discographical information about The Minnesota Orchestra, March, 1990.

Information supplied by the subject (1989 and 1990).

---

*J. Latimer is a subject in this book.

Dash, Patricia
Born August 7, 1961, Rochester, New York

Chicago Symphony Orchestra percussionist Patricia Dash has performed with conductors Abbado, Bernstein, Solti and Tilson Thomas among others. Dash earned a diploma with honors at the Preparatory Department of the Eastman School of Music in 1979, studying with *Ruth Cahn and *Gordon Stout. She enrolled at the Eastman School and received a Bachelor of Music degree with distinction from the Eastman School of Music of the University of Rochester in 1983, studying with *John Beck. Her major emphasis of study at Eastman was applied music. During summers in 1982 and 1983, Patricia Dash performed with the National Repertory Orchestra in Colorado; the orchestra at that time was named the Colorado Philharmonic.

In 1983, Dash moved to Cincinnati, Ohio, and attended the graduate school in the College-Conservatory of Music at the University of Cincinnati, studying with Richard Jensen, Allen Otte and William Platt. In 1984, she participated in the Aspen Music Festival in Colorado, studying with *Doug Howard. Dash attended a timpani workshop presented by *Cloyd Duff in 1989.

As a percussion teacher, Patricia Dash has taught at American Conservatory of Music and at Northwestern University. As a professional percussionist, she performed part-time in the Rochester Philharmonic Orchestra in 1982-83. In 1983-84, she performed as an extra percussionist with the Cincinnati Symphony Orchestra and the Cincinnati Pops Orchestra. In 1985-86, Dash worked as principal percussionist in the Philharmonic Orchestra of Florida. She became a member of the Chicago Symphony Orchestra in 1986 and has remained in that position. Also, she has toured as percussionist with the Summit Brass Ensemble and with the Virtuoso di Landolfi Chamber Ensemble. Orchestral percussion instruments with which

---

*R. Cahn, G. Stout, J. Beck, D. Howard and C. Duff are subjects in this volume.

Patricia Dash has recorded include clash cymbals and snare drum. She is clearly a leader in her field.

DISCOGRAPHY

Chicago Symphony Orchestra recordings since 1986, Illinois.
New Morning for the World. Eastman Philharmonia, New York.
Sousa Spectacular. Eastman Wind Ensemble, New York.

ARTICLES ABOUT SUBJECT

Green, Thomas. Announcement of faculty appointment. Chicago: American Conservatory of Music, 1990.

REFERENCE SOURCES

Information supplied by the subject (1989 and 1991).

DeJohnette, Jack
Born August 9, 1942, Chicago, Illinois

Drum set specialist Jack DeJohnette began his musical studies as a pianist. He played bass during secondary school, and finally began playing the percussion. An ensemble with which he performed is named The Association for the Advancement of Creative Musicians. He also performed with blues bands in Chicago, before moving to New York City in 1966. Musicians with whom he performed have included organist John Patton, Jackie McLean's band in 1967, and Charles Lloyd's quintet that included keyboardist Keith Jarrett.

During DeJohnette's rise to the top of his profession, he received the opportunity to perform with several well known jazz musicians including John Coltrane, Miles Davis, Bill Evans, Stan Getz, Freddie Hubbard and Hubert Laws. Since 1968, DeJohnette has performed regularly and recorded with the ensembles Directions and Special Edition. His recording participation has included work on albums that have earned Grammy awards for excellence in musical performance as well as various awards in Europe for similar accomplishments.

Jack DeJohnette has participated in several styles of music performance in his career, including avant-garde, blues and jazz musics. He approaches the drum set melodically as well as rhythmically and coloristically, and can be compared in musical style with *Max Roach. DeJohnette has also performed as a pianist, composer and synthesizer performer. His music displays advanced technique combined with musical exploration and top level improvisation within defined limits.

---

*M. Roach is a subject in this book.

DISCOGRAPHY

Album Album. ECM 25010-1.

Ancient Dynasty. With JoAnne Brackeen. Columbia 36593.

At the Montreux Jazz Festival. With Bill Evans. Verve V6-8762.

Audio-Visualscapes. MCA Records, 1988.

Batik. With Ralph Towner. ECM 1121.

Changes. With Keith Jarrett. ECM 25007-1.

Cloud Dance. With Collin Walcott. ECM 1061.

Complex. Milestone 90022.

Deer Wan. With Kenny Wheeler. ECM 1102.

Flowering of the Original Quartet. With Charles Lloyd. Atlantic 1586.

Forest Flower. With Charles Lloyd. Atlantic 1473.

Gateway One. With John Abercrombie. ECM 1061.

Gateway Two. With John Abercrombie. ECM 1105.

Have You Heard? Milestone 9029.

In A Silent Way. With Miles Davis. Columbia 9875.

In Europe. With Charles Lloyd. Atlantic 1500.

Inflation Blues. ECM 1244.

In the Soviet Union. With Charles Lloyd. Atlantic 1571.

Irresistible Forces. MCA-Impulse 5992.

Journey Within. With Charles Lloyd. Atlantic 1493.

Keyed In. With JoAnne Brackeen. Columbia 36075.

Live at the Fillmore. With Miles Davis. Columbia 30038.

Mountain in the Clouds. With Miroslav Vitous. Atlantic 1622.

New Directions in Europe. ECM 1157.

New Rags. ECM 1103.

Night. With John Abercrombie. ECM 25009-1.

Pictures. ECM 1079.

Places. With Jan Garbarek. ECM 1118.

Reel Life. With Sonny Rollins. Milestone 9108.

Rite of Spring. With Hubert Laws.

Song X. With Pat Metheny and Ornette Coleman. Geffen 24096.

Sorcery. Prestige 10081.

Sound Suggestions. With George Adams. ECM 1141.

Soundtrack. With Charles Lloyd. Atlantic 1519.

Special Edition. ECM 1152.

Standards, Volume 1. With Keith Jarrett. ECM 1255.

Standards, Volume 2. With Keith Jarrett. ECM 25023-1.

Straight Life. With Freddie Hubbard.

Supertrios. With McCoy Tyner. Milestone 55003.

Timeless. With John Abercrombie. ECM 1047.

Tin Can Alley. ECM 1189.

Trio. With Terje Rypdal and Miroslav Vitous. ECM 1125.

Untitled. ECM 1074.

Zebra. With Lester Bowie. MCA Records, 1989.

80/81. With Pat Metheny. ECM 1180.

ARTICLES ABOUT SUBJECT

Beuttler, Bill. "Jack DeJohnette Interview." Down Beat, September, 1987.

"Jack DeJohnette: Special Edition." MCA Records, 1988.

REFERENCE SOURCES

"Goings On About Town." The New Yorker, December 4, 1989.

Information supplied by the subject (1989).

"Night Life." The New Yorker, December 4, 1989.

Denov, Sam
Born December 11, 1923, Chicago, Illinois

In high school, Sam Denov was a member of the High School National Champs Band and Orchestra, and featured soloist on the snare drum. From 1938 to 1941, Denov studied percussion with Roy Knapp. Denov was a member of the United States Navy from 1942 to 1946. In the U.S. Navy, Denov graduated from the Navy School of Music in Washington, D.C., in 1943, then performed with bands of the Commander 4th Fleet and Fleet Air Wing 16.

In 1946-47, Sam Denov performed in the Civic Orchestra of Chicago. From 1947 to 1950, he was a percussionist in the San Antonio Symphony Orchestra. From 1950 to 1952, Denov was percussionist in the Pittsburgh Symphony Orchestra. From 1954 to 1985, he was percussionist and assistant timpanist in the Chicago Symphony Orchestra. Since 1985, Denov has performed part-time in the San Diego Symphony Orchestra as substitute timpanist and percussionist.

As an orchestral recording artist, Sam Denov has performed for several recordings with the Chicago Symphony Orchestra that have received Grammy awards for excellence in performance. He graduated from Roosevelt University in Chicago in 1973. Denov invented and patented a device that allows the timpani to be tuned automatically. His specialty with the Chicago orchestra was clash cymbals, in a percussion section that also featured *Albert Payson and *Gordon Peters. Denov was chairperson for an International Conference of Symphony and Opera Musicians in 1969-70, and served as chairperson of a committee that assisted in arranging the Chicago Symphony's first international concert tour in 1971. He also served as chairperson of a Chicago Symphony Members Committee that led a campaign to establish an American Federation of Musicians symphony-opera strike fund. In 1970, Sam Denov was featured in an educational film entitled

---

*A. Payson, G. Peters, A. Cirone and C. Duff are subjects in this volume.

"Cymbal Techniques" that won honorable mention at an American Film Festival in New York City. Denov has served his profession admirably at a very high level of quality, including participation as a symphony musician, committee chairperson, video presenter and author.

DISCOGRAPHY

Chicago Symphony Orchestra recordings from 1954 to 1985 on record labels RCA, Mercury, Columbia, Angel, London and Deutsche Grammophon.

David Carroll percussion pops recordings for Mercury Records.

VIDEO RECORDINGS

Concert Percussion - A Performer's Guide, Volume I. With *Anthony Cirone and *Cloyd Duff. Grand Rapids, Michigan: Yamaha EV-30I, 1989.

Concert Percussion - A Performer's Guide, Volume II. With *Anthony Cirone and *Cloyd Duff. Grand Rapids, Michigan: Yamaha EV-30II, 1989.

Cymbal Techniques, 1970.

BOOKS

The Art of Playing the Cymbals.

ARTICLES

Articles about percussion in The Instrumentalist.

REFERENCE SOURCES

Information supplied by the subject (November 1989).

---

*A. Cirone and C. Duff are subjects in this book.

DePonte, Niel B.
Born May 3, 1953, New York, New York

As a student from 1970 to 1974, Niel DePonte worked as an administrative assistant with a summer youth employment program for the Suffolk County Department of Labor in Hauppauge, New York. In 1974, he received a Bachelor of Music Education, Magna cum Laude, at the State University of New York in Fredonia, with an emphasis in percussion instruments. In 1976, he received a Master of Music in music literature and percussion performance at the Eastman School of Music of the University of Rochester. DePonte also studied conducting with Helmuth Rilling at the International Bach Academy in Germany.

Since September, 1977, Niel DePonte has served in the position Principal Percussion for the Oregon Symphony Orchestra. From 1978 to 1981, DePonte was timpanist for the Sunriver Music Festival. In 1981, he was percussionist with Chamber Music Northwest, and in 1987 performed as timpanist for a Rudolf Nureyev performance with the Paris Ballet. Since September, 1980, DePonte has served as musical director and conductor for the West Coast Chamber Orchestra.

DePonte's primary percussion teachers have been *John Beck, Ted Frazeur and *Fred Hinger. Niel DePonte performed with the Eastman Philharmonia and the Eastman Wind Ensemble, and worked as graduate assistant in percussion at the Eastman School of Music, where he earned a Performer's Certificate in percussion. He has performed with the Rochester Philharmonic Orchestra, and has appeared as a drum set performer with award winning jazz ensembles from the Eastman School and Fredonia. Other successes have included performing as a recitalist for J.C. Deagan Company, performing as a featured soloist with the Chautauqua Festival Symphony Orchestra, and winning a mock audition for symphony orchestra sponsored by the Percussive Arts Society.

---

*J. Beck and F. Hinger are subjects in this volume.

As a percussion teacher, DePonte has taught at Lewis and Clark College in Portland, Oregon, and at National Music Camp in Interlochen, Michigan. He has also taught at the University of Massachusetts in Amherst, and performed drum set for the Oregon Symphony Pops Orchestra with conductor Norman Leyden. As a student, DePonte received the opportunity to conduct the Eastman Wind Ensemble with Donald Hunsberger, and the Eastman Percussion Ensemble with *John Beck. In 1984, DePonte presented the first performance of his composition Concertino for Marimba and Orchestra with the Oregon Symphony Orchestra conducted by James DePreist.

DePonte has served as a music reviewer for Percussive Notes. His music compositions have been written for voice and chorus in addition to percussion and orchestra, and have been published by Alfred Music and Music for Percussion, receiving performances nationally and internationally. He has also written "pops" orchestral arrangements for various ensembles. As a student at Fredonia, DePonte received the Outstanding Music Educator Award in 1974, and later at Eastman he was inducted into the national honorary society Pi Kappa Lambda.

Besides music performance, Niel DePonte has participated in various professional activities. He has talked on a radio show entitled "Inside Portland's Performing Arts" for classical music station KYTE in Portland, and has worked as a contributing author for The Oregonian newspaper specializing in arts topics. He served as board president for the West Coast Chamber Orchestra from 1980 to 1985. DePonte has been a member of the Metropolitan Arts Commission Review Panel, a member of Oregon Arts Commission Committee, a member of the Oregon Symphony Orchestra Players Association Sub-committee, a member of the Oregon Arts Commission Review Panel, and chairperson of the Oregon Symphony Orchestra Players Committee in 1978-79.

Niel DePonte's numerous professional activities in various capacities allow him to participate in a wide range of endeavour. His considerable

---

*J. Beck is a subject in this book.

talents are utilized within contrasting groups of people with specific interests. DePonte's broad approach to professionalism is a good example of how one person can certainly make a significant, positive difference within a large community.

DISCOGRAPHY

Bravura. Oregon Symphony Orchestra conducted by James DePreist. N. DePonte performing snare drum and keyboard percussion. Delos Records.

"Forest Rain." Percussion at Fredonia. Fort Lauderdale, Florida: Music for Percussion ADP-075S.

Tchaikovsky: 1812 Overture. Oregon Symphony Orchestra conducted by James DePreist. N. DePonte performing snare drum and tambourine. Delos Records.

The Sea and the Gulls. Oregon Symphony Orchestra conducted by James DePreist. N. DePonte performing snare drum and orchestral bells. Delos Records.

COMPOSITIONS

Celebration and Chorale. Fort Lauderdale: Music for Percussion.

Concertino for Marimba. With large ensemble accompaniment.

Forest Rain. Fort Lauderdale: Music for Percussion.

Thoughts for Flute and Percussion. Fort Lauderdale: Music for Percussion.

REFERENCE SOURCES

Catalog. Music for Percussion. Fort Lauderdale, Florida.

Information supplied by the subject (September 1989).

Program. The Concordia Bands. Moorhead, Minnesota: Concordia College, Music Department, November 18, 1990.

Duff, Cloyd E.
Born September 26, 1915, Marietta, Ohio

Cloyd Duff is recognized as one of the masters of the timpani in the twentieth century. He graduated from the Curtis Institute of Music in Philadelphia in 1938. After four years with the Indianapolis Symphony Orchestra, Duff became timpanist of the Cleveland Orchestra, staying with that orchestra until 1981. Conductors with whom Cloyd Duff performed in Cleveland include Arthur Rodzinski, Erich Leinsdorf, George Szell and Lorin Maazel.

As a member of the Cleveland Orchestra, Duff received the opportunity to tour many countries throughout the world. Some of the places that Duff visited as timpanist are Hong Kong, Mexico, Japan, Europe, South America, Russia, Canada, New Zealand and Australia. In his earlier years, Duff performed in the All American Youth Orchestra conducted by Leopold Stokowski. He has performed at Robin Hood Dell, and in recent years has worked as Artist-in-Residence at Colorado State University in Fort Collins. Duff has presented clinics at several Percussive Arts Society International Conventions, including those in Indianapolis and San Antonio.

During his tenure in Cleveland, Cloyd Duff taught percussion in the Conservatory of Music at Oberlin College. He returned there in June, 1990, as a member of the faculty for the Oberlin Percussion Institute directed by *Michael Rosen. In 1989, Duff received an award from Remo percussion company in California for excellence in percussion instruction. He is a member of Pi Kappa Lambda honorary music society, and is listed in Who's Who in America. As an artist at Colorado State University, Duff has presented a timpani symposium and workshop several times for students of all levels of ability.

One of the associated musical activities of Cloyd Duff has been to produce timpani mallets and triangles. He has also taught several places

---

*M. Rosen is a subject in this book.

during his career on a part-time basis, including the Cleveland Institute of Music, the Cleveland Music School Settlement, Case Western Reserve University, the Aspen Music School and Baldwin-Wallace College. Clinics and master classes that Duff has presented have been at Indiana University, the University of California at Davis, the University of Calgary, Emory University, the University of Northern Colorado, the Manhattan School of Music, Northwestern University, the University of Wyoming, Rice University, University of Mexico City and Saint Louis Conservatory. Duff has worked as a timpani clinician for Yamaha musical instrument company. Certainly Cloyd Duff's performances with the Cleveland Orchestra leave a beautiful listening legacy in the repertoire of orchestral music. In addition, his teaching has been influential in his field.

DISCOGRAPHY

Recordings with the Cleveland Orchestra from 1942 to 1981 for Columbia, Victor, Angel, Epic, Telarc and London-Decca.

Szell Conducts Wagner. Richard Wagner: "Overture to the Flying Dutchman," "A Faust Overture," "Prelude to Act I of Lohengrin," "Overture to Rienzi." Cleveland Orchestra conducted by George Szell. Columbia MS-6884.

The Blue Danube. Cleveland Orchestra conducted by George Szell. New York: Columbia Records YT-30053.

Hary Janos Suite by Zoltan Kodaly and Lieutenant Kije Suite, Op. 60 by Sergei Prokofiev. Cleveland Orchestra conducted by George Szell. New York: CBS Records MY-38527, 1983.

VIDEO RECORDINGS

Concert Percussion: A Performer's Guide, Volume I. With *Anthony Cirone and *Sam Denov. Co-produced for Yamaha and Zildjian companies by MasterPlan Video Productions. Grand Rapids, Michigan: Yamaha EV-30I, 1989.

---

*A. Cirone and S. Denov are subjects in this book.

Concert Percussion: A Performer's Guide, Volume II. With *Anthony Cirone and *Sam Denov. Grand Rapids: Yamaha EV-30II, 1989.

ARTICLES ABOUT SUBJECT

"Cloyd Duff." Catalogs of the Aspen Music School, Aspen, Colorado, 1989 and 1991.

Cloyd Duff Masterclass. Fort Collins: Colorado State University Department of Music, Theatre and Dance, 1990.

"Cloyd Duff Masterclass." Percussive Notes (Spring 1990), page 47.

Oberlin Percussion Institute. Oberlin, Ohio: Oberlin College Conservatory of Music, 1990.

REFERENCE SOURCES

"EPPI Awards." Remo Rimshots (Winter 1990), 5.

Information supplied by the subject (October 1989).

"PASIC '88." Percussion News (August 1988).

Dupin, Francois
Born September 25, 1931, Marcq-en-Baroeul, France

Francois Dupin's family has contained eight generations of professional musicians since the early eighteenth century. Dupin worked in a general course of study in French schools until the age of sixteen. At that time, he enrolled in the National Conservatory of Music in Paris. At the National Conservatory, Dupin concentrated on a percussion curriculum, studying with Felix Passerone. In 1949, Francois Dupin was granted honors in percussion at the Paris Conservatory. A year later, he received honors in percussion chamber music. In 1961, Dupin earned honors in music composition at the National Conservatory, following studies with Tony Aubin, Darius Milhaud and Jean Rivier.

Dupin has held several professional percussion positions in his career. He was timpanist in the Orchestra of Strasbourg from 1951 to 1955. From 1955 to 1961, Dupin taught percussion at the Conservatory of Le Mans. In 1961, he became a keyboard percussionist for the Philharmonic Orchestra of the French Radio, until 1967. Since October, 1967, Francois Dupin has served as percussionist and assistant timpanist in the Orchestre de Paris. Additionally since 1981, Dupin has taught percussion at National Superior Conservatory in Lyon.

During his career in percussion, Dupin has performed many places in various ensembles. He has played percussion at festivals in Aix en Provence, Cannes and Vichy. He has played in symphony orchestras at Colonne, Lamoureux and Pasdeloup. Dupin has performed for the Societe des Concerts du Conservatoire, the National Orchestra of the French Radio, and orchestras of Opera de Paris and Opera-comique de Paris.

Francois Dupin has written articles for publication, as well as method books and music compositions. Publishers for whom he has written include Hachette, Leduc, Revue Musicale, and the international Percussive Arts Society. Dupin unquestionably has a professional record of being one of France's leading percussionists in the twentieth century.

DISCOGRAPHY

Marim'Bach. Transcriptions of music composed by Johann Sebastian Bach, including Brandenburg Concertos and others, for keyboard percussion. EMI CO64-12836, 1975.

Percussions de l'Orchestre de Paris. With Marius Constant, Jacques Delecluse and Nguyen Thien. EMI CO69-11326, 1970.

COMPOSITIONS

Aaron. Xylophone and piano. Alphonse Leduc via Bryn Mawr, Pennsylvania: Theodore Presser.

Kyakou. Percussion and piano. Alphonse Leduc.

Le Mammouth Debonnaire. Xylophone and piano. Alphonse Leduc.

Le Roi Igor. Timpani and piano. Alphonse Leduc.

Prelude et Rude. Timpani. Paris: Alphonse Leduc, 1987.

BOOKS

Courtes Pieces Vol. 1. Snare drum. Alphonse Leduc via Bryn Mawr, Pennsylvania: Theodore Presser.

Courtes Pieces Vol. 2. Timpani. Alphonse Leduc.

Courtes Pieces Vol. 3. Timpani. Alphonse Leduc.

Courtes Pieces Vol. 5. Drum set. Alphonse Leduc.

Courtes Pieces Vol. 6. Drum set. Alphonse Leduc.

Courtes Pieces Vol. 7. Drum set. Alphonse Leduc.

Methode Rapide Vol. 1. Xylophone. Alphonse Leduc.

Methode Rapide Vol. 2. Xylophone. Alphonse Leduc.

Parcours du Timbalier. Alphonse Leduc.

7 Moments Musicaux. Co-authored with M. Jorand. Percussion and piano. Alphonse Leduc.

28 Miniatures Vol. 1. Snare drum. Alphonse Leduc.

28 Miniatures Vol. 2. Snare drum. Alphonse Leduc.

REFERENCE SOURCES

Information supplied by the subject (September 1989).

Fink, Ron
Born August 14, 1937, Emden, Illinois

Ron Fink has performed, taught, and written for publication during his career as a percussionist, specializing in drum set. Fink earned a Bachelor of Music Education degree at the University of Illinois in 1960. A year later, he earned a Master of Music degree from that school. Fink's percussion teachers at the University of Illinois included *Albert Payson, Paul Price and Jack McKenzie.

From 1960 to 1962, Fink taught at the University of Illinois in the summer school program and at the Youth Music Camp. From 1961 to 1963, Ron Fink worked as music supervisor for the Hartsburg-Emden Public Schools in Illinois. During the 1963-64 school term, Fink taught percussion at Northern Illinois University in DeKalb. Since 1964, he has taught at the University of North Texas in Denton.

As a professional performer, Ron Fink has served as principal percussionist in the Fort Worth Symphony Orchestra. Additionally, Fink has performed in the Fort Worth Opera Orchestra and in the Dallas Symphony Orchestra. He has recorded with composer Larry Austin, and has played drum set for several big band recordings.

Ron Fink has performed in various freelance capacities during his career. Fink has played for Ice Capades ensembles since 1966 in the Dallas-Fort Worth area, and has performed with the Disney On Parade show. He has played for Miss Texas beauty pageants, and for Miss Teen Age America televised contests. Ron Fink performed for the 1984 Republican National Convention in Dallas, and has played in musical theater orchestras at Casa Manana. Fink has worked as percussionist for several tour shows in Texas, playing for featured entertainers Joel Gray, Tom Jones, Rita Moreno, Anthony Newley, Ginger Rogers and others.

---

*A. Payson is a subject in this volume.

Fink has aided his profession by serving in various volunteer positions. He has been a member of the Board of Directors for the Percussive Arts Society, and has served as a vice president of that organization. Fink was a member of the Greater Denton Arts Society, and has worked as an officer for the Denton Festival Foundation. Ron Fink was percussion editor for The Instrumentalist, and has written articles for Percussive Notes. Fink's keyboard percussion ensemble arrangements have been published in California; he has published several compositions himself, written for drum set, snare drum, timpani and vibraphone. Ron Fink's many valuable contributions have been effective in advancing the art form in the latter half of the twentieth century.

BOOKS

Drum Set Reading. Alfred Publishing Company.
Keyboard Percussion Ensemble Arrangements. Studio 4.
Latin American Rhythms for the Drum Set. Glenview, Illinois: Creative Music, 1971.

REFERENCE SOURCES

Information supplied by the subject (November 1989).

Fink, Siegfried
Born February 8, 1928, Zerbst, Germany

Siegfried Fink is known as a very successful teacher of percussion in the latter half of the twentieth century. His many students have transported his influences to the United States, Spain, Brazil, Sweden, Egypt, Norway, The Netherlands, Portugal, Argentina, Bulgaria, England and throughout Germany. Additionally, Fink has written much percussion music for publication.

Fink's formal education in music took place from 1945 to 1951. Fink studied composition with Helmut Riethmuller. He studied drums and timpani with Hans Wrede in Zerbst, Germany, then studied percussion and timpani with Alfred Wagner at Franz Liszt Hochschule in Weimar.

From 1951 to 1958, Siegfried Fink was principal percussionist for the Magdeburg Opera Orchestra while teaching in Georg Phillip Telemann Conservatory there. From 1958 to 1965, Fink taught at the academy in Lubeck, and performed as timpanist in the Lubeck Opera Orchestra. He taught from 1962 to 1966 at the Musikhochschule Hannover. From 1959 to 1972, he participated in the Ensemble fur Neue Musik for Radio Hannover. Siegfried Fink then instructed percussionists of the World Youth Orchestra from 1972 to 1985. Since 1965, Professor Fink has taught at the Hochschule fur Music in Wurzburg, Germany.

As a percussion performer, Siegfried Fink has presented solo performances around the world including Rome, Madrid, London, Tokyo, Lisbon, Hong Kong, Istanbul, Budapest, Cairo, Pretoria, Amsterdam, Chicago, Seoul, Berlin, Brussels, Munich and Barcelona. Fink's numerous publications feature sound pedagogy and variety within a disciplined approach to percussion performance.

DISCOGRAPHY

Art of Percussion. Thorofon CTH-2085.

Drums. Wurzburg Percussion Ensemble. Thorofon CTH-2003.

Fink I El Seu Grup de Percussio. Edigsa AZ 70-06.

Neue Geistliche Musik. With K.M. Ziegler. Cantate 658-225.

Ruzicka. Wergo WER 60-071.

Sound Sculptures. Wurzburg Percussion Quartet. Wergo SM 1049/50.

Talking Drums. Thorofon MIG-124.

COMPOSITIONS

Concertino fur Vibrafon und Klavier. Wiesbaden: Otto Wrede.

Concertino fur Vibrafon und Streichorchester. Wiesbaden: Otto Wrede.

Conversation for Tape and Percussion. Musikverlag Zimmermann.

Darabukka Suite. Musikverlag Zimmermann.

Dialog fur Xylofon, Bass Klarinette und 1 Perc. Wiesbaden: Otto Wrede.

Game for Two. Akkordeon and Percussion. Musikverlag N. Simrock.

Images para Percusion. Impressionen nach Antoni Gaudi fur 4 Schlagzeuger und Flote (altern. Sopranstimme). Frankfurt: Zimmermann.

Interactions fur Variable Besetzung. Munchen: Edition Pro Nova.

Jongo for Solo Snare Drum. Baltimore: Smith Publications.

Kanonade fur Trommelquartett. Wilhelmshaven: Heinrichshofen.

Motion Pictures I fur Soloschlagzeug und Tonband. Musikverlag Zimmermann.

Papillon: 4 Encores fur Vibrafon und Marimba. Musikverlag Zimmermann.

Pauken Suite. Musikverlag Zimmermann.

Pictures for Percussion. Impressionen nach Victor Vasarely fur 4 Schlagzeuger. Musikverlag Zimmermann.

Sonata for Snare Drum. Richard Schauer via Bryn Mawr, Pennsylvania: Theodore Presser.

Tablature 72. Percussion Ensemble. Richard Schauer.

Tangents fur Schlaginstrumente. 4-8 Spieler, mit Schallplatte. Musikverlag Zimmermann.

Vibrafon Suite. Frankfurt: Zimmermann.

ARRANGEMENTS

Green, G.H.: Triplets. Percussion Sextett oder Quartett. Musikverlag Zimmermann.

Haydn, J.: Divertimento. Vibraphon und Marimba. Musikverlag Zimmermann.

Joplin, S.: Ragtime Dance. Percussion Quartett. Musikverlag Zimmermann.

Suite I, BWV 1007 by J.S. Bach. Arranged for marimba by Kamp and Fink. Frankfurt: Zimmermann.

Suite V, BWV 1011 by J.S. Bach. Arranged for marimba by Lutz and Fink. Frankfurt: Zimmermann.

Suite VI, BWV 1012 by J.S. Bach. Arranged for marimba by Joaquin and Fink. Frankfurt: Zimmermann.

Telemann, G.Ph.: Allegro aus Opus 13. Vibraphon und Marimba. Musikverlag Zimmermann.

BOOKS

A. Dvorak: Ouverturen, Sl. Tanze, Konzerte. Paukenstimmen. Musikverlag N. Simrock.

Antonin Dvorak: Sinfonien 3-9. Paukenstimmen. Musikverlag N. Simrock.

Etudes in Jazz. Impressionen fur Drum Set. Musikverlag N. Simrock.

Machine Drums. Studie fur Jazzschlagzeug. Mainz: B. Schott's Sohne.

Mahler, G.: Orchesterstudien fur Pauken. Musikverlag Zimmermann.

Orchesterstudien fur Pauken. A. Dvorak: Bd. I, Sinfonien. Hamburg: Musikverlag N. Simrock, 1989.

Solobuch fur Drum Set. Musikverlag N. Simrock.

Solobuch fur Kleine Trommel. Musikverlag N. Simrock.

Solobuch fur Pauken. Musikverlag N. Simrock.

Solobuch fur Pauken, Band II. Musikverlag N. Simrock.

Studien fur Drum Set, Unterstufe. Musikverlag N. Simrock.

Studien fur Drum Set, Mittelstufe. Musikverlag N. Simrock.

Studien fur Drum Set, Oberstufe. Musikverlag N. Simrock.

Studien fur Kleine Trommel, Progressiv Etuden. Musikverlag N. Simrock.

Studien fur Pauken, Elementarubungen. Musikverlag N. Simrock.

Timing for Percussion - Patterns fur Schlagzeugquartett. Munchen: Edition Modern.

REFERENCE SOURCES

Information supplied by the subject (July 1990).

Albert, M. et al. 25 Jahre Perkussions-Studio Hochschule F. Musik Wurzburg. Wurzburg, Germany: Hochschule fur Musik, 1990.

Firth, Everett J. (Vic)
Born June 2, 1930, Winchester, Massachusetts

Vic Firth's career has been marked not only by success, but also by high quality performance, good appearance and variety. Firth earned a Bachelor of Music with honors at New England Conservatory of Music in Boston. From 1952 to 1975, Vic Firth performed and recorded with the Boston Pops Orchestra. Since 1952, he has been principal timpanist for the Boston Symphony Orchestra in Massachusetts. Other positions that Firth has held include playing with the orchestra of the Boston Opera Company, and with Boston Symphony Chamber Players.

His orchestral recording experience has encompassed work for Mercury, RCA Victor, Philips, Polydor, and Columbia record companies. Of course he has performed at Tanglewood, the summer residence of the Boston Symphony Orchestra, and has presented clinic demonstrations in various locations such as Toho School in Tokyo.

As a teacher, Vic Firth is one of the most respected members of the percussion profession. Firth has served as chairperson of the percussion area of study at New England Conservatory and at the Tanglewood school. In addition, he has written for publication articles and method books that specifically guide the percussion student through etudes or repertoire. Third, he operates a manufacturing company that offers the percussion field high quality drum sticks and timpani mallets for the student and for the professional. Fourth, as a member of the highly visible and often televised Boston orchestras, Vic Firth has through the decades served as an obvious example of correct percussion performance for any student who would happen to be watching.

As a member of the international Percussive Arts Society, Firth has been in the positions of treasurer and member of the executive committee. As a composer, Firth's Encore in Jazz for percussion ensemble has been a most performed composition in that medium for some time. Vic Firth is a member of Pi Kappa Lambda music honorary society.

DISCOGRAPHY

Recordings of the Boston Pops Orchestra from 1952 to 1975.

Recordings of the Boston Symphony Orchestra since 1952.

Sibelius: Symphony No. 1 and Finlandia. Boston Symphony Orchestra conducted by Colin Davis. Philips 9500-140, 1975.

COMPOSITIONS

Encore in Jazz. Percussion ensemble including drum set.

BOOKS

Percussion Symposium. New York: Carl Fischer, 1966.

ARTICLES

"Etude for Playing Softly." Modern Percussionist I/2 (March 1985), 44.

"Orchestral Etude." Modern Percussionist II/1 (December 1985), 34.

"Sound." Modern Percussionist I/1 (December 1984), 48.

"Stickings." Modern Percussionist II/3 (June 1986), 48. Includes Firth's recommendations for specific stickings used in the performance of music compositions written by Barber, Bartok, Bernstein, Hindemith, Prokofiev and Stravinsky.

"Tuning and Pitch." Modern Percussionist I/3 (June 1985), 42.

"Tuning Etude for Two Timpani." Modern Percussionist I/4 (September 1985), 26.

"Tuning Problems." Modern Percussionist III/2 (March 1987), 32.

REFERENCE SOURCES

Information supplied by the subject (September 1989 and June 1990).

"Premier Elite . . . Firth Class Timpani." Advertisement. Modern Percussionist II/4 (September 1986), 4.

Friedman, David
Born March 10, 1944, New York, New York

Vibraphonist David Friedman received his higher education in music at The Juilliard School in New York City. Friedman's teachers have included *Gary Burton and Saul Goodman. As a jazz music performer, David Friedman has specialized in the keyboard percussion instruments, including both marimba and vibraphone.

One of Friedman's collaborators through the years has been *David Samuels. The two percussionists have performed together professionally for some time, called variously The Mallet Duo and Double Image, an ensemble that involved an entire band. The Friedman-*Samuels Duo present clinics, concerts and recitals regularly. Other professional performers with whom Friedman has played include pianist Geri Allen, bassist Anthony Cox, and drummer Ronnie Burrage. Ensembles with whom Friedman has collaborated in concert include the Stuttgart Radio Orchestra and the Taiwan Symphony Orchestra. David Friedman has also performed professionally with Horacee Arnold, Jane Bloom, Peter Erskine, Daniel Humair, Marc Johnson, David Lahm, Hubert Laws, and Harvie Swartz.

As a busy leader in his field, Friedman has performed widely and well. He is in the forefront of developments artistically and electronically with his instrument. Friedman's specialty is improvised music with modern tonalities and techniques. He can be classified as a member of the American avant-garde in jazz. In this role, David Friedman performs at significant occasions, for example Percussive Arts Society International Conventions, jazz festivals and concerts in Geneva, Berlin, and elsewhere in Europe.

---

*G. Burton and D. Samuels are subjects in this book.

DISCOGRAPHY

Composition by Ulrich Susse for vibraphone and orchestra, Stuttgart Radio Orchestra, Europe.

Dawn. ECM-1146, 1978.

Double Image. Enja 2096, 1977.

Educational recording with *David Samuels as a duo. Includes notated music from the recording. New York: Marimba Productions.

Of the Wind's Eye. Enja 3089, 1981.

Recording with flutist Hubert Laws.

Shades of Change. Contains "Shades of A Labyrinth," "Out of A Labyrinth," "3 + 1 = 5," "The Search," "Ibrahim." Enja 5017.

BOOKS

Vibraphone Technique: Dampening and Pedaling. Foreword by *Gary Burton. Boston: Berklee Publications, 1973.

ARTICLES ABOUT SUBJECT

Mattingly, Rick. "David Friedman." Modern Percussionist II/1 (December 1985), 8.

Theroux, Gary. "Friedman, David." The New Grove Dictionary of Jazz, Volume One, 1988.

---

*D. Samuels and G. Burton are subjects in this volume.

Frock, George A.
Born July 16, 1938, Danville, Illinois

George Frock first studied the percussion instruments with his father from 1948 to 1956. From 1954 to 1956, Frock studied percussion with Roy Knapp. At the University of Illinois, George Frock studied percussion with Jack McKenzie from 1956 to 1960. As a university student, Frock performed as featured marimba soloist with the University of Illinois Percussion Ensemble.

At the University of Kansas, George Frock taught in the music department from 1960 to 1963. From 1963 to 1966, Frock taught in the music department at Memphis State University, and concurrently performed as timpanist in the Memphis Symphony Orchestra. During the 1966 summer session, he taught in the School of Music at the University of Illinois. Since 1966, George Frock has taught percussion at the University of Texas, and has played timpani in the Austin Symphony Orchestra. In 1989-90, Frock served as interim associate chairperson in the music department at the University of Texas.

For the Percussive Arts Society, George Frock has worked in the position of chairperson of the Contest and Audition Procedures Committee. He has regularly written reviews of new music for Percussive Notes magazine. One of his honors is having received an Austin A. Harding Award from the University of Illinois bands.

As a freelance percussionist, George Frock has performed in musical theater orchestras, and for shows in Memphis and Austin. Frock has played timpani in the orchestra of the Austin Lyric Opera, and percussion for the Ice Capades. Major entertainers whom Frock has backed as a percussionist include Roger Miller and Dionne Warwick. Musicals that he has performed include "Camelot," "Sugar Babies," "Hello, Dolly," and "How To Succeed in Business Without Really Trying." George Frock's consistency and service to the profession have been apparent nationally during the latter half of the twentieth century.

DISCOGRAPHY

Extended Saxophone: Albert Regni.   Karl Korte: "Symmetrics." University of Texas Percussion Ensemble conducted by G. Frock. CRI 431.

Robert Kelly: Toccata for Marimba.   G. Frock, featured marimba soloist. University of Illinois Percussion Ensemble, 1960.

The Music of Karl Korte. "Gestures" for Percussion and Band. G. Frock, featured percussion soloist. Golden Crest Records CRS 4141.

COMPOSITIONS

Two Structures.   Percussion ensemble.   Fort Lauderdale, Florida: Music for Percussion.

REVIEW ARTICLES

Frenzy for snare drum by Michael Varner. Percussive Notes 29/3 (February 1991), 65.

Kaleidoscope for flute and percussion by H.J. Buss. Percussive Notes 29/3 (February 1991), 63.

Plane Dancing by Erik Lund. Percussive Notes 29/3 (February 1991), 63-64.

The Echo for snare drum by James Jurrens. Percussive Notes 29/3 (February 1991), 65.

Top Flight by Thomas Brown. Percussive Notes 29/3 (February 1991), 64.

REFERENCE SOURCES

Information supplied by the subject (November 1989).

Lambert, James, editor. "Selected Reviews of New Percussion Literature and Recordings." Percussive Notes 29/3 (February 1991), 63-65.

Gadd, Stephen (Steve)
Born c. 1945, Rochester, New York

Steve Gadd is a most successful drum set performer in the latter part of the twentieth century. Gadd attended the Manhattan School of Music in New York City, and the Eastman School of Music in Rochester. As an undergraduate student at the Eastman School, Steve Gadd received the opportunity to play not only jazz music and the drum set, but also classical percussion with the Rochester Philharmonic Orchestra. His control of drumming fundamental technique is an important ingredient in his success.

As a drum set specialist, Gadd performed professionally with Gap Mangione in 1971-72, following service as a percussionist in the United States Army Field Band. Steve Gadd has toured Europe and recorded with jazz flugelhorn performer Chuck Mangione. From 1975 to 1981, Gadd performed regularly with Chick Corea in New York. Other performers with whom Steve Gadd has worked include Roland Hanna, Bob James and Quincy Jones. Gadd has toured with Al DiMeola, Tom Scott, Richard Tee and Sadao Watanabe. As a supporting percussionist, Steve Gadd has performed with James Brown, Steely Dan, Aretha Franklin and Paul Simon. Gadd's playing is exciting, precise and rhythmic.

DISCOGRAPHY

Alive! With Chuck Mangione and small ensemble. Mercury SRM 1-650, 1972.

Main Squeeze. With Chuck Mangione and small ensemble. A & M Records SP-4612, 1976.

The Leprechaun. With Chick Corea. Polydor 6062, 1975.

VIDEO RECORDINGS

In Session. Educational video. Grand Rapids, Michigan: Yamaha EV-7.

Up Close. Educational video. Grand Rapids: Yamaha EV-1.

ARTICLES ABOUT SUBJECT

Braman, Chuck. "Gadd, Steve." The New Grove Dictionary of Jazz, Volume One, 1988.

Mattingly, R. "Gadd." Modern Drummer VII/7 (1983), 8.

Pitt, D. "Gadd about Town." Down Beat XLIX/7 (1982), 14.

Santelli, R. "Steve Gadd." Modern Drummer X/1 (1986), 19.

Tomkins, L. "Drummer of the Decade: Steve Gadd." Crescendo International XIX/7 (1981), 20.

REFERENCE SOURCES

Beck, John. Sonata for Timpani. Boston: Boston Music, 1971.

Gauger, Thomas
Born December 20, 1935, Wheaton, Illinois

Thomas Gauger has served his profession as an orchestral performer, chamber music performer, teacher, composer, and manufacturer of bass drum mallets. Gauger's undergraduate study was at the University of Illinois from 1955 to 1959, where he studied with Jack McKenzie and Paul Price.

From 1959 to 1963, Thomas Gauger worked in the position of principal percussion in the Oklahoma City Symphony Orchestra. Since 1963, Gauger has been a member of the Boston Symphony Orchestra. He has taught at Boston University since 1965, being in charge of percussion instruction and directing the percussion ensemble. Additionally, Thomas Gauger has been on the faculty of the Boston University Tanglewood Institute, and has performed as percussionist with the Boston Pops Orchestra.

During his collegiate study at Illinois, Gauger received the opportunity to perform and record with composer Harry Partch. After graduating from the university, Thomas Gauger performed at a summer music festival in Saskatoon, Saskatchewan, in Canada. While performing in Oklahoma, Gauger also taught at Oklahoma City University and played jazz music with Ray Eberly and others. In Boston, Thomas Gauger has played with The Wuz, a jazz ensemble, and with Collage, a contemporary music ensemble founded by Gauger's colleague Frank Epstein. Gauger began manufacturing percussion sticks, mallets and accessories in 1969. He has received several commissions to compose music. Thomas Gauger has served his profession at a high level of quality in several different roles.

DISCOGRAPHY

Aisle Seat: Great Film Music. Boston Pops Orchestra conducted by John Williams. Philips 6514-328, 1982.

American Classics: Great Moments of Music. Boston Pops Orchestra conducted by Arthur Fiedler. Time-Life Records STLS-7001.

Other recordings with the Boston Symphony Orchestra and the Boston Pops Orchestra since 1963 with various conductors.

Sibelius: Symphony No. 1 and Finlandia. Boston Symphony Orchestra conducted by Colin Davis. Philips 9500-140, 1976.

Paul Price Plays: Snare Drum Solos. "Snare Drum Solo No. 1" by T. Gauger. Fort Lauderdale: Music for Percussion, MFP-513.

COMPOSITIONS

Doubles. Duo for marimbas in two movements. Brookline, Massachusetts: Tom Gauger.

Gainsborough. Percussion quintet. Southern Music Company.

Nomad. Solo jazz march for multipercussion including wood block, tom-toms, triangle, suspended cymbal and tambourine. Brookline: T. Gauger.

Round Trip. Jazz/rock trio for vibraphone, timpani and drum set, with optional parts for piano and bass. Brookline: T. Gauger, 1990.

Snare Drum Solo No. 1. Fort Lauderdale: Music for Percussion.

ARTICLES ABOUT SUBJECT

Announcement of Percussion Faculty. Boston University School of Music. Percussive Notes 29/3 (February 1991), 16.

Announcement of Percussion Faculty. Boston University School of Music. Percussive Notes (Spring 1990), 25.

REFERENCE SOURCES

Information supplied by the subject (December 1989 and June 1990). "Fun Music." Advertisement. Percussive Notes (Spring 1990), 9.

Hampton, Lionel
Born c. 1909, Louisville, Kentucky

Vibraphonist Lionel Hampton is unique in his success as both a drum set performer and a vibraphone performer in the jazz area of the percussion music field. Hampton is a member of the generation of American musicians who did not necessarily attend music schools, but who essentially founded them.

Lionel Hampton's family moved to Chicago in 1916. In the late 1920s, Hampton was based in Culver City, California. In 1930, he took part in several recording sessions with legendary trumpet performer Louis Armstrong. In 1936, Hampton performed with clarinetist and band leader Benny Goodman. Hampton performed and recorded with small ensembles led by Goodman until 1940. In that year, Lionel Hampton organized an ensemble that included variously Cat Anderson, Clifford Brown, Quincy Jones and Illinois Jacquet. In the 1950s, Hampton toured Africa, Australia, Europe, Japan, and the Middle East, including a performance in Royal Festival Hall in London. In 1978, Lionel Hampton performed at the White House in Washington, D.C., with President Carter in the audience. That year, Hampton began publishing his own recordings. He has also been recorded as a singer and as a pianist. The vibraphone tremolo that is displayed in Hampton recordings is often heard at a fast speed, since many of the instruments in the early twentieth century were built with a capability of only one speed of tremolo.

Lionel Hampton's vibraphone performance exhibits excellent control of the instrument's damper pedal, with duration of sound being well controlled by the performer. His playing is at times virtuosic in music of both fast and slow rhythmic pulse. His four-mallet performance on vibraphone, or vibraharp, is often chordal with the four notes sounding at once. Hampton's improvisations contain a specific type of thoughtfulness that seems consistent with his often light-hearted approach.

Specifically, a Hampton recorded improvisation may include extension of one rhythmic idea followed by presentation of a contrasting rhythmic idea. At other times, his improvisation may include several rhythmic ideas consecutively, with some repetition of musical motives among the contrasts. This form compares with historical forms in music of the western world. Hampton's recorded harmonies sometimes alternate major chords with minor chords. One of his recorded musical ideas is the reiteration of a single note in a drumming style on the vibraphone: at times this reiteration serves as a kind of theme for further improvisation. Notably, Hampton's blues style does not seem sad. His preference for the insertion of "double-time" passages in his music, that is, improvisation with notes twice as fast as those having been performed immediately preceding, compares with military drum music from recent centuries. Hampton's playing exhibits fine art in both rhythmic and melodic characteristics.

DISCOGRAPHY

Air Mail Special. Decca 18880, 1946.

Down Home Jump. Victor 26114, 1938.

Drum Stomp. Victor 25658, 1937.

Flying Home. Decca 18394, 1942.

Golden Vibes. Personnel include woodwinds and rhythm section. Columbia CL-1304.

Lionel Hampton - Carnegie Hall Concert, 1945. Decca DL-8088.

Lionel Hampton's Jazz Giants. Norgran 1080, 1955.

Many-Splendored Vibes. Epic 16027.

Midnight Sun. Decca 24429, 1947.

Other recordings on labels of RCA, RCA-Camden, MGM, Verve, GNP and Decca.

Together Again. Reunion of Benny Goodman Quartet. RCA 2698.

COMPOSITIONS

Flying Home.
Israeli Suite.
Midnight Sun.
Vibraholiday.

ARTICLES ABOUT SUBJECT

Aldam, J. "The Lionel Hampton Band." Jazz Monthly III/1 (1957), 5.

Feather, Leonard. The Book of Jazz. New York: Horizon Press, 1965.

Feather, Leonard. The Encyclopedia of Jazz in the Sixties. New York: Horizon Press, 1966.

"Hampton, Lionel." Who's Who in America, Volume 1, 45th edition (1988), 1296.

"Hampton Receives Honorary Doctorate." Modern Percussionist II/3 (June 1986), 60.

Harrison, M. "Lionel Hampton on Victor." Jazz Monthly IX/1 (1963), 3.

Jones, C. "The Illustrious Past and Present of Lionel Hampton." Crescendo International XVI/7 (1978), 10.

Larrick, Geary. "Letters to the Editor." Musical Heritage Review 13/5 (1989), 22.

Roach, Hildred. Black American Music. Boston: Crescendo Publishing, 1973.

Robinson, J. Bradford. "Hampton, Lionel." The New Grove Dictionary of Jazz, Volume One, 1988.

Townsend, Irving. Record jacket notes. Golden Vibes. Columbia CL-1304.

REFERENCE SOURCES

Photograph of Lionel Hampton. Catalog. Selmer, Ludwig-Musser (1990), 20.

Hinger, Fred D.
Born February 9, 1920, Cleveland, Ohio

Timpanist Fred Hinger graduated with a Bachelor of Music degree in percussion and education at the Eastman School of Music in Rochester, New York. His teachers included Ned Albright, Benjamin Podemski, Frank Tichy and *William Street.

From 1942 to 1948, Hinger was a member of the United States Navy Band in Washington, D.C. With the Navy Band, Fred Hinger performed as percussionist and featured xylophone soloist. In 1948, Hinger became a member of the Philadelphia Orchestra in Pennsylvania. In Philadelphia, Hinger served as principal percussionist, then became timpanist in 1951 until 1967. While in Philadelphia, Fred Hinger taught percussion at the Curtis Institute of Music.

In 1967, Hinger became timpanist for the orchestra of the Metropolitan Opera. He remained in this position until 1983. While playing for the Metropolitan Opera in New York City, Fred Hinger taught at Yale University in Connecticut, and at the Manhattan School of Music in New York. During the summer of 1974, Hinger was timpanist with the Aspen Festival Orchestra in the Colorado mountains.

Other performances by Fred Hinger have included work with the Rochester Philharmonic Orchestra. He has presented clinics and demonstrations of performance technique in many locations, for example in 1969 in Hanover, New Hampshire, in Europe, and in Israel in 1976 at the request of conductor Zubin Mehta. Other work that Hinger has performed includes founding a company that manufactures and distributes snare drum sticks, snare drums, timpani mallets, and timpani. Further, he has authored several method books and repertoire books with commentary about performance interpretation.

---

*W. Street is a subject in this volume.

Recent presentations by Fred Hinger include teaching at the Oberlin Percussion Institute in Ohio in 1989, and writing an introduction for George Hamilton Green's keyboard percussion method book for a Florida publisher. In 1991, Hinger is employed as a part-time faculty member at the University of Alabama in Huntsville.

DISCOGRAPHY

Finlandia. The Philadelphia Orchestra conducted by Eugene Ormandy. Columbia ML-5596.

George Frederick Handel: Messiah. Philadelphia Orchestra conducted by Eugene Ormandy. Columbia M2L-263.

Invitation to the Dance. Philadelphia Orchestra conducted by Eugene Ormandy. Columbia ML-5641.

Orff: Carmina Burana. Philadelphia Orchestra conducted by Eugene Ormandy. New York: CBS Records MYK-37217, 1981 (originally recorded in 1960).

Other recordings with the Philadelphia Orchestra, 1948-67.

The Blue Danube: A Johann Strauss Festival. Philadelphia Orchestra conducted by Eugene Ormandy. Columbia ML-5617.

BOOKS

Solos for the Virtuoso Tympanist. Hackensack, New Jersey: Jerona Music Corporation.

Technique for the Virtuoso Tympanist. Hackensack: Jerona Music.

The Timpani Player's Orchestral Repertoire, Volume 1: Beethoven Symphonies. Hackensack: Jerona Music, 1982.

The Timpani Player's Orchestral Repertoire, Volume 2: Brahms Symphonies. Hackensack: Jerona Music.

The Timpani Player's Orchestral Repertoire, Volume 3: Tchaikovsky. Hackensack: Jerona Music.

The Timpani Player's Orchestral Repertoire, Volume 4: Sibelius. Hackensack: Jerona Music.

The Timpani Player's Orchestral Repertoire, Volume 5: Richard Strauss. Hackensack: Jerona Music.

ARTICLES ABOUT SUBJECT

"Fred D. Hinger." Brochure. Oberlin Percussion Institute. Oberlin College Conservatory of Music, 1989.

Mattingly, Rick. "Fred Hinger: Individuality." Modern Percussionist II/2 (March 1986), 18.

REFERENCE SOURCES

Information supplied by the subject (September 1989).

Larrick, Geary. "Addendum." National Association of College Wind and Percussion Instructors Journal XXXV/1 (Fall 1986), 38.

"Timpani Books by Fred D. Hinger." Advertisement. Modern Percussionist (March 1986), 47.

Howard, Douglas
Born c. 1948, Greeneville, Tennessee

Douglas Howard learned rudimental drumming from a teacher of the marching band percussion section he played in during his secondary school attendance, and became interested in classical music around that time. In 1966, Howard enrolled at the University of Tennessee in Knoxville, studying percussion music and instruments in addition to his general university studies. Howard graduated from the University of Tennessee in 1970.

In 1970, Douglas Howard became a member of the United States Air Force Band in Washington, D.C. He was accepted as a percussionist in the Louisville Orchestra in Kentucky in 1974, and attended the Aspen Music Festival in Colorado also that year. After one year in Louisville, Howard auditioned and was accepted for the position of principal percussion in the Dallas Symphony Orchestra in Texas. Douglas Howard's percussion teachers have included Butch Legg, Chet Hedgecoth, Michael Combs, Alan Abel, *Cloyd Duff, *Charles Owen, and Tony Ames. As a service band percussionist in Washington, D.C., Howard worked toward a Master's degree at Catholic University.

Douglas Howard has played with the Dallas Symphony Orchestra since 1975. He has performed in the Aspen Music Festival several times, including the roles of timpanist in the Aspen Chamber Symphony and Aspen Festival Orchestra, and his present position as principal percussionist in the Festival Orchestra.

With the U.S. Air Force Band, one of Douglas Howard's many appearances was at an American Bandmasters Convention in Austin, Texas. With the Dallas Symphony Orchestra, he has performed in Mexico, France, England and Germany in addition to the United States. Howard has taught percussion at Southern Methodist University and at the Aspen Music School. He has also served on the faculty of Ludwig International Percussion

---

*C. Duff and C. Owen are subjects in this book.

Symposium, and as clinician at Percussive Arts Society International Convention. As a timpanist, in addition to his performances in Aspen since 1982, Douglas Howard has performed in the Air Force Concert Band, and as assistant timpanist in the Dallas Symphony Orchestra. His knowledge of orchestral percussion repertoire is outstanding.

DISCOGRAPHY

Recordings with the Dallas Symphony Orchestra since 1975 for RCA, Pro Arte, Telarc and Angel-EMI record companies.

Recordings with the Louisville Orchestra, 1974-75, for First Edition Records.

ARTICLES ABOUT SUBJECT

"Faculty." Catalog. Aspen Music School. Aspen, Colorado (Summer 1990), 36.

"Faculty." Catalog. Aspen Music School (Summer 1991), 43.

Vogel, Lauren. "Doug Howard." Modern Percussionist III/2 (March 1987), 8.

Hutcherson, Bobby
Born January 27, 1941, Los Angeles, California

Bobby Hutcherson studied the piano at an early age, then moved on to the keyboard percussion instruments. He is a most successful musician and vibraphonist within much of the twentieth century.

Early musical experiences for Hutcherson included lessons with Dave Pike, and performance on the west coast with Curtis Amy, Al Grey, Charles Lloyd and Billy Mitchell. Around 1961, Bobby Hutcherson resided in New York City and performed with several musicians, including Eric Dolphy, Grant Green, Herbie Hancock, Andrew Hill, Jackie McLean, Charles Tolliver, McCoy Tyner, and Tony Williams. In 1965, Hutcherson performed at the Monterey Jazz Festival with Gil Fuller's ensemble.

From 1967 to 1971, Hutcherson led a quintet with Harold Land that included pianists Chick Corea, Stanley Cowell and Joe Sample, bassists Reggie Johnson and Albert Stinson, and drum set performers Donald Bailey and Billy Higgins. In the 1970s, Hutcherson moved to San Francisco, California, and toured internationally during the 1980s. His performance is characterized by consistency and competency regardless of the medium being performed.

DISCOGRAPHY

Color Schemes. With M. Miller, J. Heard, B. Higgins and Airto. Landmark LLP-1508.

Components. Blue Note 84213, 1966.

Dialogue. Blue Note 84198, 1965.

Happenings. With H. Hancock, B. Cranshaw and J. Chambers. Blue Note originally recorded in 1966. Hollywood, California: Capitol Records CDP 7 46530 2, 1987.

Highway One. Columbia 35550, 1978.

Joe Henderson: Mode for Joe. Hollywood: Capitol Records, Blue Note Series, 1985.

Knucklebean. Blue Note LA-789, 1977.

Montara. Blue Note LA-551, 1975.

Solo/Quartet. Contemporary 14009, 1982.

Waiting. Blue Note LA-615, 1976.

COMPOSITIONS

Aquarian Moon.

Bouquet.

Head Start.

Rojo.

The Omen.

When You Are Near.

ARTICLES

"About the Vibes." Crescendo International IX/9 (1971), 24.

"Bobby Hutcherson." Master Technique Builders for Vibraphone and Marimba, compiled and edited by *Anthony J. Cirone. U.S.A.: Belwin-Mills Publishing (1985), 23.

ARTICLES ABOUT SUBJECT

Jeske, Lee. "Hutcherson, Bobby." The New Grove Dictionary of Jazz, Volume One, 1988.

Miller, William F. "Bobby Hutcherson." Modern Percussionist I/3 (June 1985), 69.

Reich, Howard. "Sweet and Exuberant All-Stars Never Miss A Beat." Chicago Tribune, Thursday, November 8, 1990, Section 1, page 16.

Tolleson, Robin. "Bobby Hutcherson: Street Vibes." Modern Percussionist I/2 (March 1985), 12.

---

* A. Cirone is a subject in this volume.

REFERENCE SOURCES

Egart, Richard. "Recordings." <u>Modern Percussionist</u> II/4 (September 1986), 55.

Feather, Leonard. Record jacket notes. <u>Happenings</u>. Capitol Records Blue Note Series CDP 7 46530 2, 1987.

Jackson, Milt

Born January 1, 1923, Detroit, Michigan

Like *Bobby Hutcherson, vibraphonist Milt Jackson began his musical studies on an instrument other than the percussion. Jackson began playing the guitar at age seven, and began playing the piano at age eleven. During his teen years, he began playing the xylophone and vibraphone. His first public appearance in performance was as a tenor in a vocal quartet that performed religious music in concert and on tour.

About 1945 in Detroit, Milt Jackson performed with a jazz group that accompanied a Dizzy Gillespie concert. In 1946, Jackson was performing with Gillespie's ensembles in New York City. In 1948 and 1949, Jackson worked with Woody Herman, Howard McGhee, Thelonius Monk, and Charlie Parker among other jazz artists. In 1950-52, Jackson performed regularly with Dizzy Gillespie.

In the latter part of 1952, Jackson organized a combo that was called Milt Jackson Quartet. The ensemble was re-named Modern Jazz Quartet that year, and remained intact for twenty years. Original members of the Modern Jazz Quartet, besides Jackson, were bassist Ray Brown, drum set performer Kenny Clarke, and pianist John Lewis. In 1974, Jackson started performing individually as a solo artist, including tours, and recently has rejoined the Modern Jazz Quartet for an annual concert tour.

Typically, the tremolo of the vibraphone that Milt Jackson performs runs at a rather slow speed, in contrast to the often fast speed of tremolo in recordings of *Lionel Hampton and usually no tremolo in performances by *Gary Burton. It can be mentioned that the vibraphone gets its name from the electricity-driven tremolo, or "vibrato," that characterizes the instrument along with a damper pedal that functions similarly to the damper pedal on the

---

*B. Hutcherson is a subject in this book.

*L. Hampton and G. Burton are subjects in this book.

piano. The vibraphone is thus an invention of the twentieth century in its use of electricity and aluminum alloy bars, with a musical instrument ancestry centuries old.

Milt Jackson's performance is characterized by expression and a wide range of dynamics. His two-mallet approach is often virtuosic in achievement. Jackson's playing with the Modern Jazz Quartet is often philosophically abstract in contrast to the more obvious exclamations of rock and other popular musics. Although Jackson is capable of prodigious technical display, often his playing exhibits the ability to say much with few notes sounding.

Jackson has performed with many top level jazz musicians during his career. Some of these people are Percy Heath, Connie Kay, Freddie Hubbard, Ron Carter, Billy Cobham, Joe Pass, Tommy Flanagan, Virgil Jones and Kenny Dorham. Milt Jackson's playing has been favorably reviewed in publication numerous times.

DISCOGRAPHY

Ballad Artistry. Atlantic 1342, 1959.

Blues at Carnegie Hall. Atlantic 1468, 1966.

Bluesology. Dee Gee 3702, 1951.

Brother Jim. Pablo 2310-916, 1985.

European Concert. Atlantic 1385-6, 1960.

It Don't Mean A Thing If You Can't Tap Your Foot to It. Pablo 2310-768, 1976.

Milt Jackson + Count Basie + The Big Band. Pablo 2310-822-3, 1978.

Milt Jackson: Opus de Funk. Prestige P-24048, 1975.

Milt Jackson Sunflower. CTI Records 6024, 1972.

MJQ Live at the Lighthouse. Atlantic SD-1486, 1967.

Soul Brothers. Atlantic 1279, 1957.

The Big 3. With Ray Brown and Joe Pass. Pablo 2310-757, 1975.

Third Stream Music. Atlantic 1345, 1957.

Three Windows. Modern Jazz Quartet with the New York Chamber Symphony. Atlantic 81761-1.

What's New? Blue Note 1592, 1952.

COMPOSITIONS

Bluesology.
For Someone I Love.
I've Lost Your Love.
Novamo.
Poom-a-Loom.
Ralph's New Blues.
Stonewall.
The Cylinder.
The Sealer.

ARTICLES ABOUT SUBJECT

Albright, Thomas. Record jacket notes. Milt Jackson: Opus de Funk. Prestige P-24048, 1975.

Balliett, W. "Like A Family." Improvising: Sixteen Jazz Musicians and Their Art. New York, 1977.

Blum, J. "Milt Jackson: Vibes Original." Jazz Times (July 1984), 13.

Burns, J. "Good Vibes." Jazz and Blues II/5 (1972), 7.

DeMicheal, Don. Record jacket notes. MJQ Live at the Lighthouse. Atlantic SD-1486, 1967.

Egart, Richard. "Modern Jazz Quartet: Three Windows." Modern Percussionist III/4 (September 1987), 54.

Feather, L. "The Evolution of Milt Jackson." Los Angeles Times Calendar (September 2, 1984), 55.

Hentoff, N. "Jazz Reviews: Modern Jazz Quartet." Down Beat XX/22 (1953), 16.

Hentoff, N. "The Modern Jazz Quartet." High Fidelity V/3 (1955), 36.

Lyons, L. "Milt Jackson: Dollars and Sense." Down Beat XLII/9 (1975), 14.

Owens, Thomas. "Jackson, Milt." The New Grove Dictionary of Jazz, Volume One, 1988.

Owens, Thomas. "Modern Jazz Quartet." The New Grove Dictionary of Jazz, Volume Two, 1988.

130

Owens, T. "The Fugal Pieces of the Modern Jazz Quartet." <u>Journal of Jazz Studies</u> IV (1976), 25.

*Samuels, Dave. "Milt Jackson." <u>Modern Percussionist</u> III/4 (September 1987), 1.

---

*D. Samuels is a subject in this book.

Jenks, Vicki P.
Born July 18, 1952, Devils Lake, North Dakota

Vicki Jenks was valedictorian of the senior class at Wolford High School in North Dakota in 1970. She enrolled at Minot State University, attending that school for two years. Jenks then enrolled at the University of Wisconsin - Stevens Point, graduating there with a baccalaureate degree in music education in 1974. She received a graduate assistantship at Baylor University in Texas that year, and earned a Master of Music degree at Baylor in 1975. Her graduate study emphasized music literature and percussion performance. Vicki Jenks' percussion teachers from 1970 to 1975 included Geary Larrick, Stanley Schleuter, and Larry Vanlandingham.

Professional experience of Vicki Jenks includes symphonic playing and educational coaching in addition to private teaching. Organizations with which she has performed are the Central Wisconsin Symphony Orchestra, the American Waterways Wind Orchestra, the Waco Symphony Orchestra, the Madison Symphony Orchestra, the Wisconsin Chamber Orchestra, the Minot Symphony Orchestra, and the Madison Community Orchestra. Other ensembles in which she has performed are percussion ensembles at Baylor University and the University of Wisconsin in Stevens Point, the Madison Municipal Band, Oakwood Chamber Players, El Paso Pro Musica Chamber Orchestra, the marimba ensemble Repercussion, and the percussion trio Array.

Since May, 1989, Vicki Jenks has worked as a percussion performer and clinician for the band and orchestra division of Yamaha Corporation of America. She has taught at the University of Wisconsin in Whitewater since 1987. Jenks has been a member of the percussion section of the Madison Symphony Orchestra in south-central Wisconsin since 1981.

Other work that Jenks has performed include service as a director of education for Ward-Brodt Music Company from 1980 to 1987, and freelance teaching. Specific teaching appointments have included assignments at International Music Camp, the Institute of the Arts in El Paso, Lakeland

College Summer Music Camp, University of Wisconsin - Madison Summer Music Clinic, and the University of Wisconsin - Stevens Point Summer Music Camp. In addition, Jenks has worked with the Musicians' Forum of Dane County, the Wisconsin Percussive Arts Society, the Wisconsin School Music Association, the Fine Arts Department of the Madison Metropolitan School District, and summer theater programs in Minot and Stevens Point.

Professional associations of Vicki Jenks include Pi Kappa Lambda and Sigma Alpha Iota societies. She has worked as a percussion artist for El Adobe Recording Studios in El Paso, Texas. Jenks was percussion instructor at the University of Texas - El Paso from 1976 to 1980. She has served as an advisory board member for the International Ambassadors of Music, and has directed the Percussion Ensemble of the Wisconsin Youth Symphony Orchestra. Vicki Jenks was cited for excellence by the Wisconsin Band Association in 1987 and 1991. She has also received awards from the International Music Camp, the International Ambassadors of Music, and the Mid-West International Band and Orchestra Clinic of Chicago. Jenks has performed and lectured in the United Kingdom and in other parts of Europe.

DISCOGRAPHY

Post-European tour albums with the International Music Camp and the International Ambassadors of Music in 1970, 1974, 1980, 1984 and 1985.

What Kind of Man. Accessory percussion, keyboard percussion and timpani. El Paso, Texas: El Adobe, 1978.

VIDEO RECORDING

1989 Scotland Tour. Wisconsin Youth Symphony Orchestra. Madison: High Road Productions.

ARTICLES

"Expecting and Receiving the Best from the Orchestral 'Drummers' via the Percussion Ensemble Experience." Wisconsin Percussive Arts Society Newsletter 19/1 (January 1991), 2.

ARTICLES ABOUT SUBJECT

*Latimer, James, editor. "Directory of Wisconsin Percussive Arts Society Percussionists." <u>Newsletter</u> 19/1 (January 1991), 9.

"Vicki P. Jenks." Wisconsin Youth Symphony Orchestras. Madison: Humanities Building.

REFERENCE SOURCES

Information supplied by the subject (February 1991).

"Percussion Excellence Ensures Success for U.S. Youngsters." Scotland: <u>Aberdeen Press and Journal</u>, August 14, 1989.

Phillips, Roddy. "Wisconsin Youth Symphony Orchestra at the Music Hall." Scotland: <u>Aberdeen Evening News</u>, August 14, 1989.

---

*J. Latimer is a subject in this volume.

Jones, Elayne
Born January 30, 1928, New York, New York

Elayne Jones received a specialized education at the Music and Art High School in New York City from 1942 to 1945. She enrolled at The Juilliard School in New York in 1945, and graduated from there in 1949. Jones attended the Tanglewood summer music school also in 1949. Her teachers at Juilliard included percussionist-author Morris Goldenberg, and timpanist-author Saul Goodman.

From 1945 to 1951, Elayne Jones was a member of the National Orchestra Association directed by Leon Barzin. Her performance competencies encompass both percussion and piano. For several years in New York City following her graduation from Juilliard, Elayne Jones led a very active professional career. Her professional preparation was aided financially in the names of Duke Ellington and Serge Koussevitsky at Juilliard and Tanglewood, respectively. One of her early jobs was performing with the New York City Opera Orchestra. Other orchestras with which she has performed include the San Francisco Symphony, the American Symphony Orchestra, the San Francisco Opera Orchestra, the New York City Ballet Orchestra, the New York All-City Orchestra, and the New York Philharmonic.

As a resident of New York City and San Francisco during her career, Elayne Jones has had the opportunity to perform with many ensembles and people within major metropolitan areas. Jones is one of nine persons who founded the Symphony of the New World in New York. She has performed with the American Ballet Theatre, the New Jersey Symphony Orchestra, the Caramoor Summer Festival, the Metropolitan Opera Orchestra, the Brooklyn Philharmonic, and the Westchester Symphony Orchestra. Jones has performed for the New York City Light Opera, and for many Broadway productions of musical theater. She played for the opening of Disney World in Florida, and for the opening of the Kennedy Center in Washington, D.C. Elayne Jones has performed in Carnegie Hall in New York City.

In 1956, Jones performed for a National Education Television special. In 1976, she was featured in a half hour television program aired over station KQED in San Francisco; the program was entitled "Echoes of Africa in the Symphony." In 1977, Elayne Jones performed with two other artists for an hour television program that was produced by Channel 21 in San Mateo, California.

As a teacher, Jones has worked in many locations. She has instructed timpani and percussion at the San Francisco Conservatory, has lectured and taught piano at Bronx Community College, has taught at Marti Christi High School on Long Island, and has instructed at the Westchester Conservatory of Music.

Elayne Jones has lectured and performed at schools and resorts on Long Island and in New York, New Jersey, and Connecticut. She has given presentations for the National Music Teachers Guild and at music camps in New York state. Jones was invited to participate in a Scholars-in-Residence program in Nassau county, helping to enlighten youngsters in understanding and appreciating the arts by having personal contact with practicing artists.

Broadway productions that Jones has played include "Porgy and Bess," "Raisin," "Chorus Line," "Baker's Wife," "West Side Story." Also "Purlie," "Greenwillow," "On A Clear Day You Can See Forever," "Kelly," "All Hail the Conquering Hero," and "Carnival!" New York City Light Opera productions that Elayne Jones has played include "Milk and Honey," "Most Happy Fella," "South Pacific," Gilbert and Sullivan operettas, and Johann Strauss operettas. Jones has played at The Melody Tent in Hyannis, and with the CBS Symphony Orchestra conducted by Antonini. She has performed for Mineola Playhouse productions of "Stop the World, I Want to Get Off," "Annie, Get Your Gun," "Flower Drum Song" and "Oklahoma!"

Elayne Jones is an example of a very busy percussion professional performer who has played in many ensembles with many musicians and conductors. A partial list of the surnames of conductors with whom she has performed follows: Stokowski, Fiedler, Adler, Fischer, de Waart, Buckley, Ozawa, Levine, Macal, Martinon, Tillson Thomas, Delacote, Rudel, Rostropovich, Lewis, Pritchard, Gavezzari, Hollreiser, Gardelli, Pelosi, Rennert, Minde, Navarro, Minor, Mund, Kord, Kubelik, Mauceri,

Loposcopos, Shapirra, Variso, Schermerhorn, Simmons, Sanzogno, Suitner, von Dohnanyi, Steinberg, Leinsdorf, Stravinsky, Serafin, Irving, Rosenstock, Barzin, Bernstein, Copland, Halasz, Morel, Landau, Wallenstein, Boulez, Previn, Casals, Dixon, Henderson, Henze, Iturbi, Krips, Kletsky, Reiner, Walton, Otterloo, Joachim, Imbal, Menuhin, Golshmann, Lee, Walter, Pretre, Horenstein, Fjelstadt, Schmidt-Isserstedt, Monteux. Jones has presented more than three hundred solo lecture-demonstrations of percussion instruments in schools and colleges, beyond her regular perfoming appointments.

DISCOGRAPHY

Recordings with the San Francisco Symphony Orchestra, 1972-75, conducted by Seiji Ozawa.

ARTICLES ABOUT SUBJECT

Commanday, Robert. "Analysis and Opinion: Players' Committee Repeats an Injustice." The San Francisco Chronicle, August 27, 1975.

Field, Sidney. "Only Human: Drums Are Her Beat." The New York Daily News, Wednesday, December 1, 1965.

"Meet: Elayne Jones." San Francisco, California: The Opera Companion.

Tircuit, Heuwell. "Show of Symphony Pride." San Francisco Chronicle, Thursday, July 6, 1972.

Zakariasen, Bill. "Frisco Rumblings." New York Daily News, September 9, 1975.

REFERENCE SOURCES

Information supplied by the subject (September 1989).

Jones, Elayne. "Opera Repertoire." Unpublished list.

"Leopold Stokowski Speaks." Music and Artists, January, 1972.

Kraft, William
Born c. 1930

Timpanist, composer and conductor William Kraft has performed in the Los Angeles Philharmonic Orchestra and conducted the Los Angeles Percussion Ensemble in recording. Kraft's compositions for percussion cover a wide range in pedagogy and fine art, requesting both standard and unique instrumentation. Besides performing for years in the Los Angeles Philharmonic as leader of the percussion section, principal timpanist, assistant conductor, and composer in residence, William Kraft has served as composer in residence at Chapman College in California.

Kraft's concerto entitled "Quintessence" features five percussion soloists accompanied by concert band. It was commissioned by the United States Air Force Band, and has been performed at a Percussive Arts Society International Convention. His works for percussion ensemble and multiple percussion soloist are mainstream generally, with his other chamber music being more avant-garde. William Kraft's music compositions tend to challenge the audience as well as the performer(s) in regard to outlook, ideas and sound concepts. In this way, Kraft's percussion music is like much that has been written in the twentieth century in that it is new, always new.

William Kraft has been influential in the premiering, performing, and recording of many works for primarily percussion instruments. Kraft has written for concert band, orchestra, multipercussion, snare drum, xylophone, tom-tom, glockenspiel and field drum, among other instruments. Some of his music requests acting on the part of the music performer, within a contained theatrical environment. Indeed, drama and beauty seem to be basic facets of Kraft's music.

DISCOGRAPHY

Avalanche. Soundtrack for the film (1978). Delos Del/F-25452.
Cadenze (1971). Desto 7166.

Concerto for Four Percussion Soloists and Orchestra (1976). London CS-6613.

Concerto Grosso (1961). Louisville S-653.

Contextures: Riots-Decade '60 (1967). London CS-6613.

Des Imagistes (1974). CRI Records.

Dialogues and Entertainments (1980). Crest D-81.

Double Trio (1966). Protone CSPR-163.

Encounters III: Duel for Trumpet and Percussion (1971). Protone CSPR-163.

Encounters IV: Duel for Trombone and Percussion (1972). Crystal S-641.

Evening Voluntaries (1980). Crystal S-375.

Fanfare 1969 (1969). Avant AV-1001.

Gallery '83 (1983). CRI Records.

Games: Collage I (1969). Angel S-36036.

In Memoriam Igor Stravinsky (1974). Orion ORS-76212.

Momentum (1966). Crystal S-104 and Golden Crest 4145.

Morris Dance (1963). WIM R-5.

Nonet for Brass and Percussion (1959). Crystal S-281.

Organist David Craighead. The Los Angeles Percussion Ensemble conducted by W. Kraft. Crystal Records S-858, 1977.

Recordings as timpanist with the Los Angeles Philharmonic for eighteen years.

Requiescat (1975). Townhall S-24.

Soliloquy: Encounters I (1975). Protone CSPR-163.

Theme and Variations for Percussion Quartet (1956). Crystal S-104.

Translucences (1979). Contemporary Record Society.

COMPOSITIONS

See listing immediately preceding in Discography.

ARTICLES ABOUT SUBJECT

Pershing, Karen Ervin. "William Kraft." <u>Modern Percussionist</u> II/4 (September 1986), 22.

REFERENCE SOURCES

Knaack, Donald. "Critique." <u>Modern Percussionist</u> II/1 (December 1985), 32.

Record jacket notes. <u>Organist David Craighead</u>. Crystal Records S-858, 1977.

Kuehn, Donald
Born March 3, 1947, Denver, Colorado

Donald Kuehn studied the piano privately from age six to age eighteen. From 1962 to 1965, Kuehn studied percussion instruments and performance technique with Walter Light, timpanist in the Denver Symphony Orchestra. From 1965 to 1968, Kuehn attended Boston University in Massachusetts. In Boston, he studied percussion with two Boston Symphony Orchestra percussionists, *Thomas Gauger and Charles Smith. In 1976 and 1977, Kuehn studied with timpanist *Cloyd Duff.

As a professional percussion performer, Donald Kuehn played in a musical theater orchestra at the Broadmore Hotel in Colorado Springs during the summer of 1963. In the summer of 1965, Kuehn played percussion with a trio at night clubs in the Denver area while performing with the University of Colorado Symphony Orchestra. In 1966 and 1967, he performed with a jazz band in the greater Boston area.

From 1968 to 1973, Donald Kuehn performed as percussionist and assistant timpanist in the Baltimore Symphony Orchestra in Maryland. In 1969, Kuehn began teaching at the Peabody Conservatory of Music in Baltimore, and in the Department of Music at Susquehanna University in Selinsgrove, Pennsylvania, until 1973.

In 1973, Kuehn moved to Toronto, Ontario, Canada, to perform as principal percussionist in the Toronto Symphony. He currently works in that position. Since 1976, Donald Kuehn has worked with the Toronto Symphony Education Program. Examples of the kind of work that Kuehn performs, as the principal percussionist in a major symphony orchestra, are 1) playing important snare drum parts in the orchestral repertoire and 2) preparing bass drum heads for concert performance.

Honors and awards that Donald Kuehn has been granted include receiving a performance award at Boston University, graduating with honors

*T. Gauger and C. Duff are subjects in this volume.

from the Mathews School of Music in piano, and receiving scholarships to study at Rocky Ridge Music Center in Estes Park, Colorado.

DISCOGRAPHY

Recordings with the Baltimore Symphony Orchestra, 1968-73.
Recordings with the Toronto Symphony since 1973.

REFERENCE SOURCES

Attendance at Toronto Symphony concerts, 1980 and 1990.
Information supplied by the subject (September 1990).

Kvistad, Richard T.

Born September 10, 1943, Chicago, Illinois

Richard Kvistad studied percussion privately with Frank Rullo in Chicago from 1954 to 1958. In 1959 and 1960, Kvistad studied with Jack McKenzie at the National Music Camp, Interlochen. In 1961, Kvistad enrolled at Oberlin College in Oberlin, earning a baccalaureate degree there in 1965. Kvistad's scholarly emphasis at Oberlin in the Conservatory of Music was music education, studying percussion with *Cloyd Duff. During his higher education at Oberlin, Kvistad took a year's leave-of-absence to study in Europe where he resided in Salzburg, Austria. Percussion studies in Europe for Kvistad included work with Paul Hirsh, a performer for the Mozarteum orchestra. In 1965, Richard Kvistad studied with George Gaber, percussion professor at Indiana University.

From 1966 to 1969, Kvistad attended the graduate school at the University of Illinois, studying percussion again with Jack McKenzie. In 1969, Kvistad also studied percussion with *Albert Payson, a member of the Chicago Symphony Orchestra. Richard Kvistad received a Master of Music degree from the University of Illinois in 1969. Later study for Kvistad has been in California where he studied Asian Indian drumming and Indonesian gamelan at Center for World Music in Berkeley in 1974.

Richard Kvistad's professional career started in the summer of 1965, when he was timpanist for the American Waterways Wind Orchestra in Pittsburgh, Pennsylvania. The ensemble at that time was called the American Wind Symphony Orchestra. It is conducted by Robert Austin Boudreau.

In 1965-66, Kvistad performed as percussionist for the Florida Symphony Orchestra in Orlando. In 1967 and 1968, he was principal percussionist in Chicago's Grant Park Symphony during the summers. In 1969, Richard Kvistad was timpanist at Grant Park. Later in the year, he performed as percussionist for the Lyric Opera Association in Chicago.

From December, 1969, to June, 1972, Kvistad served as principal percussionist and associate principal timpanist in the Pittsburgh Symphony

---

*C. Duff and A. Payson are subjects in this book.

Orchestra. From 1972 to 1974, he was a founding member of Blackearth Percussion Group. This chamber ensemble toured and presented lecture demonstrations nationwide, developing a new repertoire for percussion in small ensembles. The quartet worked with avant-garde composed music, with mixed media such as film and electronic tape and dance, and with classical improvised music within a modern musical language. Their touring and various performances were very influential in the development of contemporary percussion literature. The Group exists in 1991 as a trio in southern Ohio in residency at the College-Conservatory of Music at the University of Cincinnati.

From 1974 to 1980, Richard Kvistad performed freelance in San Francisco, California, as a percussionist and timpanist working in the ballet orchestra, the opera orchestra, and the symphony orchestra. Since 1980, Kvistad has served as principal percussionist and associate principal timpanist in the San Francisco Opera Orchestra. He performs annually as timpanist in the San Francisco Pops Orchestra.

Freelance jobs that Kvistad has played include work with American Ballet Theatre, the Bolshoi Ballet in 1987, the Kirov Ballet in 1989, and Dance Theatre of Harlem in 1989. Previous work was with the University of Chicago Contemporary Players in 1969, directed by Ralph Shapey. In 1971, Kvistad presented a timpani demonstration for the children's television show entitled "Mr. Roger's Neighborhood." Kvistad performed the timpani part for the film "Apocalypse Now."

In March, 1989, Richard Kvistad premiered his own music composition titled "Concerto for Timpani and Chamber Orchestra" with Sinfonia San Francisco. He has written music that has been published by M.M. Cole and Belwin-Mills, in addition to publishing some works himself.

Honors and awards that Kvistad has received include being a concerto winner at National Music Camp in 1960, with performance of Darius Milhaud's percussion concerto, being inducted into Pi Kappa Lambda honorary music society in 1969 at the University of Illinois, and performing a timpani concerto with the Pittsburgh Symphony Orchestra in 1971. Kvistad is a founding member of California Percussion Players since June, 1989.

As a teacher of percussion, Richard Kvistad has taught at Interlochen Arts Academy in 1967-68, at Carnegie Mellon University in 1971-72, at Northern Illinois University in 1973-74, and at Sonoma State University in

Rohnert Park, California, from 1978 to 1981. Kvistad has taught at San Francisco State University from 1981 to 1984. He has been composing music for percussion since 1954.

DISCOGRAPHY

California Percussion Players. Music compositions by Cage, Kraft, Kvistad, London, Reich, Rouse. R. Kvistad performing timpani and percussion, 1990.

"Dreaming of Another." Kote Kan-Percussion and Reference Recordings. R. Kvistad, composer and percussionist. RR-3.

"Ed Dugger: Intermezzi." American Contemporary. San Francisco Contemporary Music Players. R. Kvistad performing xylophone and percussion. CRI-378.

"Frederic Rzewski: Opus One Number Twenty, 'Les Mouton de Panurge'." Blackearth Percussion Group. R. Kvistad performing nabimba.

Gershwin: American in Paris. San Francisco Symphony Orchestra. R. Kvistad performing percussion and taxi horns. DGG 2530-788.

Music of Salvatore Martirano. University of Illinois. R. Kvistad performing percussion on "Ballad," and marimba on "Octet." Polydor 24-500.

"Opus One Number Twenty-Two." The Blackearth Percussion Group. R. Kvistad performing percussion and timpani.

Paul Chihara: The Tempest. San Francisco Performing Arts Orchestra. R. Kvistad performing snare drum, tabla drums, and other percussion. MMG 201-X.

San Francisco Contemporary Music Players. R. Kvistad performing snare drum in two Charles Boone compositions. Grenadilla GS-1063.

76 Pieces of Explosive Percussion. Sonic Arts Symphonic Percussion Consortium. R. Kvistad performing percussion. Direkt to Disk Records LS-11.

COMPOSITIONS

Concerto for Timpani and Chamber Orchestra. Solo part with piano reduction. R. Kvistad, 1988.

REFERENCE SOURCES

Information supplied by the subject (September 1989).

Pfaff, Timothy. "'Virtuoso'--Marred by Schubert Piece." <u>San Francisco Examiner</u>, Tuesday, March 7, 1989, D-7.

"Virtuoso Night." Program booklet. Sinfonia San Francisco. Herbst Theatre, March 6, 1989.

Lamb, Christopher S.

Born March 28, 1959, Sandusky, Ohio

Christopher Lamb studied at the Eastman School of Music in Rochester, New York, from 1977 to 1981. He earned a baccalaureate degree there, studying percussion with *John Beck. Previously, Lamb had begun percussion study with Salvatore Rabbio in 1975. From 1977 to 1978, Christopher Lamb studied percussion with *Leigh Howard Stevens. In 1982 and 1983, Lamb studied his musical instrument with Glen Velez. Privately, Christopher Lamb continues to study ethnomusicology in its practical aspects.

As a professional percussion orchestral performer, Lamb has received much valuable experience. From March, 1981, to July, 1982, Christopher Lamb was a percussionist and assistant timpanist in the Buffalo Philharmonic Orchestra. From August, 1982, to April, 1985, Lamb served as a percussionist in the Metropolitan Opera Orchestra in New York City. Since April, 1985, he has worked in the position Principal Percussion in the New York Philharmonic. Lamb was twenty-five years of age at the time that he successfully passed the audition for membership in that orchestra, and twenty-six when he performed in his first concert there.

Christopher Lamb's teaching experience includes serving as a percussion instructor at Mannes College of Music from 1986 to 1989. Since 1989, Lamb has worked as chairperson of the percussion department at the Manhattan School of Music. Since 1986, he has presented clinic demonstrations sponsored by the Sabian cymbal company. Since 1985, Christopher Lamb has been involved with the duo Lambchops, a piano and percussion chamber ensemble shared with his wife Virginia Perry Lamb.

---

*J. Beck and L. Stevens are subjects in this volume.

DISCOGRAPHY

Aaron Copland: Symphony No. 3. The New York Philharmonic conducted by Leonard Bernstein with C. Lamb performing xylophone and orchestral bells. DG-4191701, 1985.

Antonin Dvorak: Carnival Overture. New York Philharmonic conducted by Zubin Mehta with C. Lamb performing tambourine. DG, 1989.

Gustav Mahler: Symphony No. 2. New York Philharmonic conducted by Leonard Bernstein with C. Lamb performing clash cymbals. DG, 1988.

Gustav Mahler: Symphony No. 3. New York Philharmonic conducted by Leonard Bernstein with C. Lamb performing bass drum. DG, 1987.

Gustav Mahler: Symphony No. 5. New York Philharmonic conducted by Zubin Mehta with C. Lamb performing bass drum and bells. Teldec, 1989.

Gustav Mahler: Symphony No. 7. New York Philharmonic conducted by Leonard Bernstein with C. Lamb performing bass drum. DG, 1986.

Music of Zwillich. New York Ensembles with C. Lamb performing marimba and vibraphone. New World NW 372-1, 1989.

Other recordings with the New York Philharmonic since 1985.

Peter Tchaikovsky: Symphony No. 6 in B Minor. New York Philharmonic conducted by Leonard Bernstein with C. Lamb performing bass drum. DG, 1987.

Richard Wagner: The Mastersingers of Nuremberg. The New York Philharmonic with C. Lamb performing triangle. DG-4191691, 1985.

The Heroic Mr. Handel. New York Trumpet Ensemble with C. Lamb performing snare drum. Vox MW CD-7100.

ARTICLES ABOUT SUBJECT

Mattingly, Rick. "Chris Lamb: New York's Newest." Modern Percussionist I/4 (September 1985), 18.

REFERENCE SOURCES

Information supplied by the subject (October 1989).

<u>Live from Lincoln Center</u>. New York Philharmonic conducted by Zubin Mehta. Wisconsin Public Television, December 31, 1990.

<u>Program Guide</u>. Madison: Wisconsin Public Television, 1991.

Lang, Morris
Born February 2, 1931, New York, New York

Morris Arnold Lang attended New York City's Music and Art High School from 1945 to 1948. He then enrolled at The Juilliard School, studying there from 1948 to 1953. Lang earned the degree Bachelor of Science at Juilliard. One of his teachers there was timpanist Saul Goodman. In 1947 and 1948, Morris Lang studied percussion privately with Morris Goldenberg. From 1950 to 1953, Lang studied with William (Billy) Gladstone.

Morris Lang's professional playing experience began with his performing for the New York City Ballet from 1951 to 1955. From 1953 to 1955, Lang served as a substitute percussionist at Radio City in New York. During the same period, he worked as a percussionist for the New York Opera Society. From 1952 to 1955, Lang was a percussionist with the Little Orchestra Society. Since 1955, Morris Lang has performed in the positions Percussionist and Associate Timpanist in the New York Philharmonic Orchestra.

Other work that Lang has performed includes playing timpani for Gian-Carlo Menotti's "Saint of Bleeker Street" on Broadway and in Washington, D.C. He performed in Puerto Rico in 1958 as a percussionist for the Metropolitan Opera. In 1977, Morris Lang performed the percussion part to Bela Bartok's "Sonata for Two Pianos and Percussion" at a Percussive Arts Society International Convention in Knoxville at the University of Tennessee.

As a teacher of percussion, Morris Lang has worked at the Oberlin Percussion Institute in 1988 in northern Ohio during the summer. From 1965 to 1971, Lang taught at the New York College of Music. From 1969 to 1975, he instructed percussion students at the Manhattan School of Music. From 1969 to 1972, Lang taught at Kingsborough Community College in Brooklyn. Since 1973, Morris Lang has served as chairperson of the percussion department in the Conservatory of Music at Brooklyn College. In 1973 and 1976, Lang led the Brooklyn College Percussion Ensemble on a performance tour of Roumania and Hungary. He has presented master classes in many locations, including Japan, Hong Kong, and the continental United States.

Morris Lang has performed with numerous conductors, including Zubin Mehta, Leonard Bernstein, George Szell, Pierre Boulez and Bruno Walter. Lang has performed chamber music with conductors Boulez, Farberman and Waldman. Composers whose music Morris Lang has performed include Elliott Carter, Carlos Chavez, Igor Stravinsky and Edgard Varese.

Lang has served his profession as not only an orchestral performer, but also a chamber music performer, author, teacher and businessperson. As organizational leader of Lang Percussion Company, he manufactures Goodman timpani and Gladstone snare drums, publishes music, method books and a percussion dictionary, and distributes Saito percussion keyboard instruments. Morris Lang received the George Wedge Award in 1953. Lang is unquestionably a leader in his field, and a performer of high quality.

DISCOGRAPHY

All-Star Percussion Ensemble. Conducted by Harold Farberman.

Carlos Chavez: Toccata, 1954.

Edgard Varese: Ionisation. Conducted by Waldman, 1952. Conducted by Boulez, 1975.

Elliott Carter: Eight Pieces for Four Timpani. Columbia, 1975.

Gian-Carlo Menotti: Saint of Bleeker Street, 1954.

Igor Stravinsky: L'Histoire du Soldat, 1957.

Ludwig van Beethoven: Symphony No. 9. The New York Philharmonic conducted by Leonard Bernstein. New York: CBS Records MK-42224, 1969 and 1986.

Other recordings with the New York Philharmonic since 1955.

BOOKS

Dictionary of Percussion Terms. New York: Lang Percussion.

The Beginning Snare Drummer. New York: Lang Percussion, 1979.

ARTICLES

"A Talk with Marimba Virtuoso, *Keiko Abe." Interview, Part 2. Marimba Clinic, edited by *Leigh Howard Stevens. <u>Percussive Notes</u> 21/5 (July 1983), 20.

"Orchestral Percussionist: New York Philharmonic Audition." <u>Modern Percussionist</u> I/4 (September 1985), 36.

REFERENCE SOURCES

Information supplied by the subject (January 1990).

<u>Lang Percussion Inc.</u> Brochure. New York: Lang Percussion, 1988 and 1989.

<u>Live from Lincoln Center.</u> The New York Philharmonic conducted by Zubin Mehta. Wausau: Wisconsin Public Television, December 31, 1990.

---

*K. Abe and L. Stevens are subjects in this volume.

Latimer, James H.
Born June 27, 1934, Tulsa, Oklahoma

James Latimer attended Indiana University in Bloomington, earning the degree Bachelor of Music in 1956. In 1964, Latimer received a Master of Music degree at Boston University in Massachusetts. Previously, he had taught in Tulsa in 1956 and 1957, and at Florida A & M University in Tallahassee, working in the Department of Music there as percussion instructor and assistant director of bands. At Florida A & M, James Latimer founded and directed the University Percussion Ensemble.

From 1963 to 1968, Latimer worked as a freelance percussion performer in the Boston metropolitan area. He performed in the Boston Pops Orchestra from 1968 to 1974, conducted by Arthur Fiedler.

Since 1968, James Latimer has served on the faculty in the School of Music at the University of Wisconsin in Madison. Latimer has performed as timpanist in the Madison Symphony Orchestra also since that time.

Latimer's career in Wisconsin exhibits the variety that is available to a professor at a major university. He has received several university research grants. Since 1968, James Latimer has worked as a clinician for the Ludwig Drum Company. From 1972 to 1978, Latimer was conductor of the Wisconsin Youth Symphony Orchestra, including a performance at the Mid-West Band and Orchestra Clinic in Chicago.

Since 1981, James Latimer has conducted the Capitol City Band in Madison. He has worked as a guest conductor for youth orchestras since 1974. Latimer has guest conducted the Madison Symphony Orchestra, the Racine Symphony Orchestra, and the Tulsa Philharmonic. He has participated at many music and percussion conferences, and has served as President and Newsletter Editor for the Wisconsin chapter of the international Percussive Arts Society. Latimer has performed at the Ludwig International Percussion Symposium in Madison. With the Racine Symphony, he has worked as featured percussion soloist in presentations of

Darius Milhaud's multipercussion concerto and Paul Creston's marimba concerto. Latimer has composed percussion ensemble music for publication.

During the 1984-85 school term, James Latimer was a Fulbright lecturer at Cairo Conservatoire in Egypt, where he served as guest conductor of the Cairo Symphony Orchestra. Latimer also appeared as a solo percussion performer on Egyptian national television. From 1985 to 1987, he was a visiting professor at Radford University in Virginia, specializing in percussion. In January, 1990, Latimer played the Creston concerto accompanied by the Madison Symphony.

Latimer has coordinated a Duke Ellington Festival at the University of Wisconsin in Madison. Latimer has received several honors and awards, including biographical listings in Who's Who in Music, International Who's Who in Music, ASCAP Biographical Dictionary, Who's Who in the Midwest, and Dictionary of Distinguished Americans. James Latimer has been cited for musical excellence by government offices in Madison, including those of Governor, Mayor, and County Executive. He has been honored by the Wisconsin Federation of Music Clubs for outstanding music performance, and was presented an honorary membership in that organization. James Latimer regularly conducts University Percussion Ensemble concerts at the Madison campus of the University of Wisconsin.

ARTICLES

Newsletter 19/1 (January 1991). Madison: Wisconsin Percussive Arts Society.

"Nexus - Wisconsin Day of Percussion." Madison: Wisconsin Percussive Arts Society, March, 1990.

ARTICLES ABOUT SUBJECT

"Symphony Will Observe Tenth Anniversary of Civic Center Performances." Madison, Wisconsin: Madison Symphony Orchestra, January, 1990.

REFERENCE SOURCES

Information supplied by the subject (October 1989).

Lee, Garry
Born December 27, 1951, Rochford, Essex, England

Vibraphonist Garry Collin Lee has performed for fifteen years as a freelance musician and leader in Sydney, New South Wales, and in Perth, Western Australia, in the country of Australia. Lee has worked as a teacher in the jazz music curriculum at Western Australia Conservatorium of Music since 1984. Besides teaching and performing, he has been active as a composer and recording artist.

In the 1970s, Garry Lee studied jazz guitar privately in Sydney with George Golla. In 1981 and 1982, Lee studied the vibraphone with *David Samuels at the New South Wales Conservatorium of Music. A few years later, Lee received a grant to study with *Samuels and *David Friedman in New York City in early 1985.

In 1984, Garry Lee was the first Western Australia resident to receive an international study grant for jazz music. A year later, Lee was one of three composers to receive a commission from the Australian Bicentennial Authority to compose a three movement work entitled "Reflections of Western Australia," for which Lee composed the first movement. The composition received its first performance in 1988, the year of Australia's bicentenary, and was recorded at that time.

Garry Lee recorded in ensemble with several musicians in 1987. In February of that year, Lee performed as a featured vibraphone soloist with the Western Australia Symphony Orchestra. In 1989, Garry Lee led a trio called Jazz Line that was selected to tour Jakarta, Indonesia. Also in 1989, Lee's quintet called Qango performed as a support band for a concert presented by Gene Harris Superband in Perth. In 1990, Garry Lee's septet was chosen to support the Wynton Marsalis Septet in Perth.

Garry Lee's jazz playing at times sounds ethereal, natural and various. That is, his music tends to contain a considerable amount of variety and is

---

*D. Samuels and D. Friedman are subjects in this volume.

contrasted from piece to piece. At times the harmonies are complicated, while at other times they are simple. His rhythms tend to be complex. At times his playing is atonal, and at times it borders on tonality. As would be expected with a percussionist composer, there is typically a myriad of tone colors, or timbres, in his music, not always within the same piece, but certainly in his composite works.

DISCOGRAPHY

Garry Lee, 1987. Unpublished audio cassette tape. Perth, Western Australia, 1987.

Reflections of Western Australia. First movement composed by G. Lee. Australian Bicentennial Authority, 1990.

COMPOSITIONS

Dance of the Emu.
Heartvelt.
Leeward Murmurings.
Peace of Mind.
Samba de Yallingua.
Towards Fred.

REFERENCE SOURCES

Information supplied by the subject (December 1989).

Leonard, Stanley S.
Born September 26, 1931, Philadelphia, Pennsylvania

Stanley Leonard moved to Independence, Missouri, at a young age, studied at Northwestern University in Evanston, Illinois, and graduated from the Eastman School of Music in Rochester, New York. Leonard's percussion teacher at Eastman was *William Street. Stanley Leonard earned a Bachelor of Music degree at the Eastman School, with a Performer's Certificate in Percussion. Leonard's percussion teacher at Northwestern in 1950 was Edward Metzinger.

In 1953, Stanley Leonard was a member of the first Eastman Wind Ensemble. This wind and percussion group is historic in its instrumentation that is more soloistic with a chamber music nature in comparison with the traditional concert or symphonic wind band that is often twice the size of the standard wind ensemble. The concert band and the wind ensemble typically share about half of the wind band repertoire, with the other half being specifically oriented toward one or the other. Another name for the wind ensemble is "wind symphony" or "wind symphony orchestra." However, nearly all wind bands of these types usually contain the percussion as part of their instrumentation, though this fact is not often apparent in the ensemble's name. A similar confusion exists in classifying early twentieth century jazz ensembles as either bands or orchestras: often the name is not accurately descriptive of the group's content, but is merely a convenient, popularly known term.

Before pursuing his higher education, Stanley Leonard studied music in 1945 with Very McNary, principal percussionist of the Kansas City Philharmonic. The next year, Leonard studied with Ben Udell, timpanist in the Kansas City Philharmonic. In 1949, Leonard studied at National Music Camp at Interlochen, Michigan.

---

*W. Street is a subject in this book.

After graduation from the Eastman School of Music, Stanley Leonard became a U.S. Army musician, and in 1955-56 was assistant conductor of the 19th United States Army Band at Fort Dix, New Jersey. Since 1956, Stanley Leonard has worked as principal timpanist with the Pittsburgh Symphony Orchestra in Pennsylvania.

After moving to Pittsburgh, Leonard pursued graduate study at Carnegie Mellon University. With the Pittsburgh Symphony Orchestra, Stanley Leonard has performed as featured soloist for subscription concerts in 1958, 1964, 1966, 1973 and 1984. Featured solo repertoire that Leonard has performed include Darius Milhaud's "Concerto for Percussion and Small Orchestra," Werner Tharichen's "Concerto for Timpani and Orchestra," Andrzej Panufnik's "Concertino for Timpani and Percussion and Strings," Byron Mcholloh's "Symphony Concertante for Timpanist and Orchestra," and Raymond Premru's "Celebrations for Solo Timpani and Orchestra." Leonard performed as timpanist of the Pittsburgh Pops Orchestra from 1965 to 1969.

In 1958, Stanley Leonard organized the first percussion ensemble in Pittsburgh at Carnegie Mellon University. From 1965 to 1969, Leonard conducted the wind and percussion ensembles at that school during summer sessions.

Stanley Leonard has worked as a rather prolific composer of percussion music for several years, publishing much of his own work. Leonard has been active as a performer of English handbell music in addition to the concert percussion. In addition to Carnegie Mellon University, Stanley Leonard has given presentations about percussion and timpani at the University of Michigan, West Virginia University, Indiana University of Pennsylvania, the Eastman School of Music, and the Manhattan School of Music.

DISCOGRAPHY

Maurice Ravel: Mother Goose Suite. Peter Tchaikovsky: Symphony No. 4. George Gershwin: Rhapsody in Blue, Concerto in F, and American in Paris. Pittsburgh Symphony Orchestra conducted by Andre Previn. Phillips Records.

More than fifty recordings as timpanist with the Pittsburgh Symphony Orchestra since 1956, including the complete symphonies of Ludwig van Beethoven and Johannes Brahms, with William Steinberg and other conductors, for MCA and other companies.

Peter Tchaikovsky: Symphony No. 1. Nicolas Rimsky-Korsakov: Symphony No. 1. Pittsburgh Symphony Orchestra conducted by Lorin Maazel. Telarc Records.

COMPOSITIONS AND ARRANGEMENTS

A New Processional. Four-octave handbell ensemble. Columbia Pictures Publications.

Antiphonies. Two percussion quartets. Stanley Leonard Publications.

Canticle. Solo timpani. Ludwig Music Publishing.

Christmas Prelude. Three-octave handbell ensemble. Jenson Publications.

Circus. Six percussion. Columbia Pictures.

Closing Piece. Four triangles, wood blocks, snare drums and four timpani with five performers. S. Leonard.

Collage. Duo for flute and keyboard percussion with graphic notation. S. Leonard.

Continuum. Duo for keyboard percussion and timpani. S. Leonard.

Cycle for Percussion. Quartet with some construction of instruments. S. Leonard.

Dance Suite. Four percussion. S. Leonard.

Duales. Keyboard percussion with percussion accompaniment. S. Leonard.

Duet No. 1. For two timpanists. S. Leonard.

Duet No. 2. For two timpanists. S. Leonard.

Fanfare and Allegro. Duo for timpani and trumpet. N. Simrock via Theodore Presser Company.

Fanfare, Meditation and Dance. Eight percussion. S. Leonard.

Fantasia on Luther's Hymn. Timpani and organ. S. Leonard.

Forms. Timpani. Ludwig Music.

Four Canons. Percussion keyboard ensemble, arranged from music by Franz Joseph Haydn. Ludwig Music.

Four Images. Six percussion. Ludwig Music.

Genesis. Four-part chorus and five percussion. S. Leonard.

He Is Risen. Three-octave handbell ensemble. Columbia Pictures.

Incidental Music. Five percussion. S. Leonard.

Madras. Solo timpani. S. Leonard.

March and Scherzo. Percussion. S. Leonard.

March for Percussion. Six percussion. S. Leonard.

Mirror Canon. Four keyboard percussion arranged from music by Wolfgang Amadeus Mozart. Theodore Presser.

Mirrors. Six percussion. S. Leonard.

On That Day. Percussion and organ. S. Leonard.

Prelude. Four marimbas. Ludwig Music.

Processional. Four marimbas and optional percussion. S. Leonard.

Ring Hosannas. Two-octave handbell ensemble. Jenson Publications.

Scherzo. Seven keyboard percussion and timpani. S. Leonard.

Soliloquy. Three-octave handbell ensemble. Columbia Pictures.

Solo Dialogue. Multipercussion. Ludwig Music.

Sonnet. Multipercussion and pre-recorded tape. S. Leonard.

Symphony for Percussion. Nine percussion. S. Leonard.

The Music Box. Three-octave handbell ensemble. Jenson Publications.

Three Duets. Keyboard percussion, arranged from music by Johann Sebastian Bach. S. Leonard.

Three Spaces. Three percussion. S. Leonard.

Two Contemporary Scenes. Three percussion. S. Leonard.

Two Meditations. Solo percussion. S. Leonard.

Ubique. Solo multipercussion with graphic notation. S. Leonard.

Waltz. Six percussion. S. Leonard.

Word Games II. Five percussion with music theater. S. Leonard.

BOOKS

Pedal Technique for the Timpani. S. Leonard.
Seventeen Technical Studies for the Kettledrums. S. Leonard.

REFERENCE SOURCES

Information supplied by the subject (December 1989).

Lesbines, Tele
Born October 29, 1928, Middletown, Connecticut

Timpanist Tele Lesbines attended the University of Connecticut and Hartt School of Music of the University of Hartford. Lesbines earned a Bachelor of Arts degree, and studied percussion with *Vic Firth, Saul Goodman, *Fred Hinger, Alexander Lepak and Paul Price. Early study of percussion by Lesbines involved the snare drum, beginning his freshman year of high school working with his band director who accompanied him at the piano. Lesbines also studied percussion in Hartford with a show drummer who was a freelance musician.

Lesbines purchased his first set of timpani at the age of twenty-five. He performed timpani in the Hartford Symphony Orchestra before moving to Wisconsin and becoming principal timpanist in the Milwaukee Symphony Orchestra in September, 1969. Lesbines has remained in that position.

Besides performing as an orchestral timpanist, Tele Lesbines has presented lecture demonstrations variously. He served as organizational leader of the percussion section in Milwaukee for several years after becoming timpanist there. Lesbines has taught at the Wisconsin Conservatory of Music in Milwaukee. He has also helped to organize contemporary chamber music concerts at the Milwaukee Art Museum and elsewhere.

Other work for Lesbines has involved performing in a marimba ensemble at night clubs and shopping malls, and playing for recordings in Connecticut, Massachusetts, New York, Vermont and Wisconsin. Tele Lesbines has performed with the Bridgeport Symphony Orchestra and at the Brattleboro Music Festival. He has played percussion with the Milwaukee Chamber Orchestra, Pro Musica Nova and Rosewood Percussion Group. Among his many presentations are master classes at the University of Wisconsin in Stevens Point, and an address to a statewide meeting of the Wisconsin Percussive Arts Society in Milwaukee.

---

*V. Firth and F. Hinger are subjects in this volume.

Conductors with whom Lesbines has performed include Lukas Foss, Jose Iturbi and Jonel Perlea. In 1988, Tele Lesbines presented a percussion recital with piano accompaniment in Milwaukee. He is a regular attender at music and percussion conferences and conventions, as well as communicator with specific colleagues within his profession.

DISCOGRAPHY

Chamber music recordings, including Alvin Epstein's Dialogue for Double Bass and Percussion and Donald Erb's Diversions for Two.

"Stravinsky: Symphony of Psalms. Foss: Psalms. Ives: Psalm No. 67." Milwaukee Symphony Orchestra conducted by Lukas Foss and Wisconsin Conservatory Symphony Chorus directed by Margaret Hawkins. Minneapolis: Pro Arte PCD-169, 1984.

Other recordings with the Milwaukee Symphony Orchestra since 1969.

REFERENCE SOURCES

Information supplied by the subject (September 1989 and March 1990).

Attendance at Milwaukee Symphony Orchestra concerts and rehearsals, 1969-1990.

Larrick, Geary. "Guidelines for the Timpanist." Written in collaboration with T. Lesbines. National Association of College Wind and Percussion Instructors Journal XXXIX/3 (Spring 1991), 12-18.

Larrick, Geary. The Temple Garden. Five short movements for glockenspiel and piano. Dedicated to T. Lesbines. Stevens Point, Wisconsin: G and L Publishing, 1989.

Ludwig, William F.
Born 1879, Germany, Europe

William F. Ludwig, Senior, had a distinguished career as a professional percussionist and is a member of the Hall of Fame of the international Percussive Arts Society. Ludwig wrote several percussion instruction books. The Ludwig Drummer, a periodical that was distributed throughout the United States, contained many articles by leading percussionists and drummers in the era of its publication. Ludwig performed as an orchestral percussionist in the Pittsburgh Symphony Orchestra and the Chicago Symphony Orchestra and founded the Ludwig Drum Company.

Ludwig was known as an educator, manufacturer and inventor in addition to his professional percussion performance work. He was a leader in the National Association of Rudimental Drummers. In 1909, William F. Ludwig, Sr. founded a partnership with his younger brother, Theo, to form a company called Ludwig and Ludwig. Company name changes since then have been inclusive of Ludwig Drum Company and Ludwig Industries. The firm has been a leader in the manufacture of percussion equipment for much of the twentieth century.

Ludwig migrated to the United States from Germany in 1887 with his parents. The family moved to Chicago, Illinois, residing on the west side of that city. Ludwig first played a violin that his family brought from Germany to the United States. The instrument was a three-quarter size violin, and he began study of the instrument at the age of ten. After two years of study with the violin, Ludwig studied the piano for two years before studying the snare drum. One of his early teachers was rudimental drum specialist John Catlin. With a drum set, Ludwig began performing in amateur groups, then joined the Chicago Federation of Musicians Union, Local #10, in June, 1895, soon after its founding.

Ludwig's first professional playing job was that year with Wood Brothers Circus, a wagon show, at a salary of ten dollars each week. This band played fourteen shows weekly along with a daily parade, and performed under tents and in empty lots around the city during July and August. Ludwig's next playing job was with Harris Nickel Plate Show in 1896. This organization traveled by train. In 1897 and 1898, Ludwig played at dances, picnics, and for the Omaha Exposition. In 1899, he traveled with Salisbury's Concert Orchestra, playing percussion and featured xylophone solos.

In 1900, Ludwig performed at San Souci Park on the south side of Chicago. In 1908, he performed in that city at the Auditorium Theater. At about this time, he began experimenting with an improved bass drum pedal that was eventually patented and manufactured with drum sets. Ludwig also began making timpani in cooperation with his brother-in-law, Robert C. Danly, a professional designer and manager. The Ludwigs' first "factory" was on the third floor of a building at 2427 West 14th Street in Chicago. Ludwig's professional performance engagements during this era included timpani in the Pittsburgh Symphony Orchestra beginning in 1909, percussion with the Chicago Grand Opera Orchestra, and percussion with the Chicago Symphony Orchestra beginning in 1914. In 1917, however, Ludwig left professional performance to become a full time instrument manufacturer.

William F. Ludwig, Sr. has been followed in the firm by William F. Ludwig, Jr. who is presently a consultant to the Ludwig company, and by William F. Ludwig III who leads the Artist Relations Department for the organization. An example of one of the educational projects that has been sponsored and promoted by the Ludwig organization is an International Percussion Symposium that took place on campus of the University of Wisconsin in Madison for a week during the summer of 1973. Artists who gave presentations at that conference included *Gary Burton, *Albert Payson, Joe Morello, George Gaber, Fred Wickstrom, *James Latimer and Jim Sewrey. The conference consisted of master classes, recitals, lecture demonstrations and concerts. Master classes in some instances incorporated the use of several instruments on which students performed. People who attended this event included students and teachers from Wisconsin and other states, and educational percussion authority Haskell Harr.

---

*G. Burton, A. Payson and J. Latimer are subjects in this book.

BOOKS

Ludwig, Senior, William F. and Moeller, Gus. The Art of Drumming. Chicago: Ludwig Drum Company.

Other instruction books.

ARTICLES

Durrett, Ward. "An Interview with Mr. William Ludwig, Jr." Percussive Notes 29/3 (February 1991), 7.

Ludwig, Junior, William F. "Ludwig and Musser: The Education Connection." Catalog. Ludwig/Musser Division.

ARTICLES ABOUT SUBJECT

Ludwig, Senior, William F. "The Ludwig Story." Chicago: Ludwig Drum Company, 1968.

REFERENCE SOURCES

"Hall of Fame." Percussive Notes 29/1 (October 1990), 2.

"Hall of Fame." Percussive Notes 29/3 (February 1991), 2.

Pratt, John S. "Lesson 25." Dedicated to William F. Ludwig, Sr. The Solo Snare Drummer, Vol. 1. Columbus, Ohio: Permus Publications, 1985.

Mason, Harvey
Born February 22, 1947, Atlantic City, New Jersey

Drum set performer Harvey Mason attended the Berklee College of Music in Boston, Massachusetts, for nearly two years. He then earned a baccalaureate degree in music education at New England Conservatory in Boston.

In 1970, Mason toured for four months as percussionist with Erroll Garner. In 1970-71, Mason worked for thirteen months performing and recording with George Shearing.

After moving to Los Angeles, Harvey Mason performed in film and television ensembles, recording in 1973 with Quincy Jones and Herbie Hancock. In 1974, Mason performed and recorded variously with Donald Byrd, Freddie Hubbard, Gerry Mulligan at Carnegie Hall, and Grover Washington, Jr.

Mason recorded in 1977 with Lee Ritenour and in 1983 with Victor Feldman. Mason has performed with Duke Ellington, George Benson and Bob James among others. Harvey Mason was instrumental in the musical production of innovative successful recordings like "Chameleon" in 1973 with Hancock, "Mister Magic" in 1974 with Washington, and "Breezin'" in 1976 with Benson.

DISCOGRAPHY

Breezin'. With G. Benson. Warner Brothers 3111, 1976.
Headhunters. With H. Hancock. Columbia KC-32731, 1973.
Marching in the Streets. Arista 4283, 1981.
Mister Magic. With G. Washington, Jr. Kudu 20, 1974.

COMPOSITIONS AND ARRANGEMENTS

"Chameleon." Co-authored with Paul Jackson, Bennie Maupin and H. Hancock. Headhunters CBS CQ-32731, 1974.

"H. Hancock: Watermelon Man." Arranged by H. Mason. Headhunters CBS CQ-32731, 1974.

ARTICLES ABOUT SUBJECT

Potter, Jeff. "Mason, Harvey." The New Grove Dictionary of Jazz, Volume Two, 1988.

REFERENCE SOURCES

"Sound Choices." Advertisement with photograph. North Hollywood, California: Remo, U.S.A.

Miles, Charles J.
Born July 4, 1944, Ironton, Ohio

Charles J. "Butch" Miles specializes in percussion at the drum set. One of Miles' early percussion teachers was Bob Leurant, in 1957, when Miles played percussion in the Charleston Junior Symphony Orchestra. From 1959 to 1961, Miles studied with Frank Thompson. Miles graduated from Charleston High School in 1962. From 1962 to 1966, Charles Miles attended West Virginia State College. He performed keyboard percussion from 1964 to 1966 with the Charleston Symphony Orchestra.

As a freelance percussionist, Charles Miles has performed in numerous locations with many musicians. In early 1980, Miles played the percussion part for the musical "Swing." As a drum set performer, Miles has accompanied Mel Torme from 1971 to 1974, Count Basie from 1975 to 1979, Dave Brubeck in 1979 and 1980, Tony Bennett in 1980 and 1981, and Bob Wilber from 1982 to 1984. Miles has performed with Gerry Mulligan since 1982, and with Lena Horne from 1986 to 1988. Notably, Miles has performed successfully in both big bands and jazz combos.

Miles has performed at the Newport Jazz Festival in New York since 1975, and at the Grande Parade du Jazz in Nice, France, several times. He has played at the North Sea Jazz Festival in The Netherlands, at the Montreux and Bern jazz festivals in Switzerland, and in Germany for jazz music festivals in Munich, Berlin, Cologne and Stuttgart. In 1976, Miles performed a Royal Command Performance for the Queen of England. He has played on tours in Europe, Asia, North America, Central America and the Caribbean Sea region.

Other generally well known musicians and artists with whom Miles has performed include Frank Sinatra, Joe Williams, Woody Herman, Ella Fitzgerald, Clark Terry, Billy Eckstein, Eddie Davis, Harry Edison, Benny Goodman, Zubin Mehta, Richard Hyman and Sammy Davis, Jr. Miles has performed for radio and television shows. He has appeared on "60 Minutes," "The Tonight Show Starring Johnny Carson," "The Merv Griffin Show," "The

178

Dick Cavett Show," "The Mike Douglas Show," and several times for "The Jerry Lewis Telethon." Miles has appeared in two motion pictures entitled "The Australian Jazz Fest" as a member of the Dave Brubeck Quartet, and "The Last of the Blue Devils" that was filmed on location when Miles was a member of the Count Basie Orchestra. Formerly a resident of New York City, Miles presently resides in Albuquerque, New Mexico.

Charles Miles has been recorded on more than seventy record albums. He has performed with George Masso, Dave McKenna, Helen Ward, Ronny Whyte, Vic Dickenson, Dan Barrett, Glen Zottola, Jorge Anders, John Pizzerelli and Helen Humes among others. Three recordings for which he performed with the Count Basie big band won Grammy awards for excellence in musical performance.

DISCOGRAPHY

A Classy Pair--Ella and Basie. Pablo Records.
Basie at Montreux. Pablo Records.
Basie Big Band. Pablo Records.
Basie in Europe. LRC, Ltd. Records.
Basie in Japan. Pablo Records.
Basie on the Road. Pablo Records.
Blues Walk. With Warren Vache. Dreamstreet Records.
Butch and Bucky--Lady Be Good. Dreamstreet Records.
Butch's Encore. Famous Door Records.
Butch Miles Salutes Chick Webb. Famous Door Records.
Butch Miles Salutes Gene Krupa. Famous Door Records.
Butch Miles Swings some Standards. Famous Door Records.
Butch Swings some more Standards. Famous Door Records.
Christmas in Jazztime. With Glen Zottola. Dreamstreet.
Dave Brubeck Back Home. Concord Records.
Hail to the Chief. Famous Door Records.
Introducing the Jazz Express. Dreamstreet Records.
I Told You So. With Count Basie. Pablo Records.
Little Big Horn. With Gerry Mulligan. GRP Records.
Live at the Maisonette. With Mel Torme. Atlantic Records.

*<u>Milt Jackson + Count Basie + The Big Band</u>. Volumes I and II. Pablo Records.

<u>Prime Time</u>. With Count Basie. Pablo Records.

<u>Steamin'</u> Mainstream. Dreamstreet Records.

<u>The Glory of Alberta Hunter</u>. CBS Records.

REFERENCE SOURCES

Information supplied by the subject (February 1990).

---

*M. Jackson is a subject in this book.

Molenhof, Bill
Born January 2, 1954, Saint Louis, Missouri

Vibraphonist Bill Molenhof has changed from specializing at the vibraphone early in his career to performing with both marimba and vibraphone as his experience develops. Molenhof's early percussion study was with William Clark, a member of the Saint Louis Symphony Orchestra. Molenhof studied with Clark from 1967 to 1971. From 1971 to 1973, Bill Molenhof studied at Indiana University with George Gaber and Richard Johnson. In 1973 and 1974, Molenhof studied jazz with *Gary Burton and Steve Swallow at the Berklee College of Music. In 1978 and 1979, Molenhof studied voice, ear training and sight singing with Rebecca Scott at The Juilliard School. Molenhof has also studied with Ann Countryman and Angus Godwin in New York.

As a teacher, Bill Molenhof has written several method books for publication. Some of these collections contain definitive interpretative instructions and recordings. Molenhof has taught at the Berklee College of Music in 1975 and 1976, and at the Manhattan School of Music from 1979 to 1981. He was a faculty member at Ithaca College from 1987 to 1989, and taught at Temple University in 1989.

Molenhof has written more than seventy compositions for publication by Columbia Pictures, Kendor Music, Belwin-Mills, and Contemporary Music Project. These works are distributed and sold around the world.

As a professional performer, Molenhof has given presentations at Percussive Arts Society International Conventions and schools. He has toured extensively in Europe and the United States. Some of the musicians with whom he has performed are Jackie Cain, Tim Berne, Alan Dawson, Kermit Driscoll, Ed Thigpen, Danny Gottlieb, Tom Baker and David Darling. Some of the American cities in which Molenhof has performed are San Francisco, Los Angeles, Tempe, Des Moines, Boston, Cambridge,

---

*G. Burton is a subject in this volume.

Minneapolis, Miami, Atlanta, Mobile, Anchorage, Greeley, Albuquerque, Albany, Greensboro, Grand Forks, Athens, Cincinnati, Cleveland, Columbus, Oxford, Lawton, Madison and Seattle. Some of the foreign cities in which Molenhof has performed are Oslo, Toronto, Frankfurt, Ravensburg, Munich, Nurnberg, London, Linz, Copenhagen, Coburg, Wilhelmsdorf and Schramberg. Since 1982, Molenhof has been concentrating on performing marimba as well as vibraphone, and in 1987 added a synthesizer to his instrument setup. Bill Molenhof is an effective and influential contemporary percussionist.

DISCOGRAPHY

All Pass By. Cexton Records.
Beach Street Years. Mark Records.

COMPOSITIONS

A Dancer at Heart. Kendor Music.
All I Want To Do. Contemporary Music Project.
Ballad for Falling Star and Flat Tire. Kendor Music.
Busy Signal. Kendor Music.
Frowned-on Rock and Roll. Kendor Music.
Giving What You Need. Contemporary Music Project.
Grandfather Time. Chicago: Contemporary Music Project.
Kleine Albstadt. Kendor Music.
One Notch Higher. Kendor Music.
Quiet Celebration. Kendor Music.
Robby the Tiger. Kendor Music.
Soho Saturday Night. Contemporary Music Project.
Song for the New Year. Kendor Music.

BOOKS

Contemporary Marimba Solos. Kendor Music.
Music of the Day. Delevan, New York: Kendor Music, 1977.

New Works for New Times. Kendor Music.

Vibe Songs. Miami, Florida: Belwin-Mills, 1985.

ARTICLES ABOUT SUBJECT

"Bill Molenhof Trio." Promotional card with photograph. New York: Frances White, Representative.

"Music for Mallets by Bill Molenhof." Advertisement. Modern Percussionist I/3 (June 1985), 57.

Steinberg, David. "Musician Hammering Out New Jazz Marimba Sound." Albuquerque Journal, April 8, 1988, C-1.

REFERENCE SOURCES

Information supplied by the subject (January 1990).

Moore, James L.
Born May 2, 1934, Jackson, Michigan

One of James Moore's teachers is Harold Jester, who taught Moore snare drum from the piano in the fourth grade. Moore has also studied with Milton Harris, timpanist in the Detroit Symphony Orchestra, and James Salmon, percussion professor at the University of Michigan. In his first year at the University of Michigan, Moore studied the trumpet. However, he then became a percussion major and eventually earned baccalaureate and graduate degrees at that school. In 1970, James Moore received a Doctor of Philosophy degree in music theory at The Ohio State University. His doctoral dissertation is on the subject acoustics of bar and keyboard percussion instruments.

After receiving Bachelor's and Master's degrees in music education, Moore joined the military service as a percussion instructor at the United States Navy School of Music in Washington, D.C. from 1957 to 1960. He then auditioned for and was accepted as a percussionist with the Indianapolis Symphony Orchestra. For four years, Moore remained in Indianapolis, also teaching at Butler University. While in Indianapolis, he performed numerous children's concerts with the orchestra's percussion section, and founded a newsletter that would eventually become <u>Percussive Notes</u> magazine and journal associated with the international Percussive Arts Society.

In autumn, 1964, James Moore moved to Columbus, Ohio, to serve as percussion instructor and doctoral student. He performed with the Columbus Symphony Orchestra, and eventually became the full time percussion professor at The Ohio State University where he has remained. He has also founded Permus Publications, a specialty publisher dealing with music for percussion instruments. Percussionists with whom James Moore has collaborated include Charles Spohn, percussion professor at Ohio State, and two members of the percussion section in the Indianapolis Symphony, Erwin Mueller and Richard Paul. Moore served as principal percussionist in the

Columbus Symphony for seventeen years, and currently assists directors of the marching band at Ohio State University.

Moore has taught at National Music Camp at Interlochen, Michigan, and at International Music Camp near the North Dakota-Manitoba border. He founded and has directed a summer keyboard percussion camp at The Ohio State University. Moore has received a Certificate of Appreciation from the Percussive Arts Society for his work as editor of Percussive Notes, and is an honorary member of the alumni organization for The Ohio State University Marching Band. At Ohio State, he has directed the percussion program in the School of Music. These duties include private and class teaching of undergraduate and graduate students, recital performances, and conducting the University Percussion Ensembles in concerts and tours.

DISCOGRAPHY

Concepts in Percussion. The Ohio State University Percussion Ensemble. Mark Records, 1969.

COMPOSITIONS

Characters Three. Percussion Quartet. Ludwig Music.
Latisha. Solo snare drum. Ludwig Music.
Psalm Collage. Multipercussion and speaker. Permus, 1978.
Soliloquy and Scherzo. Flute and percussion. Ludwig Music.
Sonata No. 1. Solo percussion. Ludwig Music.
Two Stars. Duo for snare drums. Music for Percussion.

BOOKS

Bach for Marimba. Solos arranged by J. Moore from music by J.S. Bach. Kendor Music, 1974.

It Only Takes Two: 18 Duets for Mallet Percussion. Arrangements by J. Moore of music by Bach, Bizet, Mozart and others. Ludwig Music.

The Acoustics of Bar Percussion Instruments. Permus.

The Solo Snare Drummer, Volume 1. Co-authored with John S. Pratt and William J. Schinstine. Permus, 1985.

ARTICLES

"Marimba Research." Readers' Forum. <u>Modern Percussionist</u> I/4 (September 1985), 4.

<u>Notes from the Drum Beat</u>. Alumni newsletter. Columbus: The Ohio State University School of Music, January, 1990.

<u>Percussive Notes</u> newsletter and magazine editor, c. 1962 to c. 1980.

REFERENCE SOURCES

Information supplied by the subject (December 1989).

Larrick, Geary. "Master Lesson on 'Tam-Bas'." Music by J. Moore, photographs by John Anderson. <u>Percussive Notes</u> VIII/3 (Spring 1970), 21.

Musser, Clair Omar

Born October 14, 1901, Manheim, Pennsylvania

Clair Musser first studied the violin with his father, then studied the xylophone and piano. Musser traveled to Baltimore and Washington for much of his early music education, studying the marimba privately with Philip Rosenweig. Musser's early study also included music theory, harmony, and conducting.

In the 1920s and 1930s, Clair Musser organized and directed several keyboard percussion ensembles. In the 1920s, Musser designed a large marimba-celeste that was built at the J.C. Deagan factory in Chicago. At this time Musser resided in Reading, Pennsylvania. The first public concert featuring the marimba-celeste was in Orchestra Hall in Chicago. Clair Musser was the featured soloist, accompanied by several members of the Chicago Symphony Orchestra. In the late 1920s, Musser toured North America and Europe as recitalist and featured soloist with symphony orchestras. He was also xylophonist for Warner Brothers and leading phonograph companies. Musser performed for a season with the Los Angeles Symphony Orchestra. In 1930, he became manager of the keyboard percussion division of the Deagan company.

In 1933, Clair Musser organized the Century of Progress Marimba Orchestra that performed in summer at the Chicago World's Fair. This ensemble was followed a year later by the International Marimba Symphony Orchestra that performed in Carnegie Hall in New York City, and eventually in London, England, for the coronation of King George V in April, 1935. This marimba ensemble consisted of one hundred instruments and performers: fifty men and fifty women ages seventeen to twenty-five. Musser arranged the music in five parts, and gave each performer his or her instrument after the group disbanded. Playing capability of the performers ranged from beginners to professionals.

From 1942 to 1952, Clair Musser was a member of the faculty at Northwestern University. In 1948, Musser left the Deagan organization to form his own company that specialized in the construction and sales of keyboard percussion instruments, that is, vibraphones and xylophones and marimbas. Eventually the Musser instrument division became a part of the Ludwig Drum Company in 1966.

Clair Musser wrote many compositions and arrangements for marimba and vibraphone. Some of these are still published. He is a member of Kappa Kappa Psi national band honorary, a member of the Royal Oxford Music Society, and was inducted into the Hall of Fame of the Percussive Arts Society. Clair Musser is unquestionably one of the busiest and most successful percussionists in the twentieth century. His "etudes" for marimba unaccompanied were groundbreaking in their role in the development of marimba literature in the twentieth century. Furthermore, his arrangements for vibraphone are tasteful and precise.

DISCOGRAPHY

"Prelude in G Major, Op. 11, No. 3." "Etude in C Major, Op. 6, No. 10." "Etude in B Major, Op. 6, No. 9." "Etude in A-flat Major, Op. 6, No. 2." *Vida Chenoweth: Classic Marimbist. Epic P-17808.

COMPOSITIONS AND ARRANGEMENTS

Etude in A-flat, Op. 6, No. 2. Northridge, California: Studio 4 Productions, 1948.

Etude in B Major, Op. 6, No. 9. Van Nuys, California: Alfred Publishing.

Etude, Op. 6, No. 8. Van Nuys: Alfred Publishing.

Master Solo Arrangements for vibraphone. In four folios containing Musser arrangements of compositions by Brahms, Chopin, Dvorak, Foster, Godard, Schubert, Scott, Wagner. Chicago: Gamble Hinged Music Company, 1941.

Masterworks for the Marimba: Music of Chopin. Chicago: Forster Music Publisher, 1940.

---

*V. Chenoweth is a subject in this book.

Prelude in G Major, Op. 11, No. 3. Van Nuys: Alfred.

Prelude, Op. 11, No. 7. Northridge: Studio 4, 1976.

ARTICLES ABOUT SUBJECT

Eyler, David P. "Clair Omar Musser and His Contributions to the Marimba." Percussive Notes Focus on Research column, edited by Richard Gipson (Winter 1990), 62.

Eyler, David P. "Largest Marimba Orchestra Ever Organized." Percussive Notes 29/6 (August 1991), 39.

Eyler, David P. "The 'Century of Progress' Marimba Orchestra." Percussive Notes 29/3 (February 1991), 57.

Eyler, David P. "The Truth about the King George Marimba as Used in the International Marimba Symphony Orchestra." Percussive Notes 29/2 Focus on Performance column, edited by *Michael Rosen (December 1990), 47.

REFERENCE SOURCES

Eyler, David P. Source materials about C. Musser. Moorhead, Minnesota: Concordia College, 1990.

---

*M. Rosen is a subject in this volume.

Owen, Charles
Born September 1, 1912, Kinsman, Ohio
Died April, 1985, Ann Arbor, Michigan

Charles Owen was a percussionist and featured soloist with the United States Marine Band in Washington, D.C. for twenty years. Following that experience, he became principal percussionist in the Philadelphia Orchestra for eighteen years. While in Philadelphia, Owen taught at Temple University. Orchestral conductors with whom Owen performed included Mehta, Ozawa, Fiedler, Ormandy, Bernstein, and Stokowski.

After performing in Philadelphia, Charles Owen became a faculty member at the University of Michigan in Ann Arbor. Also during this time, he taught in summers at the Aspen Music School in Colorado, performed in the Festival Orchestra and directed the Percussion Ensemble there.

In 1981, the Percussive Arts Society elected Owen to its Hall of Fame at the annual convention in Indianapolis. As a faculty member at the University of Michigan for ten years, Owen was awarded the title Professor with Distinction in the School of Music. He was also honored with the Harold Haugh Award for excellence in studio teaching. Owen performed for several years as percussionist in the Festival Casals in Puerto Rico. Owen was honored with a concerto performance of Paul Creston's marimba concerto with the Philadelphia Orchestra conducted by Eugene Ormandy.

Percussionist colleagues of Charles Owen within specific sections included *Doug Howard, Barry Jekowsky, *Fred Hinger, Michael Bookspan, and Alan Abel. Some of his many students are *Edward Small, *Terry Smith, Tim Bartholow and Donald Hennig. Significantly, Owen's performance and recording of the Creston <u>Concertino for Marimba and Orchestra</u> took place at a time when very little of that kind of activity was available to percussion performers, although other instrument performers such as pianists and violinists would play concertos in public regularly.

---

*D. Howard, F. Hinger, E. Small and T. Smith are subjects in this volume.

As a concert percussionist, Charles Owen toured North America, South America, Europe and eastern Asia. He has been recorded on Columbia and RCA records among those of other firms. Owen performed the snare drum with both matched and traditional methods of holding the sticks. One of his strengths was beauty in sound with a pair of cymbals. Although his background was traditional, he was adventurous in selecting music to conduct with his student ensembles.

DISCOGRAPHY

Finlandia. Philadelphia Orchestra conducted by Eugene Ormandy. Columbia ML-5596.

First Chair Encores--Volume 2. C. Owen, marimba, accompanied by the Philadelphia Orchestra conducted by Eugene Ormandy, in a performance of the first movement of Paul Creston's "Concertino for Marimba and Orchestra, Op. 21." Columbia MS-6977.

Invitation to the Dance. Philadelphia Orchestra conducted by Ormandy. Columbia ML-5641.

Orff: Carmina Burana. Philadelphia Orchestra conducted by Ormandy. New York: CBS Records MYK-37217, 1981, originally recorded in 1960.

Other recordings with the Philadelphia Orchestra.

The Blue Danube: A Johann Strauss Festival. Philadelphia Orchestra conducted by Ormandy. Columbia ML-5617.

ARTICLES

"Master Lesson on Paul Creston's Concerto for Marimba." Percussive Notes 21/2 (January 1983), 62.

ARTICLES ABOUT SUBJECT

"Charles Owen." Catalog. Aspen, Colorado: Aspen Music School (Summer 1985), 42.

*Udow, Michael W. "Charles Owen." <u>Percussive Notes</u> 20/2 (February 1982), 33.

---

*M. Udow is a subject in this book.

Pangborn, Robert C.
Born December 31, 1934, Painesville, Ohio

Robert Pangborn's early music education included percussion study with William Hruby and *Cloyd Duff. At the Eastman School of Music in 1952 and 1953, Pangborn studied with *William Street. Pangborn attended the Tanglewood Festival during the summer of 1953, studying with Roman Sculz. From 1954 to 1956, Pangborn attended The Juilliard School, studying percussion with Morris Goldenberg. Pangborn studied liberal arts in 1956-57 at Western Reserve University and in 1975-76 at Oakland University.

Pangborn's professional career as an orchestral percussionist has been various and of high quality. From September 14, 1953, to June 14, 1956, Pangborn was percussionist in the United States Military Academy Band at West Point, New York. In 1956 and 1957, he performed as principal timpanist with the Indianapolis Symphony Orchestra. In August and September, 1957, Pangborn worked as a percussionist and timpanist with the Minneapolis Symphony Orchestra on a tour of the Middle East. From October, 1957, to August, 1963, Robert Pangborn was mallet percussionist with the Cleveland Orchestra. In 1963-64, Pangborn was timpanist and percussionist with the Metropolitan Opera Orchestra. Since August, 1964, he has served as principal percussionist and assistant principal timpanist in the Detroit Symphony Orchestra.

Robert Pangborn has taught percussion at the Cleveland Institute of Music from 1958 to 1963. He taught at Oakland University in Rochester, Michigan, from 1975 to 1989. He has worked as a staff percussionist for Motown Records from 1968 to 1973. Pangborn has performed at the drum set with Symphonic Metamorphosis from 1969 to 1971. Conductors with whom Pangborn has performed include George Szell, Sixten Ehrling, Louis Lane and Antal Dorati.

---

*C. Duff and W. Street are subjects in this book.

Pangborn founded and directed percussion ensembles called Four for Percussion, Detroit Percussion Trio, and the quintet Mostly Mallets. He teaches in his studio in Bloomfield Hills, Michigan. Pangborn has been featured percussion soloist accompanied by symphony orchestra in performances of Rolf Liebermann's "Geigy Festival Concerto for Side Drum and Orchestra" in Cleveland, and Donald Erb's "Concerto for Percussion and Orchestra" in Detroit. Pangborn has served on the board of directors of the support organization Friends of the Detroit Symphony Orchestra and of Orchestra Hall.

DISCOGRAPHY

Recordings for Motown Records, 1968-73.

Recordings with the Cleveland Orchestra conducted by George Szell and Louis Lane. Epic Records and Columbia Records, 1957-63.

Recordings with the Detroit Symphony Orchestra conducted by Antal Dorati. London Records 410-110-2, 411-893-2, 411-894-2, 400-084-2, 414-273-2, 414-370-2, 414-456-2, 414-457-2, and others.

Two recordings with Symphonic Metamorphosis. London Records, 1969-71.

ARTICLES ABOUT SUBJECT

Shultis, Chris. "Robert Pangborn." Interview, edited by *Charles Owen. Percussive Notes 23/4 (April 1985), 36.

Taylor, Harvey. "Concerto Night at the Symphony: Percussion Solo Steals the Show." Detroit Free Press, Saturday, December 31, 1966, 10-A.

REFERENCE SOURCES

Information supplied by the subject (September 1989).

Erb, Donald. Program note. Detroit Symphony Orchestra conducted by Sixten Ehrling. Detroit: Ford Auditorium, December 29, 1966.

---

*C. Owen is a subject in this book.

K.G.R. "Geigy Festival Concerto for Side Drum (Basel Drum) and Orchestra (A Fantasy on Basel Folk Tunes) by Rolf Liebermann." Program note. Cleveland Orchestra conducted by George Szell. Cleveland: Severance Hall, March 19, 1959.

Payson, Albert
Born January 15, 1934, Springfield, Illinois

Albert Payson received a Bachelor of Music degree at the University of Illinois in 1956. His early musical education in percussion began with the study of the snare drum at age five, study of the marimba at age twelve, and study of the timpani at age fourteen. Payson's undergraduate education was divided into two parts by his military service. Payson served in the United States Army from early 1951 to early 1953, performing in the 44th Infantry Division Band at two locations near the west coast. Albert Payson was a member of the historic University Percussion Ensemble at the University of Illinois that was conducted by Paul Price. Some of the instruments that Payson played in that ensemble are military drum, suspended cymbal, tom-tom, cymbals, vibraphone, snare drum, medium elephant bell, chimes, and sleigh bells. Composers whose music was performed by the University of Illinois Percussion Ensemble include Chavez, *Colgrass, Harrison, McKenzie, and Varese.

After graduation from the University of Illinois, Payson performed in the Louisville Orchestra in Kentucky. He then moved to the Chicago area, working as a freelance musician. In Chicago at this time, Payson performed with the orchestra of the Chicago Lyric Opera and toured with the Royal Ballet of England. He also performed part time with the Chicago Symphony Orchestra at Ravinia, and with the Grant Park Symphony Orchestra. In the summer of 1958, Albert Payson became a percussionist in the Chicago Symphony Orchestra and has stayed in that job since then. Conductors with whom he has performed include Abbado, Gould, Levine, Martinon, Ozawa, Previn, Reiner, and Solti.

As a teacher, Payson has written several effective method books, presented lecture demonstrations, and talked at public panel discussions. He has also taught in a studio located in his home, and served as faculty member

---

*M. Colgrass is a subject in this volume.

at DePaul University. With his business called Payson Percussion Products, Albert Payson has manufactured and distributed many high quality products to the music community nationwide. Some of his products include castanet machines, bass drum beaters, timpani mallets, books, records, and mallet repair kits. Other auxiliary work of Payson has been serving as a consultant for the Ludwig Drum Company. As a member of the centrally located Chicago Symphony Orchestra, Payson has been influential to the percussion world and the music education profession. His thoughtful approach to the performance of percussion music is certainly beneficial in the improvement of performance technique during the second half of the twentieth century nationwide. Some of Payson's colleagues in the Chicago Symphony Orchestra percussion section have included *Sam Denov, *Gordon Peters, and *Patricia Dash.

DISCOGRAPHY

Bartok: Concerto for Orchestra. Chicago Symphony Orchestra conducted by Solti with A. Payson performing snare drum. London/Decca L-417754-2 LM, 1981.

Beethoven: Symphony No. 9. Chicago Symphony Orchestra conducted by Solti with A. Payson performing bass drum. London/Decca L-417800-2 LH, 1986.

Berlioz: Symphonie Fantastique. Chicago Symphony Orchestra conducted by Abbado with A. Payson performing carillon. Deutsche Grammophon DG-410895-2 GH, 1983.

Falla: "Three Dances" from The Three-Cornered Hat. Chicago Symphony Orchestra conducted by Reiner with A. Payson performing snare drum. RCA V LM-LSC-2230, 1958.

Ives: "Putnam's Camp" from Three Places in New England. Chicago Symphony Orchestra conducted by Gould with A. Payson performing snare drum. RCA V LM-LSC-2959, 1967.

---

*S. Denov, G. Peters and P. Dash are subjects in this book.

Ives (arranged Schuman): Variations on "America." Chicago Symphony Orchestra conducted by Gould with A. Payson performing snare drum. RCA V LSC-2893, 1966.

Mahler: Symphony No. 5. Chicago Symphony Orchestra conducted by Solti with A. Payson performing snare drum. London/Decca L 414321-1LH, 1970.

Mahler: Symphony No. 6. Chicago Symphony Orchestra conducted by Abbado with A. Payson performing cowbells and grosse hammer. Deutsche Grammophon 2DG-2707 117, 1979.

Mahler: Symphony No. 9. Chicago Symphony Orchestra conducted by Solti with A. Payson performing carillon. London/Decca 2L-410264-1 LJ2, 1982.

Mussorgsky (arranged Ravel): Pictures at an Exhibition. Chicago Symphony Orchestra conducted by Solti with A. Payson performing snare drum. London/Decca L-LDR-10040, 1980.

Orff: Carmina Burana. Chicago Symphony Orchestra conducted by Levine with A. Payson performing snare drum. Deutsche Grammophon DG-415 136-1GH, 1984.

Payson: Snare Drum Solo No. 1. Performed by Paul Price. Fort Lauderdale, Florida: Music for Percussion MFP-513.

Prokofiev: Lieutenant Kije. Chicago Symphony Orchestra conducted by Abbado with A. Payson performing snare drum. Deutsche Grammophon DG-419603-2GH, 1977.

Ravel: Alborada del Grazioso. Chicago Symphony Orchestra conducted by Martinon with A. Payson performing snare drum. RCA V AGL1-5061, 1968.

Ravel: Bolero. Chicago Symphony Orchestra conducted by Solti with A. Payson performing snare drum. London/Decc

Respighi: The Pines of Rome. Chicago Symphony Orchestra conducted by Reiner with A. Payson performing triangle and tambourine. RCA V RCD1-5407, 1959.

Rimsky-Korsakov: Scheherazade. Chicago Symphony Orchestra conducted by Ozawa with A. Payson performing snare drum. Angel A CDC-47617, 1969.

Shostakovich: Symphony No. 5. Chicago Symphony Orchestra conducted by Previn with A. Payson performing snare drum. Angel A S-37285, 1977.

Strauss, R.: Also Sprach Zarathustra. Chicago Symphony Orchestra conducted by Solti with A. Payson performing bass drum. London/Decca L-414043-2LH, 1975.

Stravinsky: Le Sacre du Printemps. Chicago Symphony Orchestra conducted by Solti with A. Payson performing bass drum. London/Decca L-417704-2LM, 1974.

Tchaikovsky: Symphony No. 4. Chicago Symphony Orchestra conducted by Solti with A. Payson performing bass drum. London/Decca L-414192-2LH, 1984.

Varese: Arcana. Chicago Symphony Orchestra conducted by Martinon with A. Payson performing tenor drum. RCA V LM-LSC-2914, 1966.

COMPOSITIONS

Quartet. Fort Lauderdale: Music for Percussion.

Snare Drum Solo No. 1. Fort Lauderdale: Music for Percussion.

BOOKS

Beginning Snare Drum with Play-Along Cassette. Northbrook, Illinois: Payson Percussion Products, 1972.

Elementary Marimba and Xylophone Method. Northbrook: Payson Percussion, 1973.

Music Educators' Guide to Percussion. Co-authored with Jack McKenzie. Rockville Centre, New York: Belwin, 1966.

Percussion in the School Music Program. Co-authored with Jack McKenzie. Northbrook: Payson Percussion, 1976.

Progressive Studies in Double Stops for Mallet Instruments. Fort Lauderdale: Music for Percussion.

Techniques of Playing Bass Drum, Cymbals, and Accessories (Tambourine, Castanets, Triangle, Tam-tam). Northbrook: Payson Percussion, 1971.

The Snare Drum in the Concert Hall. Northbrook: Payson Percussion, 1970 and 1985.

ARTICLES

"Instructions." Timpani Mallet Repair Kit. Northbrook: Payson Percussion, 1988.

"Timpani Techniques." Chicago: Ludwig Industries, 1976.

REFERENCE SOURCES

Information supplied by the subject (October 1989).

Recordings, 1916-88. Chicago, Illinois: Chicago Symphony Orchestra, 1989.

Pershing, Karen Ervin
Born c. 1940

Karen Ervin Pershing teaches percussion and music industry courses in the music department of California State University in Northridge. Two of her percussionist colleagues there are Joel Leach and *Emil Richards. Pershing has built a career as a solo performer, recording artist, author and teacher. She has performed the marimba at Percussive Arts Society national conferences, and made important contributions to her profession.

One of Pershing's fundamental concepts is music's role as communication. Her emphasis on solo performance stresses this role, for the solo performer usually talks with one's audience in contrast to the ensemble performer who usually remains silently in the background.

Karen Ervin Pershing is an example of a professional percussionist who shares her expertise with her peers. She has written articles about *William Kraft and Earl Hatch for publication. Pershing has performed for some time as a freelance percussionist in the Los Angeles area in addition to her solo career. Some of her activities include performing with the Los Angeles Percussion Ensemble. Karen Pershing's location on the west coast of the United States offers an important perspective about music and society that is created in an environment rich in culture and population. Her individualistic outlook as reflected in her published articles presents also a background full of knowledge, experience and perception.

DISCOGRAPHY

Karen Ervin: A Marimba Recital. Van Nuys, California: Studio 4 Productions.

Karen Ervin, Percussionist. WIM-5.

Music for Winds and Percussion. Crystal S-164.

---

*E. Richards and W. Kraft are subjects in this volume.

<u>Organist David Craighead</u>. Includes Lou Harrison's "Concerto for Organ with Percussion Orchestra" performed by the Los Angeles Percussion Ensemble. Crystal Records S-858, 1977.

COMPOSITIONS AND ARRANGEMENTS

<u>Arabesque by Claude Debussy</u>. Transcribed for solo vibraphone by Karen Ervin Pershing. Van Nuys: Studio 4 and Alfred Publishing Company, 1990.

ARTICLES

"Creative Careers." <u>Modern Percussionist</u> III/2 (March 1987), 18.
"Earl Hatch." <u>Modern Percussionist</u> II/2 (March 1986), 22.

ARTICLES ABOUT SUBJECT

DB.   "Doing It Her Way: Karen Ervin Pershing."   <u>Modern Percussionist</u> II/1 (December 1985), 22.

REFERENCE SOURCES

"Fall 1990 Releases." Van Nuys: Studio 4 and Alfred Publishing, 1990.
"Features." <u>Modern Percussionist</u> II/2 (March 1986), 1.

Peters, Gordon B.
Born c. 1931, Oak Park, Illinois

Gordon Peters attended Northwestern University in 1949 and 1950. He then became a percussionist and assistant timpanist in the United States Military Academy Band at West Point, New York. From 1953 to 1959, Peters attended the Eastman School of Music in Rochester, New York, earning a baccalaureate and a graduate degree there. In Rochester, his Bachelor's degree emphasized music education, and his Master's degree emphasized music theory. Some of Gordon Peters' teachers include Jose Bethancourt, Harry Breuer, Morris Goldenberg, Saul Goodman, Roy Knapp, *Clair Musser, and *William Street.

During summers from 1955 to 1958, Gordon Peters worked as a professional percussionist in the Grant Park Symphony Orchestra in Chicago. From 1955 to 1959, he performed percussion instruments in the Rochester Philharmonic Orchestra. In September, 1959, Peters became principal percussionist and assistant timpanist in the Chicago Symphony Orchestra. He remains in that position.

For more than twenty years, Gordon Peters served as conductor and administrator with Civic Orchestra of Chicago, the training ensemble for the Chicago Symphony Orchestra. He has worked as conductor for the Elmhurst Symphony Orchestra, and as percussion editor for The Instrumentalist music education magazine.

In the 1960s, Gordon Peters taught percussion at Northwestern University in Evanston, Illinois. In Chicago, Peters has performed as a featured soloist with the Chicago Symphony Orchestra. In Rochester, he founded The Marimba Masters, a keyboard percussion ensemble that appeared in public and on national television for shows hosted by Arthur Godfrey and Ed Sullivan. The Marimba Masters were a new and unique group in the middle of the twentieth century, at a time when the college

---

*C. Musser and W. Street are subjects in this book.

percussion ensemble was in its infancy. There was very little literature for the marimba ensemble, and Peters arranged several pieces from the classical music repertoire for that instrumentation. His arrangments that were available at Frank's Drum Shop in downtown Chicago in the 1970s, often featured the concert xylophone on a melody part doubled with a lower marimba part, plus three accompanying marimba parts. The lowest marimba part is often doubled by a contrabass in his arrangements.

Peters has performed with numerous conductors, including Walter Hendl, Irwin Hoffman, Kenneth Jean, Erich Leinsdorf, Jean Martinon, Henry Mazer, Fritz Reiner, and Georg Solti. For several years, Gordon Peters studied conducting in Maine with Pierre Monteux. Other conducting teachers were Herman Genhart and Paul White. Peters' composition entitled "The Swords of Moda-Ling" has received many performances nationwide. Peters was the first president of the Percussive Arts Society.

Gordon Peters' book, entitled The Drummer: Man, is a revised version of his very large Master's thesis written at the Eastman School. The book contains photographs and information about The Marimba Masters, middle twentieth century percussion programs, pedagogical suggestions, and much historical information. It is a compendium of just about anything that an extremely active mind could create within one field of study in book form. The manuscript's first title, "Treatise," is based on similar literary collections that were produced in Europe before 1600 A.D., centuries before the invention of the typewriter or computer. The book is written in accessible form with detailed lists of its contents, and several passages that are complete individually.

DISCOGRAPHY

Eastmontage. Includes "The Swords of Moda-Ling" by Gordon Peters. The Eastman Percussion Ensemble conducted by John Beck with G. Larrick performing percussion. Rochester, New York: University of Rochester ES-72001, 1969.

Recordings with the Chicago Symphony Orchestra since 1959.

The Marimba Masters. Kendall Records c. 1958.

COMPOSITIONS AND ARRANGEMENTS

Arrangements for keyboard percussion ensemble. Chicago: Frank's Drum Shop.

The Swords of Moda-Ling. Chicago: Frank's Drum Shop.

BOOKS

The Drummer: Man. Wilmette, Illinois: Kemper-Peters, 1975.

ARTICLES

Articles in The Ludwig Drummer.

Articles as author and editor in The Instrumentalist.

REFERENCE SOURCES

Information supplied by the subject (October 1989).

Music Directors and Associate Conductors, 1891-1988. The Chicago Symphony Orchestra. Chicago, Illinois: Orchestral Association, 1988.

"Percussive Arts Society: Advisory Board of Past Presidents." Percussive Notes 29/3 (February 1991), 2.

Program. Tri-College Percussion Ensemble and Marimba Choir directed by David P. Eyler. Music Departments of Concordia College, Moorhead State University, and North Dakota State University, December 11, 1989.

Peters, Mitchell

Born August 17, 1935, Red Wing, Minnesota

Mitchell Peters received a Bachelor of Music degree at the Eastman School of Music in 1957. He received a Master of Music degree from the Eastman School in 1958. His percussion teacher at Eastman was *William Street from 1953 to 1958.

As a professional percussionist, Peters performed in the Rochester Philharmonic Orchestra from 1956 to 1958. From 1958 to 1960, he played timpani in the 7th U.S. Army Symphony Orchestra. From 1960 to 1969, Mitchell Peters served as principal percussionist in the Dallas Symphony Orchestra in Texas. Since 1969, Peters has performed as a percussionist and principal timpanist with the Los Angeles Philharmonic Orchestra. He also performs with the Los Angeles Percussion Ensemble.

As a composer, Mitchell Peters has written many works for percussion, publishing some of them himself. As an author, he wrote articles in the 1960s for The Instrumentalist. As a teacher, he has taught at Music Academy of the West, University of Southern California, California State University at Los Angeles, and at the University of California in Los Angeles. As a freelance musician, he has performed for various motion picture scores, and has played timpani in summers of 1988 and 1989 at Mozart in Monterey Festival. Mitchell Peters was a member of The Marimba Masters at the Eastman School of Music in Rochester, New York, from 1953 to 1958; this organization was directed by *Gordon Peters. Mitchell Peters earned a Performer's Certificate in percussion at the Eastman School in 1957.

As a very successful performer of percussion in the twentieth century, Peters has worked on both the east coast and west coast of the United States.

---

*W. Street is a subject in this book.

*G. Peters is a subject in this volume.

He is influential as an author and composer in addition to being a fine performer.

DISCOGRAPHY

Los Angeles Percussion Ensemble.   Organist David Craighead. Crystal Records S-858, 1977.

Miscellaneous chamber music recordings.

Recordings with the Los Angeles Philharmonic since 1969.

COMPOSITIONS

A la Naningo. Percussion quintet. Los Angeles, California: Mitchell Peters.

A la Samba. Percussion sextet. Los Angeles: Mitchell Peters.

Chant for Marimba. Solo. Los Angeles: Mitchell Peters.

Etude #1. Four tom-toms. Los Angeles: Mitchell Peters.

Etude #2. Snare drum and two tom-toms. Los Angeles: Mitchell Peters.

Introduction and Waltz. Solo. Los Angeles: Mitchell Peters.

March of the Eagles. Percussion quintet. Los Angeles: Mitchell Peters.

Perpetual Motion. Solo percussion. Los Angeles: Mitchell Peters.

Piece for Percussion. Percussion quartet. Los Angeles: Mitchell Peters.

Primal Mood. Solo timpani. Los Angeles: Mitchell Peters.

Rondino. Solo timpani. Los Angeles: Mitchell Peters.

Rondo. Solo percussion. Los Angeles: Mitchell Peters.

Scherzo. Solo timpani. Los Angeles: Mitchell Peters.

Sea-Refractions. Solo marimba. Los Angeles: Mitchell Peters.

Sonata Allegro. Marimba and piano, or marimba and string orchestra. Los Angeles: Mitchell Peters.

Storm. Solo timpani. Los Angeles: Mitchell Peters.

Study in 5/8. Percussion quartet. Los Angeles: Mitchell Peters.

Teardrops. Solo marimba. Los Angeles: Mitchell Peters.

Theme and Variations. Marimba and piano. Los Angeles: Mitchell Peters.

Three Pieces for Three Mallets. Solo marimba. Los Angeles: Mitchell Peters.

Undercurrent. Solo marimba. Los Angeles: Mitchell Peters.

Waves. Solo marimba. Los Angeles: Mitchell Peters.

Yellow after the Rain. Solo marimba. Los Angeles: Mitchell Peters.

Zen Wanderer. Solo marimba. Los Angeles: Mitchell Peters.

BOOKS

Advanced Snare Drum Studies. Los Angeles: Mitchell Peters.

Developing Dexterity for Snare Drum. Los Angeles: Mitchell Peters.

Drum Music To March By. Los Angeles: Mitchell Peters.

Elementary Snare Drum Studies. Los Angeles: Mitchell Peters.

Hard Times for Snare Drum. Los Angeles: Mitchell Peters.

Intermediate Snare Drum Studies. Los Angeles: Mitchell Peters.

Intermediate Timpani Studies. Los Angeles: Mitchell Peters.

Odd-Meter Calisthenics for the Snare Drummer. Los Angeles: Mitchell Peters.

Odd-Meter Rudimental Etudes for Snare Drum. Los Angeles: Mitchell Peters.

Rudimental Primer. Los Angeles: Mitchell Peters.

Stick Control for the Drum Set, Volume 1: Basic Triplet Patterns. Los Angeles: Mitchell Peters.

Stick Control for the Drum Set, Volume 2: Basic Sixteenths. Los Angeles: Mitchell Peters.

REFERENCE SOURCES

Information supplied by the subject (December 1990).

Catalog of Percussion Ensembles, Snare Drum and Drum Set Books, Marimba Solos, Timpani Solos and Multiple Percussion Solos. Dallas, Texas: KSM Publishing.

Catalogue of Percussion Materials. Los Angeles: Mitchell Peters (January 1991).

Piltzecker, Ted
Born May 22, 1950, Passaic, New Jersey

Vibraphonist Ted Piltzecker received a Bachelor of Music degree at the Eastman School of Music of the University of Rochester in 1972. His emphases there were in performance, composition and arranging. In 1972 and 1973, Piltzecker studied at The Ohio State University in Columbus, studying music composition at the graduate level. In June, 1985, he received a Master of Music degree at the Manhattan School of Music in New York City. His academic emphases there were in jazz, commercial music, composition, and writing for films. Some of Piltzecker's teachers have been *Warren Benson, *Gary Burton, Michael Gibbs, Ed Greene, Richard Jones, Chuck Mangione, *David Samuels, and Ray Wright.

Piltzecker toured internationally for two years with the George Shearing Quintet. He has toured North America with a piano and vibraphone duo named Pendulum. He has toured nationally with his New York based quartet, and for Affiliate Artists. At the Aspen Music Festival in Colorado, Ted Piltzecker coordinates the jazz program. In that position, he supervises faculty within the program, recruits students, assists in selecting guest artists, chooses literature for jazz concerts, conducts and directs concerts. In addition, he composes for large ensembles, performs on the vibraphone, assists in planning curricula, teaches arranging, instructs music composition, and lectures in percussion.

As an artist clinician for the Selmer Company's Musser Division of Ludwig, Inc., since 1980, Ted Piltzecker has presented master classes in jazz and percussion performance at more than forty colleges and universities. Also in this capacity, he has performed and recorded with Musser vibraphones, and has represented the manufacturer at state and national conventions as artist and teacher.

---

*W. Benson, G. Burton and D. Samuels are subjects in this book.

From 1985 to 1987, Piltzecker taught at the University of Michigan in Ann Arbor. His duties there included teaching private lessons to college percussion students, directing jazz ensembles, teaching music improvisation to undergraduate students, and advising graduate students in special projects, as well as promoting the production of music with computers. As a graduate assistant at The Ohio State University in 1972-73, Piltzecker directed one of the jazz ensembles, taught arranging, performed with one of the ensembles, and instructed writing by advanced student performers for ensembles.

Piltzecker's professional memberships include the international Percussive Arts Society, the National Association of Jazz Educators, the American Federation of Musicians, and the American Society of Composers, Authors and Publishers. He has received several grants, including awards from the National Endowment for the Arts, MacDowell Colony, New York State Arts Council, and the American Society of Composers, Authors and Publishers. He served as a national chairperson for keyboard percussion instruments with the National Association of Jazz Educators. Piltzecker has taught privately since 1980.

In addition to percussion, Ted Piltzecker has composed music for orchestra, big band, 'cello, saxophone, flute, piano, violin, clarinet, harp, voice, electronic tape, dance, horn, bassoon, and harpsichord. Places that Piltzecker has performed include Birdland in New York City, Aspen, Chicago, Tempe, Peterborough, Leavenworth, Wichita, Bowling Green, Lethbridge, Rexburg, Milwaukee, Tucson, Billings, Regina, San Antonio, Athens, Austin, Madison, Wilmington, Fresno, Eau Claire, Caldwell, Cedar Falls, Columbus, and Washington.

Ted Piltzecker has successfully combined activities as a performer, educator and composer. With his regular associations in Colorado and New York, he is able to maintain a high level of quality in his work in addition to considerable variety. His vibraphone performance is usually with four mallets, and exhibits a thorough knowledge of drumming as well as harmony and improvisation.

DISCOGRAPHY

Destinations. With guitarist Jack Wilkins, bassist Andy Simpkins, and drum set performer Ted Moore. Bryn Mawr, California: Sea Breeze Records SB-2027, 1985.

Pendulum. Recording of Vancouver concert, November 23, 1986, by CBC Enterprises, Toronto, Ontario, Canada.

COMPOSITIONS

A Child's Dream. Piano and vibraphone. Corner Mushroom Music, 1978.

Ashcroft. "Destinations." Sea Breeze Records, 1985.

Bus. Big band, harpsichord and bassoon. Kendor Music, 1972.

Columbus Avenue Strut. "Destinations." Sea Breeze, 1985.

Ghost Farm. Pre-recorded tape, voices, percussion. Corner Mushroom, 1987.

Homesick. "Destinations." Sea Breeze, 1985.

Odyssey. Pianos and percussion. Corner Mushroom, 1980.

Skirmish. Big band. Corner Mushroom, 1982.

Stepping Out. "Destinations." Sea Breeze, 1985.

Sweet Tear. Big band. Corner Mushroom, 1984.

Tango. Violin, clarinet, harp and percussion. Corner Mushroom, 1987.

Tango for an Elegant Man. Violoncelli, soprano saxophone, conga drum and big band. Corner Mushroom, 1989.

Tango Medianoche. Violoncello and piano. Corner Mushroom, 1988.

Thea. Flute and big band. Corner Mushroom, 1989.

ARTICLES

"Ted Piltzecker." <u>Master Technique Builders for Vibraphone and Marimba</u>, edited by *Anthony J. Cirone. Miami, Florida: Belwin-Mills, 1985.

"Vibraphone Pedaling and Articulation." Elkhart, Indiana: Ludwig/Musser/Selmer Company, 1988.

"Vibraphone Workshop." <u>Percussive Notes</u> c. 1987.

"Your Own Best Teacher." <u>Percussive Notes</u> (Spring 1987).

ARTICLES ABOUT SUBJECT

"Ted Piltzecker." Catalog, Aspen Music School. Aspen, Colorado (1990), 42.

"Ted Piltzecker." Catalog, Aspen Music School. Aspen, Colorado (Summer 1991), 49.

REFERENCE SOURCES

Information supplied by the subject (November 1989).

"An Evening with Ruben Gonzalez." Program, Aspen Music Festival. Aspen, Colorado, Thursday, July 2, 1987.

"PASIC '88, San Antonio, Texas: Keyboard Percussion." <u>Percussion News</u>, August, 1988.

"Percussion Day '91." Columbus, Ohio: The Ohio State University and Coyle Music, 1991.

---

*A. Cirone is a subject in this volume.

Press, Arthur
Born July 9, 1930, Brooklyn, New York

Arthur Press received a diploma in percussion at the Juilliard School of Music in New York City. In 1950 and 1951, Press performed as a professional percussionist with the Little Orchestra Society in New York. From 1952 to 1956, he played percussion at Radio City Music Hall there. Since 1956, Arthur Press has worked as a percussionist in the Boston Symphony Orchestra in Massachusetts. He has also played timpani and percussion in the Boston Pops Orchestra.

As an artist teacher, Press has recorded, authored articles and a book, and instructed at the Boston Conservatory of Music. In 1970, he founded The Percussion Academy. These various services are his way of sharing his talent and experience with colleagues and students in a direct, accurate manner.

DISCOGRAPHY

Aisle Seat: Great Film Music. Boston Pops Orchestra conducted by John Williams. Philips 6514-328, 1982.

American Classics: Great Moments of Music. Boston Pops Orchestra conducted by Arthur Fiedler. Time-Life Records STLS-7001.

Classical Percussion. Music Minus One, 1970.

Empire Brass. Percussion and timpani. Capital Records.

Other recordings with the Boston Pops Orchestra.

Recordings with the Boston Symphony Orchestra since 1956.

Sibelius: Symphony No. 1 and Finlandia. Boston Symphony Orchestra conducted by Colin Davis. Philips 9500-140, 1976.

BOOKS

Mallet Repair. Rockville Centre, New York: Belwin-Mills, 1971.

ARTICLES

"Orchestral Percussionist: Capriccio Espagnol." Modern Percussionist I/2 ((March 1985), 54.

"Orchestral Percussionist: Dvorak--Carnival Overture." Modern Percussionist II/1 (December 1985), 66.

"Orchestral Percussionist: Multiple Parts." Modern Percussionist (March 1986), 46.

"Orchestral Percussionist: Notational Problems." Modern Percussionist II/3 (June 1986), 26.

"Orchestral Percussionist: Notational Problems." Modern Percussionist II/4 (September 1986), 26.

"Orchestral Percussionist: Scheherazade." Modern Percussionist I/3 (June 1985), 26.

"Orchestral Percussionist: The Concert Snare Drum." Modern Percussionist I/1 (December 1984), 26.

"Orchestral Percussionist: The Long Tremolo." Modern Percussionist III/1 (December 1986), 26.

REFERENCE SOURCES

"Arthur Press, Percussionist." Faculty Announcement, Boston Conservatory. Modern Percussionist I/3 (June 1985), 66.

Evening At Pops. Madison and Wausau: Wisconsin Public Television, August 17, 1991.

Information supplied by the subject (September 1989).

"Orchestral Audition Coaching." Announcement, Percussion Academy. Percussion News, January, 1991.

Ptaszynska, Marta
Born July 29, 1943, Warsaw, Poland

Marta Ptaszynska has constructed a career as a freelance percussion artist. She received college degrees in Poland, and studied further in the United States. Ptaszynska studied percussion at the Poznan Higher School of Music. She received a Master's degree from the Warsaw Academy of Music, emphasizing music theory and composition in her academic endeavours. Her teachers in Poland include Jadeusz Paciorkiewicz, Witold Rudzinski, Stefan Sledzinski, and Jerzy Zgodzinski. Advanced study was done in Paris with Nadia Boulanger. In 1974, Ptaszynska received an Artist Diploma at the Cleveland Institute of Music in northern Ohio. Her teachers in Cleveland include *Cloyd Duff, Donald Erb, and Richard Weiner.

Ptaszynska has worked in both Europe and the United States. She is the co-founder of the International Percussion Workshop that is based in Bydgoszcz, Poland, and currently serves on the board of directors for that organization. In the 1960s, Marta Ptaszynska performed with various ensembles in Poland, including the National Philharmonic Orchestra and the Radio Symphony Orchestra in Warsaw. She has performed for two years with the Poznan Percussion Ensemble. Ptaszynska has also performed with the Percussion de Strasbourg at Warsaw Autumn Festivals.

From 1970 to 1972, Marta Ptaszynska taught percussion at the Academy of Music in Warsaw. Since that time, she has served residencies at many schools, including Bennington College, the University of California at Berkeley, the University of California at Santa Barbara, Indiana University, the Eastman School of Music, the Manhattan School of Music, and the San Francisco Conservatory. Ptaszynska has also made presentations at the Cleveland Institute, the University of Illinois, and the University of Cincinnati.

Ptaszynska has participated in music festivals in both Europe and the United States. From 1981 to 1984, she was a member of the board of

---

*C. Duff is a subject in this volume.

directors for the Percussive Arts Society. She has placed high in various competitions, including the Young Polish Composers Contest, Percussive Arts Society composition contests, and a Polish Radio and Television Contest for televised opera. She has received numerous awards and honors, including awards from the American Society of Composers, Authors and Publishers, a medal from the Union of Polish Composers, and an award from the office of Prime Minister of Poland for her music for young audiences. Her compositions have been performed at Warsaw Autumn Festival, ISCM World Music Days, ISME festivals, the Aspen Music Festival, and Percussive Arts Society International Conventions.

Marta Ptaszynska specializes in contemporary chamber music, and has written especially for other performers, including Keiko Abe, Wanda Wilkomirska, Jerzy Maksymiuk, Bertram Turetzky, and Nancy Allen. Ptaszynska has written for Les Percussions de Strasbourg, the Polish Chamber Orchestra, Sinfonia Varsovia, and the Cleveland Orchestra. Her influence and range of activity are international in scope, as well as high in quality.

DISCOGRAPHY

Concerto for Marimba. Polskie Nagrania SX-2709.
Other recordings by MUZA Polskie Nagrania, Warsaw, Poland.
Space Model. Germany: Pro Viva LP Bestell ISPV-152, 1988.

COMPOSITIONS

Cadenza. Flute and percussion, 1972. Krakow: Polskie Wydawnictwo Muzyczne and New York: *M. Lang Publications.
Classical Variations. Timpani and string quartet, 1976. Langhorne, Pennsylvania: M. Ptaszynska.
Colourful World of Percussion. Flutes, recorders, voice and percussion, 1978. Co-authored with Barbara Niewiadomska. Krakow: Polskie Wydawnictwo Muzyczne.
Concerto for Marimba and Orchestra, 1985. Krakow: Polskie

---

*M. Lang is a subject in this book.

Wydawnictwo Muzyczne and Bryn Mawr, Pennsylvania: Theodore Presser Company.

Concerto for Percussion and Orchestra, 1974. Krakow: Polskie Wydawnictwo Muzyczne.

Dream Lands, Magic Spaces. Violin, piano and percussion, 1979. Krakow: Polskie Wydawnictwo Muzyczne.

Epigrams. Women's choir, flute, harp, piano and percussion, 1977. Munchen, Germany: Edition Pro Nova.

Four Preludes. Vibraphone and piano, 1965. Krakow: Polskie Wydawnictwo Muzyczne and New York: E.B. Marks.

Jeu-Parti. Harp and vibraphone, 1970. Collaborated with Nancy Allen. Fort Lauderdale, Florida: Paul Price Publications.

Little Mosaic. Percussion ensemble, 1968. Krakow: Polskie Wydawnictwo Muzyczne.

Mobile. Percussion duo, 1975. Krakow: Polskie Wydawnictwo Muzyczne.

Music of Five Steps. Flutes and percussion ensemble, 1979. Krakow: Polskie Wydawnictwo Muzyczne.

Scherzo. Xylophone and piano, 1967. Krakow: Polskie Wydawnictwo Muzyczne.

Scintilla. Marimba duo, 1984. Warszawa: Agencja Autorska.

Siderals. Two percussion quintets with optional lighting projection, 1974. Krakow: Polskie Wydawnictwo Muzyczne.

Songs. Voices, piano and percussion, 1986.

Space Model. Percussion, 1975. Munchen: Edition Pro Nova.

Stress. Electronic tape and percussion, 1972. Collaborated with Elzbieta Sikora. New York: *Lang Percussion.

Suite Variee. Percussion quartet and piano, 1968. Paris: Alphonse Leduc Editions Musicales.

Synchromy. Percussion trio, 1978. Langhorne, Pennsylvania: M. Ptaszynska.

---

*M. Lang is a subject in this book.

ARTICLES ABOUT SUBJECT

"A Concert of the Works of Polish Composer/Percussionist Marta Ptaszynska." Lira Singers and Chicago Musical College of Roosevelt University, Friday, March 4, 1988.

LePage, Jane Weiner. Women Composers, Conductors and Musicians of the 20th Century, Volume II. Metuchen, New Jersey: Scarecrow Press, 1983.

"Marta Ptaszynska, Percusionista." Musica Nueva IV/490 (Abril 1980), Instituto Nacional de Bellas Artes.

Migala, Lucyna. "Polish Composer/Percussionist Marta Ptaszynska in Concert with The Lyra Singers." Chicago, 1988.

Sabins, Jany. "Four Preludes for Vibraphone and Piano by Marta Ptaszynska." Modern Percussionist I/4 (September 1985), 61.

Smolenska-Zielinska, Barbara. "A Talk with Marta Ptaszynska." Musical Movement 25, Warsaw, Poland, 1986.

REFERENCE SOURCES

Information supplied by the subject (March 1990 and April 1991).

Lambert, James. "Percussion in Poland: An Interview with *John Beck."

Ptaszynska, Marta. Catalogue. Langhorne, Pennsylvania: M. Ptaszynska.

---

*J. Beck is a subject in this volume.

Pustjens, Jan
Born October 31, 1946, Sittard, The Netherlands

Jan Pustjens attended the Maastricht Conservatory from 1964 to 1968 where he earned a diploma in orchestral percussion with honors and a teaching certificate. Pustjens studied timpani and percussion with Jan Labordus, timpanist in the Concertgebouw Orchestra of Amsterdam.

Since 1974, Pustjens has served as principal percussionist in the Concertgebouw Orchestra. Since 1969, he has taught percussion and worked as area coordinator at Sweelinck Conservatory. Jan Pustjens is founder and president of Pustjens Percussion Products in Amsterdam, one of the world's most respected percussion specialty businesses.

From 1965 to 1969, Pustjens taught percussion at several music schools. From 1966 to 1968, he worked as principal percussionist and timpanist with the orchestra of Opera Forum in Enschede. From 1968 to 1974, Pustjens served as principal percussionist in the Netherlands Philharmonic Orchestra. Another name for that orchestra is Kunstmaand Orkest.

Jan Pustjens was percussionist for the Dutch Wind Ensemble from 1970 to 1978. He founded the New Amsterdam Percussion Group in 1980. Pustjens has made several appearances as a featured soloist with the Concertgebouw Orchestra. With that symphony orchestra, he has been able to travel to many parts of the world, including the continental United States, Mexico, Brazil, Canada, and several European countries. Pustjens has served a coordinator and teacher for an international percussion course of Eduard van Beinum Foundation Holland.

In summary, professional percussionist Jan Pustjens holds one of the most prestigious percussion positions in the world. In addition, his retail percussion business communicates worldwide. Situated in a cultural hub of Europe, and in a place with a rich heritage historically, Pustjens is influential as a percussionist and businessperson. His preparation in the areas of music education and pedagogy help him to associate with various specialists, and to keep in touch with the great music of Europe and America. As an accomplished orchestral performer, Pustjens' musicianship and technique are impressive.

DISCOGRAPHY

Bela Bartok: Concerto for Two Pianos, Percussion and Orchestra. Philips 416-378-2, 1985.

  Recordings with the Concertgebouw Orchestra since 1974.

  Recordings with the Dutch Wind Ensemble, 1970-78.

  Recordings with the Percussion Group Amsterdam, 1970-78.

REFERENCE SOURCES

Information supplied by the subject (October 1989).

Periodical catalogue of Pustjens Percussion Products, Amsterdam, The Netherlands.

Remy, Jacques
Born October 25, 1931, Saint-Cloud, France

Timpanist Jacques Remy studied percussion instruments and technique with F. Passerone. In 1950, Remy was awarded honors in percussion at the Conservatoire National de Musique de Paris. From 1948 to 1956, Jacques Remy worked as a freelance musician, performing in theaters and concert halls, eventually becoming a recording artist in both audio and video media.

In 1950, Remy played timpani in the Orchestre des Concerts Colonne. He participated in the Festival de Besancon, and in a concert tour of Scandinavia under the direction of P. Paray. From 1953 to 1956, Remy was timpanist for the Orchestre de la Societe des Concerts du Conservatoire for the Festival d'Aix en Provence under the direction of C.M. Giulini and H. Rosbaud. Jacques Remy was timpanist from 1954 to 1960 for the Orchestre du Domaine Musical conducted by P. Boulez. Other conductors with whom Remy has performed include E. Ansermet, A. Cluytens, H. Knappertbusch, P. Monteux, and C. Schuricht.

From 1948 to 1953, Jacques Remy was timpanist in l'Orchestre des Cadets du Conservatoire de Paris. He has been principal timpanist for the Orchestre de Paris since its formation in 1967. In 1958, Remy followed his teacher Felix Passerone as percussion professor at l'Ecole Normale de Musique de Paris until 1964. He has authored and edited books for percussionists, in addition to performance and teaching.

Remy has performed as timpanist in many ensembles in France. Examples of these are the Radio-France Symphony Orchestra, the Paris Opera Orchestra, and the National Orchestra of France. Professional conductors with whom he has worked include, in addition to those already mentioned, D. Barenboim, S. Bychkov, A. Jordan, H. von Karajan, L. Maazel, C. Munch, and G. Solti. Jacques Remy has played at festivals in Besancon, Edimbourg, Lucerne, Orange, and Salzbourg. Under the direction of I. Markevitch, Remy performed Darius Milhaud's "Concerto for Percussion and

Small Orchestra." This historic work requires the percussionist to perform several instruments in a large space, including timpani and pedal-operated bass drum. The composition is an important early multipercussion piece, having been completed in Paris in 1930.

Remy has composed music for percussion instruments. In the 1960s, he performed in ensemble with trumpet artist Maurice Andre under the direction of J.F. Paillard. In 1965, a recording in which he participated earned the Grand Prix du Disque for excellence in musical performance. From 1967 to 1982, Remy played in several concerts with a group that specialized in the performance of music written in the sixteenth, seventeenth, and eighteenth centuries, under the direction of J.C. Malgoire. Clearly, Jacques Remy is a most important percussion figure in the twentieth century. His ideas are both aurally and literally recorded.

DISCOGRAPHY

Musique Francaise du 18e Siecle. Ensemble conducted by P. Kuentz, 1965.

Other recordings distributed by CBS, DGG, EMI, Erato and Philips record companies.

Recordings with the Orchestre de Paris since 1967.

COMPOSITIONS

Cadence pour Percussion. Paris: Alphonse Leduc, 1989.

BOOKS

Franz Schubert: Symphonies - Parties de Timbales. Revision par J. Remy. Paris: Alphonse Leduc, 1987.

Ludwig van Beethoven: Symphonies - Parties de Timbales. Volume 1 - Symphonies 1 a 5. Revision par J. Remy. Preface de Daniel Barenboim. Paris, France: Alphonse Leduc, 1983.

Ludwig van Beethoven: Symphonies - Parties de Timbales. Volume 2 - Symphonies 6 a 9. Revision par J. Remy. Preface de Daniel Barenboim. Paris: Alphonse Leduc, 1983.

<u>Robert Schumann: Symphonies and Piano Concerto - Parties de Timbales</u>. Revision par J. Remy. Paris: Alphonse Leduc, 1989.

ARTICLES ABOUT SUBJECT

Ford, Mark. Review of "Cadence pour Percussion" by J. Remy. <u>Percussive Notes</u> (Spring 1990), 78.

"Jacques Remy." Brochure. Paris: Henri Selmer, 1971.

REFERENCE SOURCES

Information supplied by the subject (December 1989 and April 1990).

Richards, Emil
Born September 2, 1932, Hartford, Connecticut

Emil Richards' formal education has included studying music theory and composition with Asher Zlotnik from 1948 to 1952. His percussion teachers have included Alexander Lepak, with whom he studied timpani, and Lou Magnani, with whom Richards studied the vibraphone. Richards attended Hillard College and the Hartford School of Music, receiving a Bachelor of Arts degree in 1953.

From 1949 to 1952, Richards performed in the Hartford Symphony Orchestra. From 1953 to 1955, he was an assistant band leader in Japan for the First Cavalry Division Band. In 1956, Richards became a regular vibraphone performer with George Shearing Quintet, playing for two years. As a freelance jazz performer in 1958 and 1959, Emil Richards received the experience of performing with C. Mingus, F. Phillips, *E. Shaughnessy, and E. Thigpen. From 1959 to 1961, Richards performed as percussionist with Paul Horn Quintet and the Shorty Rogers Big Band.

Since May, 1959, Emil Richards has been a leading percussionist for several studios in Los Angeles, California, including those operated by Columbia Pictures, Lorimar, MGM, Warner Brothers, and 20th Century Fox. Richards was honored with a Most Valuable Percussionist award in 1971 through 1974.

As a studio musician and versatile percussionist with strengths in the jazz field, Richards has performed with many well known entertainers and musicians. Examples include Stan Kenton, Roger Kelloway, George Harrison and Frank Sinatra. Movie work that Richards has done includes performance with Henry Mancini, Lalo Schifrin, John Williams, Jerry Goldsmith, Quincy Jones, Alex North, James Horner, Dave Gruson, Bill Conti, Pat Williams, and Bernard Herman. Richards' several articles written for <u>Modern Percussionist</u>

---

*E. Shaughnessy is a subject in this volume.

magazine in the 1980s are an important original source for practical information about percussion performance.

DISCOGRAPHY

Burnished Brass. With George Shearing. Capital Records.

George Harrison. Dark Horse Records.

Journey to Bliss. Uni Records.

Paul Horn Quintet. Pacific Jazz Records.

Roger Kelloway 'Cello Quartet. A & M Records.

Sinatra and Basie. Warner Brothers Records.

Spirit of 1976. Uni Records.

The Best of Louie Bellson. E. Richards performing bells, conga drums, gong and vibraphone. Pablo 2310-851, 1980.

BOOKS

Emil Richards' World of Percussion. Sherman Oaks, California: Gwyn Publishing Company, 1972.

ARTICLES

"Creating in the Studios." Modern Percussionist III/2 (March 1987), 42.

"Doubling Categories." Modern Percussionist II/1 (December 1985), 38.

"Electronics in the Studio." Modern Percussionist II/4 (September 1986), 48.

"Hints to the Percussion Section." Modern Percussionist II/3 (June 1986), 38.

"Microtonal Music in the Studios." Modern Percussionist III/1 (December 1986), 38.

"Tracking: Dynasty Session." Modern Percussionist III/4 (September 1987), 34.

"Tracking: 'When in Doubt, Give It A Clout'." Modern Percussionist II/2 (March 1986), 30.

ARTICLES ABOUT SUBJECT

Flans, Robyn. "Emil Richards." <u>Modern Percussionist</u> I/2 (March 1985), 6 and cover page.

REFERENCE SOURCES

Information supplied by the subject (October 1989).

Roach, Max
Born January 10, 1924, Elizabeth City, North Carolina

Drum set performer Max Roach began performing in public at the age of ten. He had an early involvement with religious music. Formal study was received at the Manhattan School of Music in New York City. His career is characterized by variety, seriousness and change, in addition to a great amount of originality.

In 1942, Max Roach performed with Charlie Parker. Roach later performed with Dizzy Gillespie. During the 1940s and 1950s, Roach performed with Henry Allen, Miles Davis, Coleman Hawkins, and Louis Jordan. Two locations of Roach's early career performances are Minton's Playhouse and Monroe's Uptown House.

From 1954 to 1956, Max Roach performed with Clifford Brown in a quintet. In the 1950s and 1960s, Roach worked in the area of free jazz, in contrast to earlier concentration on the bop and cool styles of jazz. Since 1960, he has composed music for both small and large ensembles of instruments. In 1970, Roach organized a ten member percussion ensemble. He has recorded with Anthony Braxton, Abdullah Ibrahim, Archie Shepp, and Cecil Taylor. Max Roach has taught at the Lenox School of Jazz, and at the University of Massachusetts.

Honors and awards that Roach has received include an honorary doctorate from The New England Conservatory in 1982. He has received commissions for musical creation from the Penfield Music Composition Project. Roach received a MacArthur Fellowship for extraordinary individual talent and in appreciation of his contributions to American scientific and cultural life. Max Roach was awarded a first place winner in polls organized by Down Beat magazine in 1955, 1957-60, and 1984. He performed at the Paris Jazz Festival in 1949, and at the Newport Jazz Festival in 1972. As a composer, one of his frequent collaborations has been with dance. Other performers with whom Max Roach has performed include Ray Bryant, Eric Dolphy, Booker Little, Thelonius Monk, Bud Powell and Sonny Rollins.

238

DISCOGRAPHY

At Basin Street. EmArcy 36070, 1956.

Birth and Rebirth. With A. Braxton. Black Saint 0024, 1978.

Bright Moments. Max Roach Double Quartet. Italy: Soul Note, 1987.

Collage. Soul Note 1093, 1984.

Deeds, Not Words. Riverside 1122, 1958.

Drum Conversation. Debut 107, 1953.

Drums Unlimited. Atlantic 1467, 1966.

Easy Winners. Soul Note 1109, 1985.

It's Time. Impulse 16, 1962.

Ko-Ko. With C. Parker. Savoy 597, 1945.

Lift Every Voice and Sing. Atlantic 1587, 1971.

Maxology. Prestige 702, 1949.

Max Roach Plus 4 at Newport. EmArcy 80010, 1958.

Move/Budo. With M. Davis. Capitol 15404, 1949.

Percussion Bitter Sweet. Impulse 8, 1961.

Study in Brown. EmArcy 36037, 1955.

Tenor Sax Stylings. With C. Hawkins. Brunswick 58030, 1943.

ARTICLES

"What Jazz Means to Me." Black Scholar III/2 (1972), 3.

ARTICLES ABOUT SUBJECT

Fish, S. "Max Roach." Modern Drummer VI/4 (1982), 8.

Howland, H. "Max Roach: Back on the Bandstand." Modern Drummer III/1 (1979), 12.

"Max Roach." Swing Journal XXXI/11 (1977), 288.

Primack, B. "Max Roach: There's No Stoppin' the Professor from Boppin'." Down Beat XLV/18 (1978), 20.

Richmond, N. "Max Roach: An Interview." Coda 172 (1980), 4.

Rusch, B. "Max Roach: Interview." Cadence V/6 (1979), 3.

Whitehead, K. "Max Roach: Drum Architect." Down Beat LII/10 (1985), 16.

Who's Who in America, 45th edition, Volume 2 (1988), 2604.

Wilson, Olly. "Roach, Max." The New Grove Dictionary of Jazz, Volume Two, 1988.

REFERENCE SOURCES

"A Tribute to Max Roach." Notes 20/6 (January 1990), Eastman School of Music of the University of Rochester, New York.

"Chapter News." Percussive Notes (Spring 1990), 89.

Egart, Richard. "M'Boom--Collage." Review of Soul Note recording SN-1059 with M. Roach, J. Chambers, R. Brooks. W. Smith, R. Mantilla, K. Abdur-Rahman, F. King, F. Waits, E. Fountain and E. Allen. Modern Percussionist I/3 (June 1985), 69.

Parks, C.A. "Self-determination and the Black Aesthetic." Black World XXIII (November 1973), 62.

Rosen, Michael
Born July 16, 1942, Philadelphia, Pennsylvania

Percussionist Michael Rosen received a Bachelor's degree in music education from Temple University in 1964. In 1966, he received a Master of Music degree from the University of Illinois. Rosen's percussion teachers have included *Cloyd Duff, *Fred Hinger, Jack McKenzie, and *Charles Owen.

From 1966 to 1972, Rosen served as principal percussionist in the Milwaukee Symphony Orchestra. Since 1972, he has been faculty percussionist in the Conservatory of Music at Oberlin College. Other work that he has done includes teaching at the Wisconsin Conservatory of Music from 1967 to 1971, and at Kent State University in 1975. In 1974, Michael Rosen performed with the Metropolitan Opera Orchestra, and since 1984 has played regularly at the Grand Teton Music Festival. Since 1972, Rosen has performed on a part time basis with the Cleveland Orchestra. From 1985 to 1987, he performed with the Cleveland Contemporary Chamber Players.

As a recitalist and clinician, Michael Rosen has appeared in Asia, Europe, and the United States. In 1976, he performed at the Jeunesses Musicales Internationale Summerkurse in Germany. He worked for six months in 1977 at the Sweelinck Conservatory in Amsterdam. In 1988, Rosen performed at Perhenimeni College in Helsinki, Finland. Other engagements for Michael Rosen have included concerts, recitals and clinic demonstrations at music schools in Paris, Lyon, Nurnberg, Wurzberg, Stuttgart, Utrecht, Enschede, Maastricht, Rotterdam, and Arnheim. He has performed with the Netherlands Wind Ensemble. Rosen has concertized at Staadlick Museum in Amsterdam, and at the Turku Music Festival in Finland. In 1980, he was a featured marimba artist for the Third International Percussion Course in Breuklen. In 1988, he was a visiting teacher at the Central Conservatory of Music in Beijing, China.

---

*C. Duff, F. Hinger and C. Owen are subjects in this book.

At Oberlin College, Rosen directs the percussion program and the summer percussion camp. He has been on the board of directors for the Percussive Arts Society, and has performed at that organization's conventions in 1974, 1981, 1984 and 1986. Rosen has presented demonstrations to conferences of the Ohio Music Education Association, Music Educators National Conference, Texas Bandmasters Association, and North Carolina Bandmasters Association. In 1988, he was a panelist for the National Endowment for the Arts. As a column editor and author for Percussive Notes, Michael Rosen has offered much detailed information to the worldwide percussion community in the latter half of the twentieth century. His mixture of high quality orchestral performance with keyboard percussion artistry and chamber music activity is exceptional.

DISCOGRAPHY

Duo Exchanges. Clarinet and percussion. Opus One 80373, 1979.

Other recordings for Bayerische Rundfunk, CRI and Lumina record companies.

Recordings with the Milwaukee Symphony Orchestra, 1966-72.

The Oberlin Percussion Group. Mizelle: "Soundscape for Percussion Ensemble." M. Rosen, conductor. Lumina L-002, 1981.

ARTICLES

"Focus on Performance: Terms Used in Percussion - L'Enfant et Les Sortileges by Maurice Ravel." Percussive Notes 29/2 (December 1990), 54.

Other "Terms in Percussion" articles in Percussive Notes magazine and journal. Lawton, Oklahoma: Percussive Arts Society.

ARTICLES ABOUT SUBJECT

"Michael Rosen." Brochure. Oberlin, Ohio: Oberlin Percussion Institute, Conservatory of Music, Oberlin College, 1989.

"The Philadelphia Connection." Percussive Notes 28/4 (Summer 1990), 54.

REFERENCE SOURCES

Information supplied by the subject (September 1989).

England, Wilber. "Programs of PAS Membership." <u>Percussive Notes</u> 29/1 (October 1990), 97.

Samuels, David
Born October 9, 1948, Waukegan, Illinois

Keyboard percussionist David Samuels studied the vibraphone with *Gary Burton. As a teacher, Samuels has taught percussion and jazz improvisation at the Berklee College of Music in Boston, Massachusetts. From 1974 to 1977, he performed various freelance work in New York City.

Samuels has performed and toured with jazz musician Gerry Mulligan, including recording sessions. In 1975, David Samuels began a collaboration with keyboard percussionist *David Friedman that continues presently. The two percussionists have further collaborated with Hubert Laws and Harvie Swartz in music recording. In 1977, *Friedman and Samuels collaborated with Swartz and Michael Pasqua to form a quartet called Double Image, making their recording debut that year for the Enja record label.

From 1977 to 1980, Samuels toured and performed in Europe, presenting various workshops and demonstrations. At this time, he also taught at the Manhattan School of Music. Samuels first recorded with the jazz ensemble Spyro Gyra in 1977, and later performed with a cooperative group called Gallery. Since 1983, Samuels has been touring and performing with Spyro Gyra, becoming a full time member of the band in 1986. His performance with that group is characterized by modal harmonies and scale material, and a quite percussive, though light, tone. Samuels' improvisations are made up of sound as well as melody, a combination that his music shares with classical percussion music of the twentieth century. This facet, perhaps, makes drummers (percussionists) "different" from other musicians in the sense that the percussion art form shares an equal balance between melody and sound, in contrast to art forms of other musical instruments.

Other musicians with whom David Samuels has performed include Paul McCandless (1979), Art Lande (1981), Anthony Davis (1983) and Bobby McFerrin (1984). Samuels made an album as an unaccompanied keyboard

---

*G. Burton and D. Friedman are subjects in this volume.

percussion soloist in 1981. He has presented clinics and workshops domestically as well as internationally, and performed at Percussive Arts Society national conferences.

DISCOGRAPHY

Access All Areas. With Spyro Gyra, D. Samuels performing vibraphone and marimba. MCA Records MCA2-6893, 1983.

Morning Dance. With Spyro Gyra. Infinity 9004, 1979.

Point of View. With Spryo Gyra, 1989.

Spyro Gyra. D. Samuels performing marimba and tabla drums. MCA Records MCA-37149, 1977.

Stories Without Words. With Spyro Gyra, D. Samuels performing marimba and vibraphone. Universal City, California: MCA Records MCAD-42046, 1987.

EDUCATIONAL VIDEOS

Mallet Keyboard Musicianship, Volume I. Grand Rapids, Michigan: Yamaha EV 28-I.

Mallet Keyboard Musicianship, Volume II. Yamaha EV 28-II.

COMPOSITIONS

"Chrysalis." Recorded with Spyro Gyra ensemble. Stories Without Words, MCA Records MCAD-42046, 1987.

"Perpetual Motion in Jazz." Co-authored with W. Zinn. Bryn Mawr, Pennsylvania: Theodore Presser Company.

BOOKS

A Musical Approach to Four Mallet Technique for Vibraphone, Volume I. Excelsior via Bryn Mawr: Theodore Presser.

A Musical Approach to Four Mallet Technique for Vibraphone, Volume II. Bryn Mawr: Theodore Presser.

ARTICLES

"Analyzing the Music You Play." <u>Modern Percussionist</u> II/2 (March 1986), 38.

"Choosing a Chord Voicing." <u>Modern Percussionist</u> I/4 (September 1985), 50.

"Learning to Articulate." <u>Modern Percussionist</u> I/2 (March 1985), 38.

"Relaxing Your Mind and Body through Warm-ups." <u>Modern Percussionist</u> I/1 (December 1984), 40.

"Rhythmic Comping." <u>Modern Percussionist</u> I/3 (June 1985), 46.

"Using the New Technology." <u>Modern Percussionist</u> II/3 (June 1986), 46.

"Vibraphone Viewpoint: Duo Playing." <u>Modern Percussionist</u> II/1 (December 1985), 56.

"Vibraphone Viewpoint: Triads for Voicings." <u>Modern Percussionist</u> III/2 (March 1987), 52.

ARTICLES ABOUT SUBJECT

"Dave Samuels." <u>Modern Percussionist</u> III/1 (December 1986), 7.

Fish, S.K. "Introducing Dave Samuels." Modern Drummer V/2 (1981), 74.

Mattingly, Rick. "Dave Samuels." <u>Modern Percussionist</u> III/1 (December 1986), 8.

Nolan, H. *"Dave Friedman and Dave Samuels: Two-Man Percussion Crusade." <u>Down Beat</u> XLIII/20 (1976), 12.

"Samuels, Dave." <u>The New Grove Dictionary of Jazz</u>, Volume Two, 1988.

Via, David. "Interview with Dave Samuels." <u>Percussive Notes</u> (September 1989), 19.

---

*D. Friedman is a subject in this book.

REFERENCE SOURCES

Baldwin, John. "Chapter News and Membership News." <u>Percussion News</u>, March, 1991.

"PASIC '88." <u>Percussion News</u>, August, 1988.

Peterscak, J. "Musically Speaking." <u>Percussive Notes</u> XIV/3 (1976), 18.

Shaughnessy, Edwin T.
Born January 29, 1929, Jersey City, New Jersey

Drum set specialist Ed Shaughnessy studied his instrument in the 1940s with Bill West in New York City. He graduated from William L. Dickinson High School in Jersey City. From 1952 to 1956 in New York, Shaughnessy studied keyboard percussion and timpani with Morris Goldenberg. In the latter 1950s, Shaughnessy studied music composition with Hall Overton in New York. Ed Shaughnessy has studied tabla drum technique with Indian percussionist Allarakha for four years.

In January, 1949, Shaughnessy performed for a recording while playing a drum set that included two bass drums, with Charlie Ventura Group. In 1950, Shaughnessy performed on tour in Europe with Benny Goodman Sextet. In April, 1954, Shaughnessy played in concert with the New York Philharmonic, conducted by Leonard Bernstein. From 1952 to 1972, Ed Shaughnessy was a very successful freelance percussionist in New York. He has played in the "Tonight Show Orchestra" since October, 1963; that ensemble is currently directed by Doc Severinsen.

Ed Shaughnessy has performed with many musicians in his career. Some of these include *John Beck, Oliver Nelson, Don Ellis, Count Basie, Duke Ellington, Mel Lewis, Teo Macero, Eric Kunzel, and Jimmy Smith. Shaughnessy has performed in concert with dancers directed by George Ballanchine. Ed Shaughnessy has performed in concert also with the Cincinnati Pops Orchestra.

Since 1972, Shaughnessy has worked as a freelance performer in Los Angeles, California. Since 1987, he has led a jazz quintet. In 1980, Shaughnessy helped to produce a drum set video recording. In March, 1991, Ed Shaughnessy appeared with the jazz ensemble of the College of Lake County in Grayslake, Illinois. In recent years, Shaughnessy has written several music compositions for large jazz ensemble. Shaughnessy's musical strengths

---

*J.H. Beck is a subject in this volume.

are versatility, dependable rhythm, virtuosic technique, and an ability to display emotion musically.

DISCOGRAPHY

Afro-American Sketches. With Oliver Nelson. Prestige Records.

A Word from Bird. With T. Charles. Atlantic 1274, 1956.

Bashin'. With Jimmy Smith. Verve Records.

Big Band Hit Parade. Cincinnati Pops Symphony Orchestra conducted by Eric Kunzel. Telarc Records.

Broadway--Basie's Way. With Count Basie. Command 905, 1966.

Happenings. With O. Nelson. Impulse 9132, 1966.

Hollywood--Basie's Way. With Count Basie. Command Records. Other recordings with Count Basie, 1966-67.

The Tonight Show Orchestra with Doc Severinsen, Volume I. Amerst Records.

The Tonight Show Orchestra with Doc Severinsen, Volume II. Amerst Records.

BOOKS

New Time Signatures in Jazz Drumming. Belwin.

ARTICLES ABOUT SUBJECT

Cook, R. "Ed Shaughnessy: Swinger on Staff." Modern Drummer II/3 (1978), 6.

"Ed Shaughnessy: The Tonight Show Orchestra." Newsbeat 1991, Sabian Cymbal Company (1991), 11.

Flans, R. "Ed Shaughnessy." Modern Drummer X/4 (1986), 17.

Lorenz, Mike. "Ed Shaughnessy Clinic November 2, 1990." Wisconsin Percussive Arts Society Newsletter 19/1 (January 1991).

Potter, Jeff. "Shaughnessy, Ed." The New Grove Dictionary of Jazz, Volume Two, 1988.

Smith, T. "Driver's Seat: Ed Shaughnessy on the Road." Modern Drummer VIII/3 (1984), 60.

Tomkins, L. "Ed Shaughnessy Talks Drums." <u>Crescendo International</u> XVIII/6 (1980), 6.

REFERENCE SOURCES

Information supplied by the subject (February 1990).

"Illinois." <u>Arts Midwest Jazz Calendar</u>. Minneapolis, Minnesota, March, 1991.

Small, Edward
Born January 17, 1942, Detroit, Michigan

Percussionist Edward Small studied privately with Sal Rabbio in 1964, and performed with the American Waterways Wind Orchestra in Pittsburgh that summer. The next year, he graduated from Michigan State University with a baccalaureate degree in music education. In 1967, Small earned a Master of Music degree at the University of Rochester's Eastman School of Music in upstate New York. For the next four years, Edward Small was a member of the percussion section of the United States Marine Band in Washington, D.C. With the Marine Band, Small toured and played featured marimba solos with the concert band. His percussion teachers have included *John Beck, *Charles Owen, and *William Street.

In 1971, Edward Small became a member of the Denver Symphony Orchestra in Colorado. His job description with that ensemble was percussion and assistant principal timpani. He has remained with that organization during its recent name change to Colorado Symphony Orchestra. Also since 1971, Small has taught in the Lamont School of Music at the University of Denver. His duties at that school have included teaching private lessons, percussion methods classes, percussion pedagogy and repertoire studies. He has directed the Lamont Percussion Ensemble and performed in the artist faculty concert series. Small has played for musicals in Denver, and presented featured marimba solos with a community wind band in that city. He has played timpani for the Central City Opera since 1986, and is a past president for the Colorado chapter of the international Percussive Arts Society.

Following secondary school, Edward Small attended Lawrence Academy preparatory school in Groton, Massachusetts. He graduated from Cooley High School in Detroit, and attended Wayne State University before enrolling at Michigan State University. From 1972 to 1974, Small directed the

---

*J. Beck, C. Owen and W. Street are subjects in this volume.

Denver Percussion Ensemble for young audience performances in the greater Denver area. Small's valuable bibliography listing percussion articles in <u>Down Beat</u> magazine, first published in 1969, is an example of the kind of sharing with his colleagues that Edward Small practices. Small is included in <u>Who's Who in the West</u>.

Some of Small's freelance performance has included work with Frontier Airlines, the Denver Center Theatre, Carousel Productions, and others. Small has presented lecture demonstrations at the University of Northern Colorado, at Colorado State University, at Adams State College, at Western State College, and at Fort Lewis College. He has made presentations to the Colorado Music Educators Association. Small has adjudicated for the concerto competition of the Jefferson County Symphony. Other adjudication work has been for the state solo and ensemble festival of the Colorado High School Activities Association, and for the collegiate level solo competition in the west-central region for the Music Teachers National Association.

Edward Small has performed with many professional musicians and entertainers. Some of these are Philippe Entremont, Newton Wayland, Yasunori Yamaguchi, Robert Austin Boudreau, Ferrante and Teicher, Judy Collins, Bob McGrath, Nelson Riddle, Henry Mancini, John Williams, Arthur Fiedler, the Canadian Brass, Aaron Copland, Sixten Ehrling, Antal Dorati and John Nelson. One of the major concert works that Edward Small has performed is Robert Kurka's marimba concerto.

DISCOGRAPHY

<u>A Touch of Fiedler</u>. Denver Symphony Pops Orchestra conducted by Newton Wayland. Pro Arte CDD-452, 1987.

<u>Bolero</u>. Denver Symphony Orchestra conducted by Philippe Entremont. Pro Arte CDD-361, 1987.

<u>George Gershwin: Rhapsody in Blue</u>. Denver Symphony Pops Orchestra conducted by Newton Wayland. Pro Arte CDD-352, 1987.

<u>Mussorgsky: Pictures at an Exhibition</u>. Denver Symphony Orchestra conducted by Philippe Entremont. Pro Arte CDD-453, 1989.

United States Marine Band. Recordings for the Department of Defense, 1967-71.

Vive la France. Denver Symphony Orchestra conducted by Philippe Entremont. Pro Arte CDD-410, 1988.

ARTICLES

"An Index of Percussion Articles Appearing in Down Beat." Percussionist VII/2 (December 1969), Lawton, Oklahoma, Percussive Arts Society.

"An Index of Percussion Articles Appearing in Down Beat." Percussionist VII/3 (March 1970).

REFERENCE SOURCES

Information supplied by the subject (August 1990).

Smith, Terry J.
Born August 5, 1952, Tulsa, Oklahoma

Terry Smith graduated from the University of Colorado in Boulder in 1973 with a baccalaureate degree in music education. In 1974, Smith graduated from the University of Michigan in Ann Arbor with a Master of Music degree. Smith graduated from the University of Colorado in 1984 with a Doctor of Musical Arts degree in percussion performance. His percussion teachers have included John Galm and *Charles Owen.

During his undergraduate studies, Smith performed a detailed study of high school percussion ensembles in the Colorado area. One of his lecture demonstrations during his doctoral study was on the topic of mallet making. Smith has played timpani and percussion with the National Repertory Orchestra, previously named the Colorado Philharmonic. A major concert work that Smith has performed is James Basta's marimba concerto.

In the late 1980s, Terry Smith was chapter president for Colorado and the Percussive Arts Society. He directed a percussion workshop several years previously in Wisconsin. Smith has taught at the University of Michigan as a graduate assistant, at International Music Camp in 1975, at the University of Wisconsin - River Falls, and at the University of Colorado. Subjects that he has taught include percussion, music theory, percussion methods, jazz ensemble, percussion ensemble, and music appreciation. Terry Smith has performed as timpanist in the orchestra of the Canary Islands Opera Festival, as timpanist for the Minnesota Opera, and as substitute percussionist and timpanist for the St. Paul Chamber Orchestra. Since 1980, Smith has been a member of the Denver Symphony Orchestra, and has remained with that ensemble since its name change to Colorado Symphony Orchestra.

As a freelance musician, Terry Smith has performed with Keith Jarrett, Roger Williams, American Ballet Theatre, and the Metropolitan Opera. Smith has performed with the Sante Fe Opera, and with the Central City

---

*C. Owen is a subject in this volume.

Opera. He has served on the faculty of an International Percussion Symposium in Texas. Additionally, Smith has led the Concerts and Lectures Committee at the University of Wisconsin in River Falls, and has coordinated the Pre-Concert Lecture Series of the Colorado Symphony Orchestra. From 1975 to 1980, Smith collaborated with Professor John Radd in a Vibe/Piano Duo, and since 1981 has worked with Don Prorak in a Vibe/Marimba Duo. Repertoire of the latter ensemble is eclectic in nature, and includes transcriptions written for KAT-MIDI controller, marimba, tenor pan and vibraphone. Terry Smith has virtuosic ability as an orchestral xylophonist. His combination of high quality performance with scholarship and administrative ability place him in a unique population of professional percussionists.

DISCOGRAPHY

A Touch of Fiedler. Denver Symphony Pops Orchestra conducted by Newton Wayland. Pro Arte CDD-452, 1989.

Bolero. Denver Symphony Orchestra conducted by Philippe Entremont. Pro Arte CDD-361, 1987.

Christmas on Campus. University of Michigan ensemble. Ann Arbor: University of Michigan SM-0001, 1974.

Concertos for Trumpet. National Repertory Orchestra with David Hickman, trumpet, conducted by Walter Charles and Carl Topilow. Denver: Clarino Records SLP-1005, 1973.

George Gershwin: Rhapsody in Blue. Denver Symphony Orchestra conducted by Newton Wayland. Pro Arte CDD-352, 1987.

La Fiesta de la Posada. St. Paul Chamber Orchestra conducted by Dennis Russell Davies including T. Smith performing marimba, pianist Dave Brubeck, bassist Richard Davis, and drum set performer Mel Lewis. CBS Masterworks IM-36662, 1979.

Mussorgsky: Pictures at an Exhibition. Denver Symphony Orchestra conducted by Philippe Entremont. Pro Arte CDD-453, 1989.

Vive la France. Denver Symphony Orchestra conducted by Philippe Entremont. Pro Arte CDD-410, 1988.

200 Years of American Marches. University of Michigan ensemble. Ann Arbor: University of Michigan SM-0002, 1975.

COMPOSITIONS AND ARRANGEMENTS

Graceful Ghost. Composed by William Bolcom, arranged by T. Smith for keyboard percussion ensemble. Van Nuys, California: Alfred Publishing Company and Studio 4 Productions, 1990.

BOOKS

Mallet Master Series. Transcriptions for vibraphone by T. Smith of solos recorded by *Gary Burton and *Milt Jackson: "Green Mountains," "John Brown's Body," "Moonchild/In Your Quiet Place." Piano accompaniments by John Radd. Shell Lake, Wisconsin: Etoile Music, 1980, now published by MMB Music, Saint Louis, Missouri.

REFERENCE SOURCES

Information supplied by the subject (September 1989 and March 1991).

"Announcement of New Publications." Shell Lake, Wisconsin: Etoile Music Publications Division, January 7, 1980.

"New Percussion Publications from Studio 4 Productions." Van Nuys, California: Alfred Publishing Company.

"Stephen F. Austin University." Percussion News, March, 1990.

"SFA International Percussion Symposium, June 23-29, 1990." Nacogdoches, Texas: Stephen F. Austin State University Band Camps, Dr. Lawrence Kaptain, Director of the 1990 Symposium.

---

*G. Burton and M. Jackson are subjects in this volume.

Steele, Glenn
Born August 23, 1944, Brooklyn, New York

Glenn A. Steele received a Bachelor of Arts degree at Glassboro State College in New Jersey. He received a Master of Music degree at Temple University in Pennsylvania. His percussion teachers have included Philadelphia Orchestra percussionists Alan Abel, *Fred Hinger, and *Charles Owen.

In 1966 and 1967, Glenn Steele was timpanist in the Oklahoma City Symphony Orchestra. From 1967 to 1970, Steele served as a percussionist with the U.S. Military Academy Band at West Point, New York. From 1970 to 1972, he taught at Settlement Music School. In 1972-73, Steele served as a visiting professor in the School of Music at Northwestern University in Illinois. Since 1973, Glenn Steele has taught at Temple University in Philadelphia.

Percussionist Steele has played an immense amount of freelance work through the years, with numerous ensembles and many musicians. He has performed with the Philadelphia Orchestra, the Opera Company of Philadelphia, the Penn Contemporary Players, the Chicago Contemporary Players, and the Smithsonian New Music Consort. Steele has played with the Philly Pops Orchestra, the Pennsylvania Ballet Company, the Grant Park Symphony Orchestra, the Philadelphia Philharmonia, the Batterie Percussion Quartet, and the Mozart Society Orchestra. Other study for Glenn Steele has included Midland Park High School in New Jersey graduating in 1962, study with Frank Malabe, and studies at the University of Oklahoma and The Juilliard School. Steele regularly attends Percussive Arts Society conferences and other academic meetings on a regional, national and international scope. Steele's areas of specialization are twentieth century performance practice, conducting, music education and percussion pedagogy. He has read a scholarly paper in Nashville, Tennessee, at a Percussive Arts Society International Convention on the topic of percussion performance and health.

---

*F. Hinger and C. Owen are subjects in this book.

Glenn Steele is a past president of the Pennsylvania chapter of the Percussive Arts Society. Other affiliations include the American Federation of Musicians, the Music Educators National Conference, and Phi Mu Alpha Sinfonia. As a university professor, Steele has served on numerous committees, including those that considered jazz music, promotion and tenure, budget review, grading and standards, recital policies and graduate policies. He has worked with faculty senate and collegial assembly.

Steele's new music activities have included working with composer George Crumb and attending a conference on time at the University of Wisconsin in Milwaukee. On February 24, 1980, Steele performed the world premiere of Ross Finney's "Chamber Piece" in Baltimore, Maryland, with the Penn Contemporary Players. He also helped present the first performance of Wilkenson's "Violin Concerto." Auxiliary percussion teaching effected by Glenn Steele includes working with the drum line at Hammonton High School. Steele is decidedly a prominent figure in the field of percussion music.

DISCOGRAPHY

George Crumb: Lux Aeterna. Columbia Records.
John Russo: Four Riffs for Percussion and Clarinet. C.R.S. Records.
Lukas Foss: Time Cycle. C.R.S. Records.
Pierre Boulez: Eclat. Candide Records.
Richard Wernick: A Prayer for Jerusalem. C.R.I. Records.
The Philly Pops with Peter Nero. Ruth Records.

ARTICLES

"Beginning Keyboard Percussion Instruction." Pennsylvania Music Educators Association Journal, May, 1984.

"Pumping Mallets: A Preliminary Investigation into Musicians' Performance-Related Injuries, Injury Prevention and Performance Enhancement." Percussive Notes 29/5 (June 1991), 26.

REFERENCE SOURCES

Information supplied by the subject (January 1990).

Popovic, Dr. Sandor and Steele, Prof. Glenn. "Ergonomic Experiment in Percussion." Philadelphia: G. Steele.

Steele, Glenn. "Pre-Task Warmups for Musicians." Philadelphia: G. Steele, 1990.

Stevens, Leigh Howard
Born March 9, 1953, Orange, New Jersey

Leigh Howard Stevens received a Bachelor of Music degree with a Performer's Certificate in 1975 at the Eastman School of Music of the University of Rochester. His percussion teachers have included xylophonist William Dorn, drum set perfomer Joe Morello, marimbist *Vida Chenoweth and timpanist *John Beck. A continuing education experience of Leigh Stevens is his constant contact with percussion students nationwide.

Stevens performed and demonstrated technical ideas at the first Percussive Arts Society International Convention in the autumn of 1976 in Rochester, New York. This has been followed by his participation at several conferences and visitation at many college campuses in the United States. As a freelance artist, Stevens performs, records, writes, publishes, and manufactures percussion implements.

Leigh Stevens has performed marimba concertos with symphony orchestras in Illinois and Colorado. His method book for the marimba is very detailed and specific in regard to outlining his particular approach to holding marimba mallets and performing challenging passages from the musical literature. His compact disc recording of music by Johann Sebastian Bach played on the marimba is convincing and beautiful in sound. The marimba mallets that he manufactures are of very good quality. Stevens' articles about marimba technique and philosophy are sprinkled with a bit of humor as well as wise advice. Of particular interest is his invention of technique based on pre-existing personal approaches. Leigh Stevens exhibits dynamic control of his resources, instrument, and repertoire.

Stevens has worked as an author of marimba columns for <u>Modern Percussionist</u> and <u>Percussive Notes</u> magazines. His performance has been reviewed in <u>Time</u>, <u>Digital Audio</u>, <u>Stereophile</u>, <u>Volkskrant</u>, <u>Ovation</u>, and other periodicals. He has toured extensively in Europe and the United States as

---

*V. Chenoweth and J.H. Beck are subjects in this volume.

recitalist and clincian. Composers whose music has been performed by Stevens, in addition to J.S. Bach, include Joseph Schwantner, John Serry, Minoru Miki, Alfred Fissinger, David Maslanka, *Clair Musser, Raymond Helbe, Robert Kurka, Robert Schumann, Wolfgang Mozart, Peter Tchaikovsky, *Gordon Stout, Robert Aldridge, John Corigliano, William Penn and Christopher Stowens. Stevens has been featured in a broadcast of National Public Radio's "All Things Considered" show, and has been interviewed by Arlene Francis on "New York, New York." Leigh Stevens has edited several works for solo marimba, and has served as a consultant for Musser Marimba Division in the Selmer Company. Stevens' specialty is classical marimba music.

DISCOGRAPHY

Bach on Marimba. Music Masters MMD 60124-F, MML 40124-H.
William Penn: Preludes. Composers Recording, CRI.

BOOKS

Method of Movement for Marimba. Asbury Park, New Jersey: Marimba Productions.

ARTICLES

"Dear Leigh." Modern Percussionist III/2 (March 1987), 40.

"Marimba Perspectives." Modern Percussionist I/2 (March 1985), 28.

"Marimba Perspectives: Accompanying on Marimba." Modern Percussionist II/3 (June 1986), 40.

"Marimba Perspectives: Accompanying on Marimba," Part 2. Modern Percussionist III/1 (December 1986), 32.

"Marimba Perspectives: Four-mallet Grip Needed." Modern Percussionist I/3 (June 1985), 30.

"Marimba Perspectives: Marididdles." Modern Percussionist II/2 (March 1986), 42.

---

*C. Musser and G. Stout are subjects in this book.

"Marimba Perspectives: Seven Super Sequential Stickings." <u>Modern Percussionist</u> II/1 (December 1985), 42.

"Marimba Perspectives: UFOs and Mummies." <u>Modern Percussionist</u> I/4 (September 1985), 44.

ARTICLES ABOUT SUBJECT

Larrick, Geary. "Leigh Howard Stevens." <u>Wisconsin Percussive Arts Society Newsletter</u> X/6 (May 1980), 7.

REFERENCE SOURCES

Information supplied by the subject (October 1989).

Hashimoto. Professional artist photograph. Asbury Park, New Jersey: Marimba Productions.

"Malletech Concert Keyboards." Brochure. Asbury Park: Marimba Productions, February, 1991.

*"Vic Firth Presents Leigh Howard Stevens Concert Marimba Mallets." Brochure. Dover, Massachusetts: Firth.

---

*E. (Vic) Firth is a subject in this volume.

Stout, Gordon B.
Born October 5, 1952, Wichita, Kansas

Classical marimbist Gordon Stout earned a Bachelor of Music degree in percussion performance at the Eastman School of Music of the University of Rochester in 1974. He received a Master of Music degree in music composition at the Eastman School in 1976. Stout's teachers have included Samuel Adler, *John Beck, and *Warren Benson. Gordon Stout presented a marimba performance and demonstration at the first international convention of the Percussive Arts Society in 1976 in Rochester, New York. Stout has also studied with *Vida Chenoweth and James D. Salmon. While attending the Eastman School of Music, Stout performed with the Eastman Marimba Band, the Eastman Percussion Ensemble, and the Rochester Philharmonic Orchestra.

From 1976 to 1979, Gordon Stout taught at St. Mary's College in Maryland. Since 1980, Stout has taught percussion at Ithaca College in upstate New York. Beginning in 1978, he has worked during summers at Birch Creek Music Center in Door County, Wisconsin. Stout has taught at *Leigh Stevens' summer marimba camps on the east coast of the United States in 1987-89. His music compositions have received many performances. He has made numerous presentations as lecturer and performer.

From 1987 to 1990, Gordon Stout was a column editor and author for Percussive Notes magazine. He has served on the board of directors for the Percussive Arts Society. Stout has authored several pedagogical articles in addition to compositions for publication. He frequently performs chamber music in addition to presenting clinics and workshops. Significantly, Stout has recorded the entire Creston marimba concerto with piano accompaniment. His influence is strong nationwide as a performer and teacher. In 1986, Stout received a Consortium Commissioning Grant from the National Endowment

---

*J. Beck, W. Benson, V. Chenoweth and L. Stevens are subjects in this book.

for the Arts in collaboration with William Moersch and *Leigh Howard Stevens for the purpose of motivating the composition of new music for solo marimba by composers Jacob Druckman, Roger Reynolds and Joseph Schwantner. One of the many clinic presentations by Gordon Stout occurred on March 24, 1990, at East Carolina University in Greenville for a North Carolina Percussive Arts Society Day of Percussion.

DISCOGRAPHY

Alec Wilder's Music for Marimba with Other Instruments. Includes "Suite for Trumpet and Marimba," "Suite for Flute and Marimba," "Sextet for Marimba and Wind Quintet." Golden Crest Records CRS-4190.

Brian Bowman, Euphonium. Includes "Four Dialogues for Euphonium and Marimba" by Samuel Adler. Crystal Records S 393.

Gordon Stout: II. Includes the entire Paul Creston marimba concerto with piano accompaniment, "Duo" by David Wheatley, "Yellow after the Rain" by *Mitchell Peters, and "Reverie" by G. Stout. Northridge, California: Studio 4 Productions S4P-R102.

Music for Solo Marimba. Includes "Two Mexican Dances" performed by the composer. Van Nuys, California: Alfred Publishing 03-2911.

Nola. Eastman Marimba Band. Mercury Golden Imports SRI-75108.

Organist David Craighead. Adler: "Xenia, A Dialogue for Organ and Percussion" with G. Stout performing multipercussion. Los Angeles: Crystal Records S-858, 1977.

COMPOSITIONS

Andante and Allegro. Van Nuys, California: Studio 4.

Duo. Van Nuys: Studio 4 Productions.

Elegy. Van Nuys: Studio 4.

Ode for Marimba. Fort Lauderdale, Florida: Paul Price Publications, 1979.

---

*L. Stevens is a subject in this book.

*M. Peters is a subject in this volume.

<u>Reverie</u>. Van Nuys: Studio 4.

<u>Suite for Solo Guitar</u>. Van Nuys: Studio 4.

<u>Triptych No. 2</u>. Marimba and percussion ensemble. University of Oklahoma Press.

BOOKS

<u>Etudes for Marimba</u>, Book III. Van Nuys: Alfred, 1990.

<u>Five Etudes for Marimba</u>, Book I. Fort Lauderdale: Paul Price Publications, 1975.

ARTICLES

"Gordon Stout." <u>Master Technique Builders for Vibraphone and Marimba</u>, edited by *Anthony J. Cirone. Miami, Florida: Belwin-Mills Publishing, 1985.

REFERENCE SOURCES

Information supplied by the subject (September 1989).

Ford, Mark. "Percussion Keyboard Literature." <u>Percussive Notes</u> (Spring 1990), 79.

Holly, Rich. "Percussion Keyboard Literature." <u>Percussive Notes</u> (Spring 1990), 79.

"North Carolina - Steel Drum Workshop." <u>Percussion News</u>, March, 1990.

"The First Annual Central Ohio Mallet Percussion Clinic." Columbus: Columbus Percussion, June, 1991.

---

*A. Cirone is a subject in this book.

Street, William
Born c. 1895, Hamilton, Ontario, Canada
Died August 2, 1973, Rochester, New York

William G. Street moved to Rochester, New York, in infancy. He began his professional career in his middle teens, playing after school in theaters in Rochester and Watertown. As a member of the Eastman Theatre Orchestra in 1922, William Street's snare drum roll was the first musical sound heard in concert for the opening of that historic auditorium. Street also performed the xylophone between movies at the Eastman Theatre.

William Street was a charter member of the Rochester Philharmonic Orchestra. He played in the Philharmonic for thirty-four years until retiring in 1956. Some of the conductors with whom Street worked are Albert Coates, Erich Leinsdorf, and Fritz Reiner. Street began in the Philharmonic as a percussionist then became timpanist early in his tenure with the orchestra. He performed with the Rochester Civic Orchestra until 1958.

Miscellaneous professional percussion performance of William Street has included performing in the Lake Placid Club orchestras under the direction of Paul White for more than thirty years. Street performed in the Eastman School's Festival of American Music from 1925 to 1958 under the leadership of composer and director Howard Hanson.

In 1927, Hanson recruited Street for the position of percussion professor at the Eastman School of Music in Rochester. William Street taught at the Eastman School until June, 1967. His teaching techniques were extremely successful, with many of his students earning important performance positions in symphony orchestras, universities, and service bands. It was this author's good fortune to spend an hour with "Mr. Street" in his teaching studio while auditioning for entrance to the graduate program at the Eastman School. Typically, the "audition" was more like a lesson and meeting of friends than any type of intense scrutinizing experience.

William Street was an honorary member of Phi Mu Alpha Sinfonia. He was honored at an Eastman School concert on January 12, 1969, by the

Rochester chapter of Mu Phi Epsilon. At that time, Street was designated "Musician of the Year" for his accomplishments as a performer and teacher. The program that afternoon consisted of music written or arranged for percussion by Bela Bartok, Dietrich Buxtehude, Carlos Chavez, Jack McKenzie, and Elliott Schwartz. Street was a member of the United States Seniors Golf Association.

On Thursday evening, April 20, 1967, the Eastman Percussion Ensemble presented a concert dedicated to William Street. On that program was music written by *John Beck, Osher Green, Robert Ludwig, and Paul Oster. William Street's brother, Stanley, was also a member of the Rochester Philharmonic percussion section. In 1923, when William Street first performed in the Rochester Civic Orchestra, George Eastman was the conductor and musical director. Street stayed with that ensemble when its name was changed to Rochester Philharmonic.

Street's early work began at a salary of fifty cents per hour, then increased to a dollar an hour. Theaters in which Street performed also include the Hippodrome and the Piccadilly. One of William Street's concepts in percussion performance involved tone with the concert snare drum. According to his ideas, the snare drum stick could produce either a pleasing or an unpleasant tone, depending upon how the performer strikes the drum head. Therefore, contrasting terms such as "legato" and "staccato" were spoken to describe actual sound and tone concepts emanating from the musician's performance. These ideas also transferred to the construction of timpani mallets for the individual performer. It is thus legitimate to refer to an Eastman type of sound, in contrast to that produced by educational products of another school. Individual talent and variance do of course come into consideration, though generally a student of William Street will sound different in performance from a student of another teacher with a contrasting sound concept. Street was an important early twentieth century performer and teacher of percussion. His ideas unquestionably are present in later generations of students and professionals in the percussion field.

---

*J. Beck is a subject in this volume.

DISCOGRAPHY

Rochester Philharmonic recordings, 1922-56.

COMPOSITIONS

Several works. Eastman School of Music, Rochester, New York: Eastman Publications Series.

ARTICLES ABOUT SUBJECT

Cooperman, Ira. "William Street--Percussion Pioneer." Rochester, New York: Eastman School of Music News Release, August 2, 1973.

Freed, Richard D. "William G. Street To Retire--At Eastman 40 Years." Rochester: Eastman School of Music Public Relations Office, April 18, 1967.

Freed, Richard D. "William Street To Be Honored by Mu Phi Epsilon on January 12." Rochester: Eastman School of Music Public Relations Office, December 19, 1968.

Goldberg, Gerald. "His Drum Roll--The First in the Eastman." Rochester Democrat and Chronicle, Friday, August 3, 1973, 4-B.

REFERENCE SOURCES

*Beck, John H. Information supplied about the subject, 1991.

Program. Mu Phi Epsilon "Musician of the Year" Concert. Rochester, New York: Eastman School of Music, January 12, 1968.

---

*J.H. Beck is a subject in this book.

Udow, Michael
Born March 10, 1949, Detroit, Michigan

Michael W. Udow attended Interlochen Arts Academy and National Music Camp during his secondary school education. Udow has received three degrees from the University of Illinois--a Bachelor of Music, a Master of Music, and a Doctor of Musical Arts. Udow's teachers have included Alan Abel, *Warren Benson, Gordon Binkerd, Herbert Brun, Frederick Fairchild, Thomas Frederickson, Russell Hartenberger, Edwin London, Jack McKenzie, Michael Ranta, Thomas Siwe and Paul Steg.

In 1971 and 1972, Michael Udow performed percussion in the New Orleans Philharmonic. Since 1968, Udow has performed in summers as principal percussionist for the Sante Fe Opera. His teaching jobs have included work at the University of Missouri in Kansas City, at Pennsylvania State University, and at the University of Michigan since 1982. In 1972, Udow was a Fulbright Scholar in Warsaw, Poland. Presently, he composes and performs chamber music concerts in collaboration with his wife who is a modern dancer. They tour and concertize domestically and internationally. Udow has recorded for Columbia, Denon, CRI, Advance, Opus One, New World, and Orion record companies.

In 1973, Michael Udow was a touring member of Blackearth Percussion Group. In 1974 and 1975, he toured with the Barton Workshop based in Devon, England. In 1976 and 1977, Udow was a Creative Performing Arts Fellow at the University of Illinois. Udow has performed for Percussive Arts Society conventions and at many colleges and universities. His percussion performance has been aired over National Public Radio. He has performed in Japan and in Lincoln Center in New York City.

The Udows are known by the name Equilibrium--a modern dance and percussion duo. A September, 1989, performance in central Wisconsin offered the audience original American music, costumes, handbells, puppets,

---

*W. Benson is a subject in this volume.

a text by Lewis Carroll, and ten settings of Japanese poetry that was translated into English. Also in that year, Udow performed in Germany at Tubingen International Percussion Days, and with the Jackson Symphony Orchestra in collaboration with *Keiko Abe. Udow has also performed in Austria and at national conventions in the United States of America.

Michael Udow has received an award for excellence in teaching at the University of Michigan. Udow has been a member of the board of directors for the Percussive Arts Society. Udow is included in International Who's Who in Music, Who's Who in America, Who's Who in the World, and Bibliographical Dictionary of American Composers.

DISCOGRAPHY

African Welcome Piece. La Scala Opera Orchestra Percussion Section. Italy: Helidore Records.

American Indian Children's Poems. "The Artistry of Nancy and Michael Udow." WKAR Televison.

Barn Burner. Radio Bremen, Germany. RTF, Paris. Danish Radio, Arhus. The Barton Workshop.

Dancing Hands. Sound score. "The Art of Rita Blitt." Documentary film by John Altman.

Dancing Hands. Tone Road Ramblers, TRR Records.

M. Udow with *Keiko Abe and University of Michigan Percussion Ensemble. Columbia/Denon Records.

Shadow Songs IV. Tone Road Ramblers, TRR Records.

Strike. Percussion Group of Cincinnati. Opus One Records.

Tacit. "The Artistry of Nancy and Michael Udow." WKAR-TV.

Threnody II. Tokyo, Japan: NHK Radio and Television.

"6 x 6 Scanning," "Tacit," "American Indian Children's Poems." Equilibrium in Concert. Tempe: Arizona School for the Deaf and KAET Television.

---

*K. Abe is a subject in this volume.

*K. Abe is a subject in this book.

COMPOSITIONS AND ARRANGEMENTS

Acoustic Composition No. 1.   Dexter, Michigan: Equilibrium Publications.

African Welcome Piece. New York: Sam Fox Publishing, 1973.

American Indian Children's Poems. Dexter: Equilibrium.

Barn Burner. Dexter: Equilibrium.

Bog Music. Dexter: Equilibrium.

Dancing Hands. Dexter: Equilibrium.

Over the Moon. Dexter: Equilibrium.

Remembrance. Dexter: Equilibrium.

Rock Etude #7. Composed by Bill Douglas, arranged by M. Udow for percussion quintet. Fort Lauderdale, Florida: Music for Percussion, 1986.

Shadow Songs I. Dexter: Equilibrium.

Shadow Songs II. Dexter: Equilibrium.

Shadow Songs IV. Dexter: Equilibrium.

Strike. Dexter: Equilibrium.

Tacit. Dexter: Equilibrium.

Threnody II. Dexter: Equilibrium.

6 x 6 Scanning. Dexter: Equilibrium.

BOOKS

The Contemporary Percussionist.   Co-authored with Chris Watts. Twenty multipercussion recital solos.   Fort Lauderdale: Meredith Music Publications.

ARTICLES

"Focus on Performance: An Interview with *Warren Benson." Percussive Notes (Winter 1989), 42.

"From Hearing and Reading to Listening and Understanding: An Attempt to Bridge the Gap." Percussionist Research Edition (Fall 1983).

----

*W. Benson is a subject in this volume.

280

"Karlheinz Stockhausen: An Interview with an Annotated Bibliography." <u>Percussionist</u> Research Edition (Fall 1985).

"Visual Correspondence between Notation Systems and Instrument Configurations." <u>Percussionist</u> Research Edition (Fall 1982).

REFERENCE SOURCES

Information supplied by the subject (September 1989).

Program. "Equilibrium - Dance and Percussion Duo: Nancy and Michael Udow." Stevens Point, Wisconsin: University of Wisconsin - Stevens Point, College of Fine Arts and Communication, Performing Arts Office, Monday, September 25, 1989.

Staff. "PAS Welcomes Newest Members of Its Board of Directors." <u>Percussive Notes</u> (Spring 1990), 4.

Wilson, Larry
Born July 1, 1948, Chicago, Illinois

Timpanist Larry Wilson graduated from Niles West High School in Skokie, Illinois, in 1966. In 1966-67, he attended Lincoln College. In 1971, Wilson earned a Bachelor of Music degree at San Francisco Conservatory in California. From 1972 to 1975, he studied the timpani with Saul Goodman in New York City. Wilson has also studied with Roland Kohloff.

As a teacher of percussion, Larry Wilson directed the San Francisco Conservatory Percussion Ensemble from 1967 to 1972. He also taught timpani and percussion performance at that school. From 1973 to 1976, Wilson instructed percussion students at Manhattanville College, Mercy College, and at the Westchester Conservatory of Music. He is presently an instrument and implement manufacturer in Wisconsin Dells, Wisconsin.

As a professional performer, Larry Wilson's experience has been wide and varied. From 1968 to 1972, he performed as timpanist and percussionist in the Oakland Symphony Orchestra, as timpanist for Western Opera Theater, and as timpanist and percussionist for musical theater productions. From 1970 to 1972, Wilson was timpanist of the San Francisco Spring Opera Orchestra, substitute percussionist and timpanist with the San Francisco Symphony, and percussionist with the San Francisco Symphony Summer Pops Orchestra conducted by Arthur Fiedler.

In 1973, Larry Wilson played percussion for educational concerts with the New York Philharmonic. Also in 1973, he was a timpanist for the National Orchestral Association and at the Festival of Two Worlds in Spoletto, Italy. In 1974, he continued as timpanist with the National Orchestral Association, and was appointed adjudicator by the Canadian Quebec government to evaluate final examinations in percussion at the Conservatory of Music in Montreal.

From 1973 to 1975, Wilson was timpanist for the Manhattan Symphony Orchestra. From 1973 to 1976, he performed as substitute percussionist with the New York Philharmonic, and as timpanist and percussionist with several other symphony orchestras in the New York metropolitan area. These ensembles include the Lyndhurst Festival Orchestra, the Orchestral Society of Westchester, the Westchester Symphony Orchestra, and recording orchestras. In 1976, Wilson performed on timpani and percussion for young audience concerts with Pippit Productions.

From 1977 to 1988, Larry Wilson performed as principal timpanist with the Melbourne Symphony Orchestra in Victoria, Australia. He also performed for the Australian Broadcasting Corporation. During this period, Wilson taught percussion at the University of Melbourne and at Victorian College of the Arts. Since 1988, Wilson has operated Wilson Percussion Products in Wisconsin. Some of his manufactured materials include custom made conducting batons, keyboard percussion mallets, bass drum mallets, triangle beaters, claves, timpani dampers, snare drum sticks, timpani mallets, jingle sticks and slapsticks.

Some of the many conductors with whom Larry Wilson has performed are Seiji Ozawa, Joseph Krips, Carlos Chavez, Morton Gould, Willem van Otterloo, Harold Farberman, James Levine, Zdenek Macal, Aaron Copland, Leonard Bernstein, Thomas Schippers, Franz-Paul Decker, Krzysztof Penderecki, Hiroyki Iwaki, and Kurt Sanderling. Featured soloists with whom Wilson has performed are Elton John, Barry Tuckwell, Idil Biret, Edith Peinemann, Kyung-Wha Chung, Michel Block, Isador Goodman, Marilyn Horne, Sonja Hanke, James Galway, John Williams, Yvonne Minton, Sylvia Rosenberg, Jorge Bolet, Paul Badura-Skoda, Zvi Zeitlin, Alicia de Larrocha, Van Clyburn, Wanda Wilkomirska, and Vladimir Ashkenazy. Larry Wilson's varied career that has taken him from the Chicago area to the west coast then to the east coast of the United States, followed by several years in Australia, has again brought him back to the middle west. Interestingly, one of his recent products for sale is a varied selection of wind chimes.

DISCOGRAPHY

Recordings for RCA, Philips, Phonart and Nonesuch-Warner record companies, and for Australian Broadcasting Corporation.

BOOKS

The Player's Choice. Catalogue with price list. Wisconsin Dells, Wisconsin: Wilson Percussion Products, 1991.

REFERENCE SOURCES

Information supplied by the subject (October 1990).

Wyre, John
Born May 17, 1941, Philadelphia, Pennsylvania

John Wyre studied percussion with *Fred Hinger in 1955. From 1959 to 1964, Wyre attended the Eastman School of Music where he studied with *William Street. Wyre earned a Bachelor of Music degree at the Eastman School in 1964.

Wyre has held many freelance and contract positions in his professional career. He has performed as timpanist with the Toronto Symphony, the Marlboro Music Festival, the Oklahoma City Symphony Orchestra, and the Milwaukee Symphony Orchestra. He has performed New Music Concerts in Toronto. Wyre has played with the San Francisco Symphony, and with the Boston Symphony Orchestra. He has performed timpani with the Canadian Opera Company, and is a founding member of Nexus percussion ensemble since 1971.

As a teacher of percussion, John Wyre has worked at the University of Toronto, and with National Youth Orchestra of Canada. Wyre has performed percussion with the Rochester Philharmonic. Since 1984, John Wyre has served as artistic director for World Drum Festivals in Australia, Calgary, Toronto and Vancouver. Some of the artist drummers with whom he collaborates in the festivals include residents of India, Russia, Denmark, Ghana, Kenya, United Kingdom, Korea, Cuba, Indonesia, Pakistan, Puerto Rico, Canada and the United States.

Some of the professional percussionists with whom Wyre has collaborated in these festivals are *Steve Gadd, Nexus, Jamey Haddad, Lapo Kabwit, Repercussion, Ed Thigpen, Glen Velez, Samul Nori, Sal Ferreras, *John Bergamo, Brian Leonard, Rampak Gandung, Themba Tana, Trichy Sankaran, Naqqara Drummers, Abraham Adzinyah, Sharda Sahai, Mark

---

*F. Hinger and W. Street are subjects in this book.

*S. Gadd and J. Bergamo are subjects in this book.

Brzezicki, the Harmonites International Steel Orchestra, and Triumph Street Pipers.

As a composer, John Wyre has received several commissions from the Canada Council, CBC, Ontario Arts Council, Festival Singers of Canada, harpist Judy Loman, and National Youth Orchestra. Wyre's works have been performed by Nexus, the New York Philharmonic and other ensembles. His music has been played at the University of Michigan and at the University of Toronto. John Wyre has appeared as a featured soloist with major orchestras, and has taught at Central State University, at the Wisconsin Conservatory of Music, at Queen's University, and at the Banff Summer School of the Performing Arts.

Percussionist John Wyre has toured as a performer to many locations, including Wisconsin, Germany, Belgium, Japan, China, Korea, England, Finland, Denmark, The Netherlands, Nova Scotia, and New Mexico. His eleven years as timpanist with the Toronto Symphony Orchestra highlight much involvement with drums, improvisation and composition.

DISCOGRAPHY

Changes. NE-05.

"Marubatoo." Nexus Now. Holcomb, New York: *William L. Cahn Publishing, Nexus 10262, 1989.

Music of Nexus. NE-01.

Nexus and Earle Birney: Musicpoetry, Vols. 1-3. NE-02, NE-03, NE-04.

Nexus Now. Holcomb: *W.L. Cahn, Nexus 10262, 1989.

Nexus Ragtime Concert. Toronto, Ontario, Canada: Nimbus 9 Productions, UMB-DD2, 1976.

Recordings with the Toronto Symphony, 1966-80.

---

*W.L. Cahn is a subject in this book.

COMPOSITIONS

Bell Cycles. For two percussion, 1971.

Bells. For string orchestra, harp, percussion and pre-recorded tape, 1970.

Bells II. For string orchestra, harp, pre-recorded tape and percussions, 1972.

Bernie. Choir-SATB, percussion, contrabass clarinet, 1976.

Cloches pour Michel. String orchestra, harp, tuba and percussion, 1982.

Connexus. Symphony orchestra and percussions, 1977.

Earth Provides. Touch Is Such. Songs, 1985.

Eddys. Percussion ensemble, 1970.

First Flower. Orchestra, 1984.

Maruba. Marimba and tuba, 1987.

Marubatoo. Percussion quintet playing three marimbas, vibraphone and crotales, 1988.

Mind the Wind. Harp and percussion with text, 1982.

Snowflake. Flute, harp and percussion, 1975.

Utau Kane No Wa. Choir-SATB and percussions, 1974.

REFERENCE SOURCES

Information supplied by the subject (January 1990).

"A Festival of Master Musicians." Toronto: World Drums.

Brooks, Iris. "The World Drum Festival." Modern Percussionist III/1 (December 1986), 14.

Ford, Mark. "Nexus Now." Percussive Notes 29/3 (February 1991), 64.

"Nexus - 1984 International Tour." Toronto: Nexus, 1984.

"Scotia Festival of Music - 1991." International Musician (Winter 1991).

"Waterbird Institute Announces Nexus, Global Music, Master Percussionists." Percussive Notes (Spring 1990), 35.

Appendix I

Specialty Classifications

Following are listings of percussionists whose biographical sketches appear in this volume, classified according to their specialty. It is understood that all those included in this book could certainly do more than one thing well, since that is an essential nature of the percussion field. In this particular listing, however, the eighty artists are categorized within one primary area of concentration.

Chamber Musicians
Keiko Abe
Bob Becker
John Bergamo
Vida Chenoweth
Clair Omar Musser
Karen Ervin Pershing
Marta Ptaszynska
Emil Richards
Leigh Howard Stevens
Gordon B. Stout
Michael Udow

Drum Set Performers
Louis Bellson
Art Blakey
Fred Buda
Jack DeJohnette
Stephen Gadd
Harvey Mason
Charles J. Miles
Max Roach
Edwin T. Shaughnessy

Jazz Keyboard Percussionists
     Gary Burton
     David Friedman
     Lionel Hampton
     Bobby Hutcherson
     Milt Jackson
     Garry Lee
     Bill Molenhof
     Ted Piltzecker
     David Samuels

Orchestral Percussionists
     Elden C. Bailey
     John R. Beck
     James Blades
     Ruth Patricia Cahn
     William L. Cahn
     Anthony J. Cirone
     Michael Colgrass
     Paula N. Culp
     Marvin Dahlgren
     Patricia Dash
     Sam Denov
     Niel B. DePonte
     Francois Dupin
     Thomas Gauger
     Douglas Howard
     Vicki P. Jenks
     Donald Kuehn
     Richard Kvistad
     Christopher S. Lamb
     Morris Lang
     William F. Ludwig
     Charles Owen
     Robert C. Pangborn
     Albert Payson
     Gordon B. Peters
     Arthur Press
     Jan Pustjens
     Michael Rosen
     Edward Small
     Terry J. Smith

Percussion Teachers
    John H. Beck
    Owen Clark
    Ron Fink
    Siegfried Fink
    George A. Frock
    James H. Latimer
    James L. Moore
    Glenn Steele
    William Street

Timpanists
    Warren Benson
    Cloyd Duff
    Everett J. Firth
    Fred D. Hinger
    Elayne Jones
    William Kraft
    Stanley S. Leonard
    Tele Lesbines
    Mitchell Peters
    Jacques Remy
    Larry Wilson
    John Wyre

Appendix II
Ensembles and Performers

Following are listings of ensembles and performers. Each ensemble is listed with the name of a percussionist from this book who has performed in it. In some instances, there are duplications or multiplicities, since many professional percussionists perform with several ensembles during their careers. It is understood that musical organizations sometimes change names, and at times are known by more than one name, for example the Rochester Philharmonic that is also called the Rochester Philharmonic Orchestra, and the Colorado Philharmonic that is presently called the National Repertory Orchestra.

Aeolian Consort
    John H. Beck

Alexandria Symphony Orchestra
    John R. Beck

All-American Youth Orchestra
    Cloyd Duff

American Music Festival Orchestra
    John H. Beck
    Ruth Patricia Cahn
    William L. Cahn
    William Street

American Symphony Orchestra
    Keiko Abe
    Elayne Jones

American Waterways Wind Orchestra
    Vicki P. Jenks
    Richard T. Kvistad
    Edward Small

Annapolis Symphony Orchestra
    John R. Beck

154th Army Ground Forces Band
    Elden C. Bailey

Arrangers' Workshop Orchestra
  John H. Beck

Aspen Chamber Symphony
  Douglas Howard

Aspen Festival Orchestra
  Fred D. Hinger
  Douglas Howard
  Charles Owen

Aspen Jazz Ensemble
  Ted Piltzecker

Aspen Percussion Ensemble
  Charles Owen

The Association for the Advancement of Creative Musicians
  Jack DeJohnette

Austin Lyric Opera Orchestra
  George A. Frock

Austin Symphony Orchestra
  George A. Frock

Baltimore Opera Orchestra
  John R. Beck

Baltimore Symphony Orchestra
  John R. Beck
  Donald Kuehn

Barnum and Bailey Circus Band
  Elden C. Bailey

Baylor University Orchestra
  Vicki P. Jenks

Benny Goodman Band
  Louis Bellson

Benny Goodman Combo
  Lionel Hampton
  Edwin T. Shaughnessy

Bill Molenhof Trio
  Bill Molenhof

Blackearth Percussion Group
    Richard T. Kvistad
    Michael Udow

Boston Ballet Orchestra
    Fred Buda

Boston Opera Company Orchestra
    Everett J. Firth
    Arthur Press

Boston Philharmonia
    Fred Buda

Boston Pops Orchestra
    Fred Buda
    Everett J. Firth
    Thomas Gauger
    James H. Latimer
    Arthur Press

Boston Symphony Chamber Players
    Everett J. Firth
    Arthur Press

Boston Symphony Orchestra
    Everett J. Firth
    Thomas Gauger
    Arthur Press
    John Wyre

Boston University Percussion Ensemble
    Thomas Gauger

Brevard Festival Orchestra
    Warren Benson

Bridgeport Symphony Orchestra
    Tele Lesbines

Brooklyn College Percussion Ensemble
    Morris Lang

Brooklyn Philharmonic
    Elayne Jones

Buffalo Philharmonic
    William L. Cahn
    Christopher S. Lamb

Cairo Symphony Orchestra, Egypt
James H. Latimer

Cal Arts Twentieth Century Players
John Bergamo

California Percussion Players
Richard T. Kvistad

Canadian Opera Company Orchestra
John Wyre

Capitol City Band
James H. Latimer

Casals Festival Orchestra
Bob Becker
Charles Owen

CBC-Montreal Opera Orchestra
Owen Clark

CBC-Winnipeg Orchestra
Owen Clark

Central City Opera Orchestra
Edward Small
Terry J. Smith

Central Wisconsin Symphony Orchestra
Vicki P. Jenks

Century of Progress Marimba Orchestra
Clair Omar Musser

Charleston Junior Symphony Orchestra
Charles J. Miles

Charleston Symphony Orchestra
Charles J. Miles
Charlie Ventura Group
Edwin T. Shaughnessy

Chautauqua Opera Company
Ruth Patricia Cahn

Chautauqua Symphony Orchestra
Ruth Patricia Cahn
William L. Cahn

Chicago Chamber Musicians
    Patricia Dash

Chicago Contemporary Players
    Glenn Steele

Chicago Grand Opera Orchestra
    William F. Ludwig

Chicago Symphony Orchestra
    Patricia Dash
    Sam Denov
    William F. Ludwig
    Clair Omar Musser
    Albert Payson
    Gordon B. Peters

Chuck Mangione Combo
    Stephen Gadd

Chuck Mangione Orchestra
    William L. Cahn

Cincinnati Pops Orchestra
    Patricia Dash
    Edwin T. Shaughnessy

Cincinnati Symphony Orchestra
    Patricia Dash

Civic Orchestra of Chicago
    Sam Denov
    Gordon B. Peters

Cleveland Orchestra
    Cloyd Duff
    Robert C. Pangborn
    Michael Rosen
    John Wyre

Clifford Brown Quintet
    Max Roach

Colorado Symphony Orchestra
    Edward Small
    Terry J. Smith

Columbus Symphony Orchestra
    James L. Moore

Concertgebouw Orchestra
    Keiko Abe
    Jan Pustjens

Corning Symphony Orchestra
    William L. Cahn

Count Basie Band
    Louis Bellson
    Milt Jackson
    Charles J. Miles
    Edwin T. Shaughnessy
    Dallas Symphony Orchestra
    Marvin Dahlgren
    Ron Fink
    Douglas Howard
    Mitchell Peters

Dave Brubeck Combo
    Charles J. Miles

Denver Percussion Ensemble
    Edward Small

Denver Symphony Orchestra
    Edward Small
    Terry J. Smith
    Leigh Howard Stevens

Detroit Percussion Trio
    Robert C. Pangborn

Detroit Symphony Orchestra
    Warren Benson
    William L. Cahn
    Robert C. Pangborn

Dizzy Gillespie Band
    Michael Colgrass
    Max Roach

Double Image
    David Friedman
    David Samuels

Duke Ellington Band
    Louis Bellson
    Harvey Mason

Dutch Wind Ensemble
    Jan Pustjens

Eastman Chamber Players
    John H. Beck

Eastman Jazz Ensemble
    Niel B. DePonte

Eastman Percussion Ensemble
    John H. Beck
    Bob Becker
    Gordon B. Peters
    Gordon B. Stout

Eastman Philharmonia
    Bob Becker
    Patricia Dash
    Niel B. DePonte

Eastman Theatre Orchestra
    William Street

Eastman Wind Ensemble
    John H. Beck
    Bob Becker
    Patricia Dash
    Niel B. DePonte
    Stanley S. Leonard

Elmhurst Symphony Orchestra
    Gordon B. Peters

English Chamber Orchestra
    James Blades

English Opera Group
    James Blades

Ensemble fur Neue Musik
    Siegfried Fink

Equilibrium
    Michael Udow

Erroll Garner Combo
    Harvey Mason

Fairfax Symphony Orchestra
    John R. Beck

Fargo-Moorhead Symphony Orchestra
    Owen Clark

First Cavalry Division Band
    Emil Richards

Fletcher Henderson Orchestra
    Art Blakey

Florida Symphony Orchestra
    Richard T. Kvistad

Ford Sunday Evening Hour Orchestra
    Warren Benson

Fort Worth Opera Orchestra
    Ron Fink

Fort Worth Symphony Orchestra
    Ron Fink

Four for Percussion
    Robert C. Pangborn

Fredonia Jazz Ensemble
    Niel B. DePonte

Gary Burton Quartet
    Gary Burton

George Shearing Quintet
    Gary Burton
    Harvey Mason
    Ted Piltzecker
    Emil Richards

Gerry Mulligan Combo
    Charles J. Miles

Gil Fuller Band
    Bobby Hutcherson

Grant Park Symphony Orchestra
    Richard T. Kvistad
    Albert Payson
    Gordon B. Peters
    Glenn Steele

Guarneri Jazz Quartet
    John Bergamo

Harry James Band
    Louis Bellson

Hartford Symphony Orchestra
    Tele Lesbines
    Emil Richards

Herbie Hancock Combo
    Harvey Mason

Ice Capades Orchestra
    Fred Buda
    William L. Cahn
    Owen Clark
    Marvin Dahlgren
    Ron Fink
    George A. Frock

Indianapolis Symphony Orchestra
    Paula N. Culp
    Cloyd Duff
    James L. Moore
    Robert C. Pangborn

International Marimba Symphony Orchestra
    Clair Omar Musser

Japan Philharmonic
    Keiko Abe
    John Wyre

The Jazz Messengers
    Art Blakey

Jerry Hoey Ensemble
    James Blades

Lake Placid Club Orchestra
    William Street

Lamont Percussion Ensemble
    Edward Small

Lionel Hampton Band
    Lionel Hampton Band

Little Orchestra Society
    Elden C. Bailey
    Morris Lang
    Arthur Press

London Symphony Orchestra
    James Blades

Los Angeles Percussion Ensemble
 Karen Ervin Pershing
 William Kraft
 Mitchell Peters

Los Angeles Philharmonic
 William Kraft
 Mitchell Peters

Los Angeles Symphony Orchestra
 Clair Omar Musser

Louis Bellson Band
 Louis Bellson
 Emil Richards

Louisville Orchestra
 Douglas Howard
 Albert Payson

Lubeck Opera Orchestra
 Siegfried Fink

Lyric Opera Association of Chicago
 Richard T. Kvistad
 Albert Payson

Madison Symphony Orchestra
 Vicki P. Jenks
 James H. Latimer

Maelstrom Percussion Ensemble
 John Bergamo

Magdeburg Opera Orchestra
 Siegfried Fink

The Mallet Duo
 David Friedman
 David Samuels

Manhattan Symphony Orchestra
 Larry Wilson

Manitoba Opera Company Orchestra
 Owen Clark

The Marimba Masters
 Gordon B. Peters

Maryland Symphony Orchestra
  John R. Beck

Melbourne Symphony Orchestra
  Larry Wilson

Melos Ensemble
  James Blades

Memphis State University Band
  John H. Beck

Memphis Symphony Orchestra
  George A. Frock

Metropolitan Opera Orchestra
  Fred D. Hinger
  Elayne Jones
  Christopher S. Lamb
  Robert C. Pangborn
  Michael Rosen

Miles Davis Combo
  Max Roach

Mills Brothers Circus Band
  Elden C. Bailey

Milwaukee Chamber Orchestra
  Tele Lesbines

Milwaukee Symphony Orchestra
  Tele Lesbines
  Michael Rosen
  John Wyre

Minneapolis Pops Orchestra
  Marvin Dahlgren

Minneapolis Symphony Orchestra
  Marvin Dahlgren
  Robert C. Pangborn

Minnesota Orchestra
  Paula N. Culp
  Marvin Dahlgren

Modern Jazz Quartet
  Milt Jackson

Mozart Society Orchestra
    Glenn Steele

National Arts Centre Orchestra
    Owen Clark

National Gallery Orchestra
    John R. Beck

National Philharmonic Orchestra, Poland
    Marta Ptaszynska

National Repertory Orchestra
    Terry J. Smith

National Symphony Orchestra
    John R. Beck

Nazareth College Percussion Ensemble
    Ruth Patricia Cahn

Netherlands Philharmonic Orchestra
    Jan Pustjens

New Diaphony
    Ruth Patricia Cahn

New Hampshire Music Festival Orchestra
    Ruth Patricia Cahn

New Jersey Symphony Orchestra
    Elayne Jones

New Orleans Philharmonic
    Michael Udow

New York City Ballet
    Morris Lang
    Edwin T. Shaughnessy

New York Opera Society
    Morris Lang

New York Philharmonic
  Elden C. Bailey
  Michael Colgrass
  Elayne Jones
  Christopher S. Lamb
  Morris Lang
  Edwin T. Shaughnessy
  Larry Wilson
  John Wyre

Nexus
  Keiko Abe
  Bob Becker
  John Bergamo
  William L. Cahn
  John Wyre

Oakland Symphony Orchestra
  Larry Wilson

Oakwood Chamber Players
  Vicki P. Jenks

Oberlin Percussion Group
  Michael Rosen

The Ohio State University Percussion Ensemble
  James L. Moore

Oklahoma City Symphony Orchestra
  Thomas Gauger
  Glenn Steele
  John Wyre

Opera de Paris
  Francois Dupin

Opera Forum Orchestra
  Jan Pustjens

Orchestra of Strasbourg
  Francois Dupin

Orchestre de Paris
  Francois Dupin
  Jacques Remy

l'Orchestre des Cadets
  Jacques Remy

Orchestre du Domaine Musical
  Jacques Remy

Oregon Symphony Orchestra
  Niel B. DePonte

Oscar Peterson Combo
  Louis Bellson

Paris Opera Orchestra
  Jacques Remy

Paul Horn Quintet
  Emil Richards

Paul Winter Consort
  Bob Becker
  William L. Cahn

Pendulum
  Ted Piltzecker

Penn Contemporary Players
  Glenn Steele

Pennsylvania Ballet Company
  Glenn Steele

Percussion Group, Amsterdam
  Jan Pustjens

Les Percussions de Strasbourg
  Keiko Abe
  Marta Ptaszynska

Philadelphia Orchestra
  Fred D. Hinger
  Charles Owen
  Glenn Steele

Philadelphia Philharmonia
  Glenn Steele

Philharmonic Orchestra of Florida
  Patricia Dash

Philharmonic Orchestra of the French Radio
  Francois Dupin

Pittsburgh Symphony Orchestra
    Richard T. Kvistad
    Stanley S. Leonard
    William F. Ludwig

Portland Symphony Orchestra, Maine
    Elden C. Bailey

Qango
    Garry Lee

Racine Symphony Orchestra
    James H. Latimer

Radio-France Symphony Orchestra
    Jacques Remy

Ringling Brothers Circus Band
    Elden C. Bailey

Rochester Chamber Orchestra
    John H. Beck
    Ruth Patricia Cahn
    William L. Cahn

Rochester Civic Orchestra
    William Street

Rochester Marimba Band
    Ruth Patricia Cahn

Rochester Philharmonic
    John H. Beck
    Bob Becker
    Ruth Patricia Cahn
    William L. Cahn
    Patricia Dash
    Niel B. DePonte
    Stephen Gadd
    Fred D. Hinger
    Gordon B. Peters
    Mitchell Peters
    Gordon B. Stout
    William Street
    John Wyre

Rosewood Percussion Group
    Tele Lesbines

Royal Winnipeg Ballet Orchestra
    Owen Clark

Salisbury's Concert Orchestra
　　William F. Ludwig

San Antonio Symphony Orchestra
　　Sam Denov

San Francisco Conservatory Percussion Ensemble
　　Larry Wilson

San Francisco Opera Orchestra
　　Elayne Jones
　　Richard T. Kvistad

San Francisco Pops Orchestra
　　Richard T. Kvistad
　　Larry Wilson

San Francisco Symphony
　　Anthony J. Cirone
　　Elayne Jones
　　Richard T. Kvistad
　　Larry Wilson
　　John Wyre

Sante Fe Opera
　　Terry J. Smith
　　Michael Udow

Sauter-Finegan Jazz Orchestra
　　Elden C. Bailey

Spyro Gyra
　　David Samuels

Stan Getz Quartet
　　Gary Burton

Steve Reich and Musicians
　　Bob Becker

St. Paul Chamber Orchestra
　　Marvin Dahlgren
　　Terry J. Smith

Symphony of the New World
　　Elayne Jones

Syracuse University Wind Ensemble
　　John H. Beck

Tokyo Marimba Group
    Keiko Abe

Tokyo Metropolitan Orchestra
    Keiko Abe

Tokyo Philharmonic
    Keiko Abe

Toledo Symphony Orchestra
    William L. Cahn

Tommy Dorsey Band
    Louis Bellson

The Tonight Show Orchestra
    Edwin T. Shaughnessy

Toronto Symphony
    Bob Becker
    William L. Cahn
    Donald Kuehn
    John Wyre

United States Air Force Band
    Douglas Howard

19th United States Army Band
    Stanley S. Leonard

United States Army Field Band
    Stephen Gadd

United States Army 44th Infantry Division Band
    Albert Payson

7th United States Army Symphony Orchestra
    Mitchell Peters

United States Marine Band
    John H. Beck
    John R. Beck
    Bob Becker
    Charles Owen
    Edward Small

United States Military Academy Band
    Robert C. Pangborn
    Gordon B. Peters
    Glenn Steele

United States Navy Band
    Fred Buda
    Fred D. Hinger

University of Chicago Contemporary Players
    Richard T. Kvistad

University of Colorado Summer Band
    Terry J. Smith

University of Colorado Symphony Orchestra
    Donald Kuehn

University of Illinois Percussion Ensemble
    Michael Colgrass
    George A. Frock
    Albert Payson

University of Michigan Percussion Ensemble
    Charles Owen
    Michael Udow

University of Southern California Percussion Ensemble
    Mitchell Peters

University of Texas Percussion Ensemble
    George A. Frock

University of Wisconsin - Stevens Point Jazz Ensemble
    Louis Bellson

Ventnor Music Festival Orchestra
    William L. Cahn

Waco Symphony Orchestra
    Vicki P. Jenks

Washington Opera Orchestra
    John R. Beck

Westchester Symphony Orchestra
    Elayne Jones
    Larry Wilson

West Coast Chamber Orchestra
    Niel B. DePonte

Western Opera Theater
    Larry Wilson

<u>Wisconsin Chamber Orchestra</u>
Vicki P. Jenks

<u>Wood Brothers Circus Band</u>
William F. Ludwig

<u>Woody Herman Band</u>
Charles J. Miles

<u>World Youth Orchestra</u>
Siegfried Fink

<u>Xebec Marimba Trio</u>
Keiko Abe

Appendix III

Awards and Recipients

By definition, all percussionist subjects in this book are successful in their field. They would not be included here if they were not. It is true, however, that some individuals are awarded honors beyond the usual. Following is a listing of important awards and their recipients whose sketches are included in this volume.

Afro-American Society of Oakland Award - Elayne Jones, 1976

Alumnus of the Year, University of Southern California - Lionel Hampton, 1983

Arts and Letters Citation of France - Clair Musser, c. 1935

Award for Classical Percussion, Modern Drummer Publications - Anthony J. Cirone, 1986-89

Citation of Excellence, National Band Association - Warren Benson, 1976

Chicagoan of the Year - Sam Denov, 1971

DeMoulin Prize, National Band Association - Michael Colgrass, 1985

Down Beat Album of the Year, Special Edition - Jack DeJohnette, 1989

Down Beat, America's Finest All-round Drummer - Edwin Shaugnessy

Down Beat, Best Record of the Year - Max Roach, 1956

Down Beat Number One Vibist - Gary Burton, 1968-87

Fanfare Award for Education, Rochester Philharmonic League - Ruth Cahn and William L. Cahn, 1988

Grammy Awards - Gary Burton, 1971, 1979, 1980

Hilroy Award for Innovative Teaching - Owen Clark, 1985

Honorary Doctor of Humane Letters, Bellarmine College - Lionel Hampton, 1986

Institute of Music Technology Honorary Fellow - James Blades, 1986

International Who's Who in Music - Vida Chenoweth

Lillian Fairchild Prize for Musical Composition - Warren Benson, 1971

Medaille de la Ville de Paris - Jacques Remy, 1978

Meet the Composer Award, State University of New York at Buffalo - John Bergamo, 1988

Modern Drummer, Best Big Band Drummer - Edwin Shaughnessy

Musician of the Year, Mu Phi Epsilon - John H. Beck, 1976

National Association of Business and Professional Women Award - Elayne Jones, 1977

Oklahoma Hall of Fame - Vida Chenoweth, 1985

Order of the British Empire - James Blades, 1971

Oregon Arts Commission Award - Niel DePonte

Percussive Arts Society Hall of Fame - Louis Bellson, James Blades, Gary Burton, Michael Colgrass, Cloyd Duff, Lionel Hampton, Fred D. Hinger, William F. Ludwig, Sr., Clair Musser, Charles Owen, Max Roach, William Street

President's Scholar, State University of New York at Fredonia - Niel DePonte

Prize for Excellence, Tokyo Arts Festival - Keiko Abe, 1968-69, 1971, 1974, 1976

Pulitzer Prize for Music Composition, Deja Vu - Michael Colgrass, 1977

Theodore Thomas Medallion, Chicago Symphony Orchestra - Sam Denov

Toronto Arts Award - Bob Becker, 1989

Who's Who in American Music - Vida Chenoweth

Who's Who in Religion - Vida Chenoweth

Who's Who of American Women - Vida Chenoweth

Wisconsin Artist of Distinction - James Latimer, 1978

Bibliography

Dictionaries and Encyclopedias

Adato, Joseph and Judy, George. <u>The Percussionist's Dictionary</u>. Melville, New York: Belwin-Mills, 1984.

Apel, Willi. <u>Harvard Dictionary of Music</u>. Cambridge, Massachusetts: Harvard University Press, 1968.

Feather, Leonard. <u>The Encyclopedia of Jazz in the Sixties</u>. New York: Horizon Press, 1966.

Harris, William H. and Levey, Judith S., Editors. <u>The New Columbia Encyclopedia</u>, Fourth Edition. New York: Columbia University Press, 1975.

<u>The New Grove Dictionary of Jazz</u>, Volumes One and Two, 1988.

<u>The Random House Dictionary</u>, Concise Edition. New York: Random House, 1980.

Books

Grout, Donald Jay. <u>A History of Western Music</u>. New York: W.W. Norton, 1960.

Grout, Donald Jay. <u>A History of Western Music.</u> Third Edition with Claude V. Palisca. New York: W.W. Norton, 1980.

Larrick, Geary. <u>Analytical and Biographical Writings in Percussion Music</u>. New York: Peter Lang, 1989.

Meza, Fernando A. <u>Percussion Discography: An International Compilation of Solo and Chamber Percussion Music</u>. Westport, Connecticut: Greenwood Press, 1990.

Roach, Hildred. <u>Black American Music</u>. Boston: Crescendo Publishing, 1973.

Salzman, Eric. <u>Twentieth-Century Music: An Introduction</u>. Englewood Cliffs, New Jersey: Prentice-Hall, 1967.

Booklets

Encore. Program booklet of the Milwaukee Symphony Orchestra. Milwaukee, Wisconsin: Milwaukee Symphony Orchestra, 1991.

Larrick, Geary. Mechanics of the Timpani. Edited by John Beck, artwork by Herbert Sandmann. Stevens Point, Wisconsin: G and L Publishing, 1989.

Music Directors and Associate Conductors, 1891-1988. The Chicago Symphony Orchestra. Chicago: Orchestral Association.

Recordings Booklet, 1916-88. Chicago, Illinois: Chicago Symphony Orchestra, 1989.

Directories

Clark, J. Bunker, Editor. Membership Directory. Lawrence, Kansas: The Sonneck Society for American Music, 1990.

Directory of Music Faculties in Colleges and Universities, U.S. and Canada, 1986-88. Boulder, Colorado: The College Music Society, 1987.

Directory of Music Faculties in Colleges and Universities, U.S. and Canada, 1988-90. Boulder: College Music Society, 1989.

Directory of Music Faculties in Colleges and Universities, U.S. and Canada, 1990-92. Missoula, Montana: CMS Publications, 1990.

Who's Who in America, 45th Edition, 1988.

Maps

Universal World Atlas, Third Edition. Chicago: Rand McNally, 1987.

Catalogs

Catalog. Aspen, Colorado: Aspen Music School, 1989.

Catalog. Fort Lauderdale, Florida: Music for Percussion.

Catalogs. Bryn Mawr, Pennsylvania: Theodore Presser, 1991.

Catalogue. Langhorne, Pennsylvania: Marta Ptaszynska.

Catalogue. Los Angeles: Mitchell Peters, January, 1991.

Periodicals

Arts Midwest Jazz Calendar, March, 1991.

Chicago Tribune, Thursday, November 8, 1990.

International Musician 89/6 (December 1990).

Latimer, James H., Editor. Wisconsin Percussive Arts Society Newsletter, 1990.

Modern Percussionist III/4 (September 1987).

National Association of College Wind and Percussion Instructors Journal XXXIV/3 (Spring 1986).

National Drum Association Magazine 2/10 (October 1991).

News. Minneapolis: Arts Midwest, January, 1991.

Percussion News. Lawton, Oklahoma: Percussive Arts Society, 1991.

Percussive Notes 29/6 (August 1991).

The New Yorker, December 4, 1989.

Television Shows

Evening at Pops. Wisconsin Public Television, 1990.

Sesame Street. Wausau: Wisconsin Public Television, 1991.

INDEX